—FOUR VIEWS—
ON
ETERNAL SECURITY

Books in the Counterpoints Series

Are Miraculous Gifts for Today?

Five Views on Law and Gospel

Five Views on Sanctification

Five Views on Apologetics

Four Views on Eternal Security

Four Views on Hell

Four Views on Salvation in a Pluralistic World

Four Views on the Book of Revelation

Three Views on Creation and Evolution

Three Views on the Millennium and Beyond

Three Views on the Rapture

Two Views on Women in Ministry

Stanley N. Gundry (S.T.D., Lutheran School of Theology at Chicago) is vice president and editor-in-chief at Zondervan. He graduated summa cum laude from both the Los Angeles Baptist College and Talbot Theological Seminary before receiving his M.S.T. degree from Union College, University of British Columbia, and his S.T.D. degree from Lutheran School of Theology at Chicago. With more than thirty-five years of teaching, pastoring, and publishing experience, he is the author of *Love Them in: The Proclamation Theology of D. L. Moody* and coauthor of *The NIV Harmony of the Gospels*.

► COUNTERPOINTS ◄

—FOUR VIEWS—
ON
ETERNAL
SECURITY

Contributors:

Michael S. Horton
Norman L. Geisler
Stephen M. Ashby
J. Steven Harper

J. MATTHEW PINSON
General Editor

STANLEY N. GUNDRY
Series Editor

GRAND RAPIDS, MICHIGAN 49530

ZONDERVAN™

Four Views on Eternal Security
Copyright © 2002 by J. Matthew Pinson

Requests for information should be addressed to:

Zondervan, *Grand Rapids, Michigan 49530*

Library of Congress Cataloging-in-Publication Data

Four views on eternal security / J. Matthew Pinson, general editor.
      p. cm.—(Counterpoints)
    Includes bibliographical references and indexes.
    ISBN 0-310-23439-5 (pbk.)
      1. Salvation. 2. Assurance (Theology). 3. Perseverance (Theology).
  I. Pinson, J. Matthew, 1967-   II. Counterpoints (Grand Rapids, Mich.).
BT752.F68 2002
234—dc21   2001046639

Printed in the United States of America

02 03 04 05 06 /❖ DC/ 10 9 8 7 6 5 4 3

CONTENTS

INTRODUCTION

J. Matthew Pinson

Among the most hotly debated topics in the history of Christian theology has been the perseverance of the saints. Perhaps the reason for the intense interest in this subject is that the doctrine of perseverance relates closely to the assurance of salvation. Christians often associate the questions "How can I be sure I am saved?" and "Am I eternally secure in my salvation?" One's answer to one of those questions often affects his or her answer to the other. Perhaps because of this very practical reason—because it cuts to the heart of Christian experience—perseverance has been a chief source of controversy among Christians.

Besides the subject's long history and integral connection with Christian spirituality, the doctrine of perseverance serves as a handy gauge of one's theological vantage point. Perseverance touches so many other doctrinal themes—free will, grace, predestination, atonement, justification, sanctification, spirituality. Thus, the way people handle this subject tells a great deal about where they locate themselves on the theological spectrum. When we look at how theologians present the doctrine of perseverance, we can get a glimpse into the way they do theology.

A book like this is needed. Encountering the doctrines of perseverance from theological traditions other than our own should help us better understand the biblical picture of salvation in Christ. It should free us from undue reliance on and recourse to our own traditions. Furthermore, it should help us refine our own positions in light of the criticisms of other doctrinal traditions. Finally, seeing four views on perseverance compared and contrasted with each other will help clear up muddy thinking that too often characterizes popular evangelical teaching on this subject.

The views debated here are four historical Protestant positions—two Calvinist and two Arminian. Each of these perspectives is rooted in a particular set of intellectual, historical, and cultural circumstances, and each has been molded by centuries of theological debate as well as the spiritual experience of Christian communities. All these views draw from the broad stream of Reformation theology. The Classical Calvinist view arises from the thought of John Calvin and his Reformed successors on the continent and in Britain. The moderate Calvinist approach emerges from nineteenth- and twentieth-century appropriations of the Calvinist theological heritage, particularly among Calvinist Baptists and other free-church groups. The Reformed Arminian perspective traces itself to the Dutch Reformed theologian Jacobus Arminius and to the General Baptist movement that originated in seventeenth-century England. The Wesleyan Arminian position finds its roots in the teaching of John and Charles Wesley and early Methodist thinkers in eighteenth-century England.

The contributors to this volume were selected to represent their respective theological traditions. That does not imply, however, that everyone from a particular tradition will agree with what the contributor from that tradition says. It does mean that each contributor will attempt to set forth a position that is within the bounds of mainstream scholarly opinion within his own tradition. In what remains of this introduction, I will briefly discuss the historical and theological background of each view and summarize each contributor's basic approach.

CLASSICAL CALVINISM

The Classical Calvinist approach to the doctrine of continuance in salvation finds its origin in the thought of the sixteenth-century Swiss Reformer John Calvin. He developed a doctrinal system, with roots in Augustine, that posited the sovereignty of God as a key organizing principle in Christian thought. Because

God is sovereign over his creation, Calvin argued, he must be the sole actor in the salvation of his human creatures. Any response, prior to regeneration, from a depraved human being would make God less than sovereign in human redemption.

Thus, divine grace is an expression of divine sovereignty. In his grace God chooses, or predestines, whom he wills to be saved (the elect) and whom he wills to be damned (the reprobate). Those whom God predestines to salvation, he irresistibly draws to himself and regenerates. In them he effects faith in Jesus Christ, and through faith the regenerate are justified by the imputed righteousness of Christ. Calvin's picture of God's redemptive plan results in a perspective that sees the elect preserved—and thus persevering—in faith and holiness until death. For Calvin, election to salvation is unconditional, and therefore perseverance in salvation is unconditional. Those God effectually calls to himself will be irresistibly preserved in a state of grace.

A generation after Calvin, official disagreement on the doctrine of predestination began to surface in the Reformed churches on the continent. This controversy centered on Jacobus Arminius, who developed an approach to predestination and grace that differed starkly from Calvin's. In opposition to Arminius and his followers, the Reformed churches held the Synod of Dort in 1618–19, which expelled the Remonstrants, Arminius's followers. That synod systematized and crystallized Calvin's theology of salvation into what people have since called the "five points of Calvinism" or the "doctrines of grace." Many people have remembered these doctrines with the help of an acronym, TULIP:

T - Total depravity
U - Unconditional election
L - Limited atonement
I - Irresistible grace
P - Perseverance of the saints

Contemporary Calvinists debate whether Calvin taught "double predestination." This doctrine holds that God unconditionally chooses the elect for salvation without regard to his foreknowledge of their faith or good works. He unconditionally predestines the reprobate to damnation without regard to his foreknowledge of their unbelief or sin. In other words, did God simply "pass over" the nonelect, allowing them to be damned for their sin, or did he foreordain people to damnation without regard to their sin?[1]

Calvinists also disagree on whether Calvin believed in a particular/limited atonement (that Christ died only for the elect) or a general/unlimited atonement (that Christ died for all humanity). Yet Classical Calvinism, as it took shape in the scholastic theology of the sixteenth and seventeenth centuries, subscribed to particular redemption and thus limited atonement. Many advocates of what is popularly known as "four-point Calvinism" think of themselves as Classical Calvinists as well. This view found its first expression in the thought of the seventeenth-century French Reformed theologian Moise Amyraut. His system, known as Amyraldism, taught the universality of the atonement while still maintaining the other doctrines of the Canons of Dort. Amyraut and his colleagues insisted that they were simply recapturing the spirit of Calvin himself, who, they said, held a universal atonement. Amyraut was tried for heresy three times, yet was never condemned. However, the Formula Helvetic Consensus (1675) staunchly opposed his system.[2]

Though Amyraldism played a minor role in the Reformed theological scene,[3] the Calvinism of Dort became entrenched in seventeenth- and eighteenth-century Reformed scholastic theology. It lives on in confessions such as the Westminster Confession of Faith, which appeared in the middle seventeenth century and exerted an unparalleled effect on the development of Reformed theology.[4] This approach to salvation influenced the Reformed churches on the continent and in Britain (particularly Puritans, Presbyterians, Independents, and Separatists). It also became the belief of the Particular Baptists, who originated in mid-seventeenth-century England from the Independents. These

---

[1]Joel E. Hampton presents a convincing case for Calvin's belief in the latter option in "The Equal Ultimacy Question in Calvin's View of Reprobation: Is Predestination Really 'Double'?" *Integrity: A Journal of Christian Thought* 1 (2000): 103–13.

[2]See Brian Armstrong, *Calvinism and the Amyraut Heresy* (Madison, Wis.: Univ. of Wisconsin Press, 1969).

[3]Amyraldism influenced the development of Protestant theology in America, particularly among Baptists and dispensationalists.

[4]One of the best succinct treatments of Classical Calvinist soteriology is J. I. Packer's "Introductory Essay" to the Puritan John Owen's *The Death of Death in the Death of Christ* (London: Banner of Truth, 1959).

Calvinistic Baptists revised the Westminster Confession (excising paedobaptist and presbyterial ecclesiology) in the Second London Confession of 1689.[5]

In chapter 1, Michael S. Horton offers a contemporary interpretation of the Classical Calvinist viewpoint. Because Scripture teaches that election to salvation is unconditional, he argues, necessary perseverance follows. Since believers did nothing to get into a state of grace, they can do nothing to get out. If grace is irresistible before conversion, then it remains irresistible after conversion. Final perseverance is a certain and necessary part of Paul's order of salvation (*ordo salutis*) in Romans 8:29–30. Those whom the Father has elected and whom the Son has purchased through his death and whom the Holy Spirit has irresistibly drawn to himself must of necessity persevere.

Horton contends that this is the teaching of Holy Scripture. He uses covenant theology as an explanatory grid for interpreting the "eternal security" passages and the warning passages in the New Testament. To understand these texts, we must presuppose the biblical paradigm of the covenant of redemption, the covenant of works, and the covenant of grace. By so doing, Horton says, we can make better sense of the seemingly contradictory verses on eternal security and apostasy to which Calvinists and Arminians respectively appeal. Then, he argues, it becomes clear that warning passages in the New Testament do not address believers. Rather, they caution unbelievers who have participated in the covenant by virtue of their baptism and church membership. Thus, Horton fits squarely in the tradition of Calvinistic covenant theology.

MODERATE CALVINISM

Moderate Calvinism is the phrase I have chosen to designate those who come out of a Calvinist heritage but have significantly moderated their Calvinism, especially its predestinarian elements. Most Baptists today fit this description, as well as a host of evangelicals in free-church congregations, denominations,

---

[5]See Thomas J. Nettles, *By His Grace and for His Glory: A Historical, Theological, and Practical Study of the Doctrines of Grace in Baptist Life* (Grand Rapids: Baker, 1986), and Samuel Waldron, *A Modern Exposition of the 1689 Baptist Confession of Faith* (Durham, Eng.: Evangelical Press, 1989).

and parachurch groups. The most common form of moderate
Calvinism holds to a Moderated version of total depravity and
to the perseverance of the saints. Yet it either jettisons the middle
three points of TULIP or reinterprets them in a way that differs
radically from Classical Calvinism.

Curiously, the first people to hold such views started as
General Baptists, the Arminian Baptists who originated in early
seventeenth-century England. A group of General Baptists in the
late seventeenth century began to moderate their Arminianism.
They did so to the point that it changed from a belief in the possibility of apostasy from the Christian life to the unconditional
perseverance of the saints. They, like other General Baptists, had
always affirmed total depravity. After the shift to unconditional
perseverance, they continued to hold to election conditioned on
foreseen faith, general (unlimited) atonement, and resistible
grace. They articulated this perspective in a confession of faith
entitled "The Orthodox Creed" (1689).[6]

It is doubtful, however, that these early general-atonement
Baptists had any connection with later Moderate Calvinists in
the Baptist tradition. Moderate Calvinism is a nineteenth- and
twentieth-century phenomenon. Some historians argue that Baptists in North America began to soften the hard edges of traditional Calvinism in the nineteenth century. This doctrinal shift,
they maintain, coincided with the spread of the Separate Baptist
movement and the wide acceptance of the New Hampshire Confession of Faith.[7]

Baptist theologians in both the North and South held as
strenuous a brand of Calvinism as that of their Princeton Presbyterian colleagues. However, Baptists in the pew, aflame with
the fires of frontier revivalism, began to moderate the strict
Calvinism of their forebears.[8] Other historians place the erosion
of traditional Baptist Calvinism in the early twentieth century
with teachers such as E. Y. Mullins and L. R. Scarborough.[9] At

---

[6]"The Orthodox Creed," in William L. Lumpkin, ed., *Baptist Confessions of Faith*
(Valley Forge, Pa.: Judson, 1959), 297–334.

[7]Lumpkin, ed., *Baptist Confessions of Faith*, 360; H. Leon McBeth, *The Baptist Heritage: Four Centuries of Baptist Witness* (Nashville: Broadman, 1987), 210–11, 704, 774.

[8]W. Wiley Richards, *Winds of Doctrines: The Origin and Development of Southern
Baptist Theology* (Lanham, Md.: Univ. Press of America, 1991), 45–59, 124–27, 193–94.

[9]Nettles, *By His Grace and for His Glory*, 246–64; Tom Nettles, "The Rise and
Demise of Calvinism Among Southern Baptists," *The Founders Journal* 19/20:6–21.

any rate, Moderate Calvinism became the majority view among Baptists in the late nineteenth and early twentieth centuries. Many dispensationalists in groups like the Plymouth Brethren and the Bible church movement also moderated their Calvinism considerably.

Some of those I am calling Moderate Calvinists have recently begun to refer to themselves as moderate Arminians.[10] Others within the Southern Baptist Convention, for example, now espouse a full-blown Arminianism, complete with the possibility of loss of salvation.[11]

In chapter 2, Norman Geisler presents the Moderate Calvinist perspective. He argues that Classical Calvinism's understanding of predestination, the extent of the atonement, and effectual calling have no scriptural support. He stresses that the New Testament teaches that God will preserve in grace the one who has once been regenerate. Thus, the loss of salvation is impossible. Christians are eternally secure, based on the imputation of Christ's righteousness and God's unconditional promises to the believer. Rather than merely discarding the traditional TULIP formulation, however, Geisler reinterprets it, arguing that each point of Calvinism can be held in either a strong or moderate sense.

He also distinguishes himself from Classical Calvinism and Arminianism in his understanding of assurance. He argues that, while strong Calvinism offers security for the believers, it cannot offer present assurance that one is indeed elect. While Arminianism can offer present assurance, it cannot offer security.

Cf. Clark R. Youngblood, "Perseverance and Apostasy," in *Has Our Theology Changed? Southern Baptist Thought Since 1845* , ed. Paul Basden (Nashville: Broadman & Holman, 1994), 114–34.

[10]See, e.g., W. Wiley Richards, *Why I Am Not a Calvinist* (Graceville, Fla.: Hargrave, 1999).

[11]See Dale Moody, *Apostasy: A Study in the Epistle to the Hebrews and in Baptist History* (Greenville, S.C.: Smyth & Helwys, 1997). (The late Dale Moody was fired from Southern Baptist Theological Seminary owing to his belief in the possibility of apostasy. A number of Southern Baptists have since accepted his views on perseverance. This shows the importance of the doctrine of eternal security in the nation's largest Protestant denomination.) These are interesting developments, given the resurgence of Classical Calvinism in the Southern Baptist Convention, which is evidenced by the growth of the Founders Conference, a fellowship organized for the promulgation of orthodox Calvinism (see Youngblood, "Perseverance and Apostasy," 124–28).

Moderate Calvinism, he contends, has the "best of both worlds" in that it alone offers true assurance and security. Geisler presents a model that holds in tension the freedom of human beings to resist the grace God offers them before conversion and the absolute eternal security of the individual who has received Christ through faith. In this way, he attempts to strike a balance between Classical Calvinism and Arminianism.

REFORMED ARMINIANISM

Reformed Arminianism has its roots in the thought of the Dutch theologian Jacobus Arminius, the central anti-Calvinist figure in the Dutch Reformed Church at the turn of the sixteenth century. Most interpreters of Arminius have seen him as a once-supralapsarian Calvinist who rejected Reformed theology after an attempt to refute the anti-Calvinist Dirck Coornheert. Yet Carl Bangs has correctly argued that Arminius simply reflected and systematized an anti-Calvinist undercurrent that had been present in the Reformed churches since the time of Calvin, particularly among the laity.[12]

This position is called Reformed Arminianism because Arminius claimed to be a Reformed theologian within the bounds of both the Heidelberg Catechism and Belgic Confession of Faith.[13] Bangs presents "Arminius as a Reformed Theologian," positing a milieu within the continental Reformed churches in the late sixteenth century that was broader than Calvinist predestinarianism.[14] This perspective goes against the common tendency to read later Arminian themes into Arminius. It sees his theology as a development of Reformed theology rather than a departure from it. Many people confuse later Arminianism with Arminius's Arminianism. They therefore fail to recognize that while he veered from Calvinism on the question of how one *comes to be* in a state of grace (predestination, free will, and

---

[12]Carl Bangs, "Arminius and the Reformation," *Church History* 30 (1961): 155–60; idem, *Arminius: A Study in the Dutch Reformation* (Grand Rapids: Zondervan, 1985), 141–42. This anti-Calvinist posture evidenced itself most among the laity and magistrates but was not absent among the clergy.

[13]Carl Bangs, "Arminius As a Reformed Theologian," in *The Heritage of John Calvin*, ed. John H. Bratt (Grand Rapids: Eerdmans, 1973), 216–17.

[14]In addition to the above-cited works, see Carl Bangs, "Arminius and Reformed Theology" (Ph.D. diss., University of Chicago, 1958).

grace), he retained Reformed categories on the *meaning* of sin and redemption.

There has been confusion on whether Arminius believed it was possible for a once-regenerate person to apostatize, owing to statements he made in his *Declaration of Sentiments*. Yet all agree that Arminius at least laid the groundwork for the Arminian teaching that it is possible for the Christian to fall from grace. Arminius believed that not all regenerate persons are elect. He defined the elect as only those regenerate persons who persevere in a state of grace to the end of life: "Since *Election to salvation* comprehends within its limits not only Faith, but likewise perseverance in Faith ... believers and the elect are not correctly taken for the same persons."[15]

This position shows that Arminius believed apostasy is possible; otherwise, he would have said that all regenerate persons are also elect. Statements like these have led scholars like Bangs and R. T. Kendall to conclude that Arminius believed in the possibility of apostasy.[16] Yet his position does not imply that sin causes loss of salvation in a believer. The only way a Christian can lose salvation is by renouncing his or her faith in Christ. Arminius stated that it is "impossible for believers, *as long as they remain believers*, to decline from salvation."[17]

Reformed Arminians take their cues from Arminius himself and thus diverge from the mainstream of subsequent Arminianism. They are Reformed in their understanding of original sin, depravity, human inability, the nature of atonement, justification, sanctification, and the Christian life. Reformed Arminians subscribe to the penal satisfaction understanding of atonement and justification by the imputation of Christ's active and passive obedience to the believer. Thus, only by departing from Christ through unbelief—a decisive act of apostasy—can a Christian lose his or her salvation. Furthermore, they argue, apostasy is an irrevocable condition.[18] These perspectives mark

---

[15]James Arminius, *The Works of James Arminius*, trans. James Nichols and William Nichols, 3 vols. (Grand Rapids: Baker, 1986), 2:68.

[16]Bangs, "Arminius and Reformed Theology," 186–87; see also R. T. Kendall, *Calvin and English Calvinism to 1649* (Oxford: Oxford Univ. Press, 1978).

[17]Arminius, *Works*, 1:742 (italics added).

[18]The Reformed Arminian views that loss of salvation results only from apostasy through unbelief and such apostasy is irrevocable are shared by such recent scholars as Dale Moody, I. Howard Marshall, and Scot McKnight.

Reformed Arminians off from the mainstream of Arminian thought, since most Arminians disavow Reformed understandings of atonement, justification, and sanctification.

The views of Arminius were picked up by the English General Baptists, who arose in the early seventeenth century under the leadership of Thomas Helwys. He left his early compatriot John Smyth, because the latter had come to reject the doctrines of original sin, penal satisfaction, and the imputation of Christ's righteousness alone for justification. Theologians such as Thomas Grantham and John Griffith carried on the tradition of Helwys's Reformed Arminianism. Most Arminian thought was influenced more by John Wesley and others than by Arminius or the General Baptists. However, the General Baptist tradition persists in Arminian Baptist groups such as Free Will Baptists.

In chapter 3, Stephen M. Ashby defines and defends the Reformed Arminian perspective. He begins by explaining what the phrase means and how Reformed Arminians differ from Calvinists and other Arminians. He then shows how Arminius's soteriological presuppositions result in an approach to security that allows for the resistibility of grace after conversion. Ashby probes the biblical materials, thereby setting forth a case for the possibility of apostasy. He then describes how Reformed Arminianism differs from Wesleyan and other forms of Arminianism on how one can lose his or her salvation.

WESLEYAN ARMINIANISM

Wesleyan Arminianism is the theological system that arose from John Wesley's critical appropriation of the myriad theological traditions at his disposal in the eighteenth-century Church of England. It is so named not only because it is an anti-Calvinist approach to the doctrine of salvation but also because Wesley chose to identify himself with the name of Jacobus Arminius. Desiring a way to assert a non-Calvinist posture in the predestination controversies then raging in early Methodism, Wesley launched *The Arminian Magazine* in 1778. Yet the use of the word "Arminian" does not necessarily indicate Wesley's reliance on the writings of Arminius.[19] Wesley's doctrine of sal-

---

[19]See Luke L. Keefer Jr., "Characteristics of Wesley's Arminianism," *Wesleyan Theological Journal* 22 (1987): 88–100. One evidence of this is the fact that, despite

vation was a creative amalgamation of sources from his Anglican upbringing. While we can assume Wesley read some Arminius, there is more evidence of the influence of seventeenth-century English anti-Calvinism.

Wesley inherited Anglican Arminianism from his parents, Samuel and Susanna, as seen in numerous letters and discussions.[20] Samuel Wesley recommended Hugo Grotius, who had come to England from Holland, as his favorite biblical commentator. Grotius turns out to be a greater theological source for Wesley and his circle at Oxford University than Arminius was.[21] Susanna Wesley encouraged her son to read Jeremy Taylor and other authors from the Anglican "Holy Living" school. Wesley began reading Taylor in 1725, and he spoke of the latter's inestimable influence on him. Indeed, Taylor can be said to have been the vehicle through which Wesley was introduced to seventeenth-century English anti-Calvinism.[22]

Wesley was also heavily influenced by the Independent theologian John Goodwin.[23] In his writings, Wesley made numerous positive references to Goodwin, and in 1765 he republished Goodwin's *Imputatio Fidei, or, A Treatise of Justification* (1642). In this work Goodwin diverged radically from Arminius and appropriated Hugo Grotius's governmental understanding of atonement and justification. Goodwin had perhaps more influence on Wesley's doctrine of justification in the last thirty years of his life than any other single thinker.

Wesley's fondness for publishing condensed versions of earlier theological writings for common consumption, he never reprinted anything from Arminius. He did, however, republish some of the soteriological writings from earlier English anti-Calvinists, such as the Independent John Goodwin.

[20]Martin Schmidt, *John Wesley: A Theological Biography*, 3 vols. (New York: Abingdon, 1960), 1:44., While it is more technically accurate to speak of "Anglican anti-Calvinism" rather than "Anglican Arminianism," since Anglican Arminianism did not rely on Arminius, I will use the latter term here because of its wide use.

[21]See Richard P. Heitzenrater, ed., *Diary of an Oxford Methodist: Benjamin Ingham, 1733–34* (Durham, N.C.: Duke Univ. Press, 1985).

[22]*The Works of John Wesley*, ed. Thomas Jackson, 14 vols. (London: Wesley Methodist Book Room, 1872; repr., Grand Rapids: Baker, 1986), 11:366; Richard P. Heitzenrater, *The Elusive Mr. Wesley*, 2 vols. (Nashville: Abingdon, 1984), 2:23; John Deschner, *Wesley's Christology: An Interpretation* (Dallas: Southern Methodist Univ. Press, 1960), 197.

[23]"Independent" is the word used to describe Puritans whose congregations were independent from the Church of England.

Given the diverse sources of Wesley's "Arminianism," it is not surprising that Wesleyan Arminianism is somewhat different from the original Arminianism of Arminius. Still, Wesley and his followers shared many beliefs with Arminius, such as conditional election, universal atonement, the resistibility of grace, and the possibility of apostasy. However, despite the general agreement in the outlines of Arminian belief, Wesley and early disciples such as Adam Clarke, John Fletcher, and Richard Watson nuanced their theology in ways that diverged from Arminius's thought and in many ways agreed more with later Remonstrant thought.

Arminius, for example, held strenuously to a penal satisfaction theory of atonement (cf. the above section). Wesley, however, melded this concept with governmental and other atonement motifs. Clarke, Fletcher, Watson, and nineteenth-century Methodist theologians affirmed the governmental theory of atonement, rejecting the notion of the imputation of Christ's righteousness to believers in justification. This approach to atonement and justification, together with the doctrines of the "second blessing" and entire sanctification, resulted in an approach to the Christian life, assurance, and perseverance in salvation that differed from that of Arminius. While for Arminius loss of salvation came only through ceasing to believe in Christ, Wesleyans held that it could result from either unbelief or unconfessed sin. Yet apostasy could be remedied through renewed repentance.

Wesleyan Arminianism can be found today in the various Methodist bodies, in Holiness groups such as the Church of the Nazarene, the Wesleyan Church, and the Salvation Army, as well as in most traditional Pentecostal-charismatic denominations, who largely have a Wesleyan theological heritage.[24]

In chapter 4, Steve Harper provides insight into the Wesleyan Arminian view of security. He does this by probing the writings of John Wesley, thereby allowing Wesley to "speak for

---

[24]Anabaptists (e.g., Mennonites, Brethren) and Restorationists (e.g., the Churches of Christ, Christian Churches, Disciples of Christ) have traditionally tended toward doctrines of salvation similar to that of Wesleyan Arminianism—without affirming a "second blessing" and entire sanctification. There have always been some in these groups, however, who have espoused a view more akin to Reformed Arminianism. Many traditional Lutherans also affirm the possibility of apostasy and reconversion.

himself." After dealing with aspects of Wesley's historical and theological context, Harper investigates the background doctrines of depravity, grace, atonement, and justification. Then he launches into a discussion of the Wesleyan approach to apostasy, arguing that believers can lose their salvation through one of two means: (1) apostasy through unbelief and (2) unconfessed sin. Believers have the freedom to reject Christ, Harper suggests, and deliberate, voluntary sins, as violations of God's known law, become mortal if not repented of. Because of the radical graciousness of God, loss of salvation can be remedied through renewed repentance and faith.

These four views do not exhaust all the Christian approaches to the doctrine of eternal security. However, they are the perspectives that best represent what most Protestants have traditionally believed about perseverance. I have made every effort to give each contributor considerable freedom in setting forth the case for his view in the way he thinks is most effective. The result is a lively, and sometimes surprising, interchange that I hope will stimulate more productive dialogue on the questions of perseverance and apostasy.

Chapter One

A CLASSICAL CALVINIST VIEW

Michael S. Horton

A CLASSICAL CALVINIST VIEW

Michael S. Horton

"This grace [God] placed 'in Christ in whom we have obtained a lot, being predestined according to the purpose of Him who worketh all things.' And thus as He worketh that we come to Him, so He worketh that we do not depart."[1] As part of his *Predestination of the Saints*, Augustine patiently explained and passionately defended the radical graciousness of God in Christ. The recipients of this epistle were two leading monks who had expressed acute anxiety over the debates on these questions in their monasteries. Some feared that the good news was just too good to be true; others were convinced that Scripture itself cautioned against confidence in an already certain and secure salvation.

The topic before us has its origins not in Calvin or in the Synod of Dort, nor indeed even in Augustine. It is a perennial question for anyone who wrestles with the Word of God, seeking a unified biblical teaching on the most practical and self-involving question of all: What is the basis for hoping in God's promised salvation? In the brief compass of this chapter, we will argue that covenant theology explains the full range of the biblical witness more consistently than either the Arminian or eternal security positions have done.

Many of us who have been reared in evangelical circles know a lot of people who designate themselves Calvinists simply

---

[1] Augustine, "On The Gift of Perseverance," chap. 16 in Philip Schaff, ed., *A Select Library of the Nicene and Post-Nicene Fathers of the Christian Church*, vol. 5: *Anti-Pelagian Writings* (Edinburgh: T. & T. Clark, repr. 1991).

because they believe in eternal security, even if they do not accept total depravity, unconditional election, particular redemption, and irresistible grace. For instance, Norman Geisler identifies himself as a "Moderate Calvinist," while his stated positions, most recently in *Chosen But Free*, largely represent classic Arminianism: "God's grace works synergistically on free will.... Put in other terms, God's justifying grace works cooperatively, not operatively."[2] Elsewhere he writes, "Indeed, God would save all men if He could.... God will achieve the greatest number in heaven that He possibly can.... Each creature is free to accept or reject the grace of God in salvation. Of course, God determinately knew from all eternity who would and who would not believe."[3] Those who actually embrace the so-called five points of Calvinism, however, Geisler repeatedly labels "extreme Calvinists."

While this approach may be rhetorically effective, it represents a considerable misunderstanding of the historical positions. Those who embrace eternal security are not for that reason Calvinists—even Moderate Calvinists. In fact, eternal security itself is not a Calvinistic doctrine but, at least in the expressions with which I am familiar, rests on Arminian presuppositions concerning grace and free will. If this is the case (as I hope will become more apparent as we progress), then our editor has wisely distinguished the Reformed position on this subject from both Arminian and eternal security perspectives.

What, then, is a Calvinistic or Reformed account of the believer's perseverance? We will first examine the passages proponents of the eternal security position use, followed by analysis of those texts Arminians adduce; then we will conclude with the covenantal approach.

THE "ETERNAL SECURITY" PASSAGES

Lewis Sperry Chafer introduces his defense of eternal security by referring to the Calvinist-Arminian debate, the former representing (according to Chafer) the eternal security position.[4] One

[2]Norman L. Geisler, *Chosen But Free* (Minneapolis: Bethany House, 1999), 233.

[3]Norman Geisler, "God, Evil, and Dispensations," in *Walvoord: A Tribute*, ed. Donald K. Campbell (Chicago: Moody, 1982), 102, 108.

[4]Lewis Sperry Chafer, *Major Bible Themes*, rev. by John Walvoord (Grand Rapids: Zondervan, 1981), 220.

might assume, therefore, that Chafer identifies himself with Calvinism. But just pages later, in the discussion of election, he writes, "God chose the plan as a whole, not piecemeal. He knew in advance, before the choice of a plan, who in this plan would be saved and who would not be saved. By faith we must assume that God chose the best possible plan." He expressly adds that "election may be seen to proceed from [the] omniscience of God."[5]

How then does Chafer understand the security of the believer? While referring its solidity to the Father's work, the Son's work, and the Spirit's work, he does not refer to election in the first case or to effectual grace in the third. Instead, a somewhat mechanical view of salvation emerges, in which Chafer argues that once a person is regenerated (which is the result of human decision),[6] the process cannot be reversed. On one hand, Chafer insists that such security rests on the fact that salvation is God's work from beginning to end. Yet on the other hand, he argues that it rests on the fact that God foreknows human response and responds to human decision by granting new life. Thus, the more consistent Arminian, it seems to me, is perfectly justified in asking how the new birth is irreversible if it rests at least in part on the human will. If we placed ourselves in God's hands, surely we can place ourselves outside of them.

Nevertheless, Chafer appeals to many solid proof texts for the security of salvation. John's Gospel is replete with such firm and famous promises: Believers are given "eternal life" (John 3:16). "I tell you the truth," Jesus says, "whoever hears my word and believes him who sent me has eternal life and will not be condemned; he has crossed over from death to life" (5:24). "All that the Father gives me will come to me, and whoever comes to me I will never drive away.... And this is the will of him who sent me, that I shall lose none of all that he has given me, but raise them up at the last day" (6:37–39). Merely to read Romans 8:29–39 is apparently to lay the whole debate to rest: Sight of the unbroken chain of salvation leads the apostle himself to doxological heights. That God is able to keep believers is defended from John 10:29; Romans 4:21; 8:31, 38–39; 14:4; Ephesians 1:19–21; 3:20; Philippians 3:21; 2 Timothy 1:12; Hebrews 7:25; Jude 24.

---

[5]Ibid., 232–33.

[6]Regeneration "is entirely a supernatural act of God in response to the faith of man" (ibid., 99).

Furthermore, to admit the possibility of losing one's salvation is tantamount to denying the sufficiency of Christ's saving work (Rom. 3:25–26; 1 John 2:2).[7] Christ has carried away all sins for all time—there is no out-sinning divine grace (Rom. 5:20–21). Beyond this, the resurrection of Jesus secured everlasting new life (Rom. 6:23; Col. 2:12; 3:1), and the believer who is "in Christ" is no longer under any condemnation since Jesus is no longer under condemnation (Rom. 8:1). Chafer also refers to Christ's present intercession as our advocate, a role in which Jesus would be a failure were any of those for whom he interceded to be lost. The Spirit's regenerating work cannot be reversed (John 1:13; 3:3–6; Titus 3:4–6; 1 Peter 1:23; 2 Peter 1:4; 1 John 3:9), and the Spirit is the permanent possession of every believer (John 7:37–39; Rom. 5:5; 8:9; 1 Cor. 2:12; 6:19; 1 John 2:27).

Of course, more texts could be adduced, but these are surely sufficient to make the point that God's salvific work on behalf of sinners is indefectible. Believers have every confidence to approach God's throne knowing that their salvation is settled in the heavenly places (Eph. 2:1–5). But then there are the other passages.

THE "ARMINIAN" PASSAGES

Citing Wesley, Wakefield, and others, Arminian theologian H. Orton Wiley recognizes that Arminianism denies the notion of the imputation of Christ's obedience to believers. Wesley said, "The judgment of an all-wise God is always according to truth; neither can it ever consist with His unerring wisdom to think that I am innocent, to judge that I am righteous or holy because another is so. He can no more confound me with Christ than with David or Abraham."[8] Wiley himself concludes, "The personal acts of Christ were of too lofty a character to be imputed to mankind," and those who claim to be robed in "the glorious attire of the Divine Redeemer" are accused of possessing an attitude that "is not characteristic of the humility of the genuine Christian."[9]

---

[7]Ibid., 225.

[8]Cited in H. Orton Wiley, *Christian Theology*, 3 vols. (Kansas City, Mo.: Beacon Hill, 1952), 2:396–97.

[9]Ibid., 2:397.

Despite comments from Wesley that appear to support the evangelical doctrine of justification, such comments as those above represent the criticisms of the Council of Trent against the Reformers' teaching. From the Reformed standpoint, the Arminian denial of the perseverance of the saints is an implication of its synergism (that is, viewing salvation as a process of cooperation between God and the believer). For many of the same reasons that Rome had difficulty with the Reformers' insistence on the objectivity of a divinely effected salvation, Arminian theology regards a full doctrine of justification by Christ's imputed righteousness as "antinomian."[10]

The fifth point of the Remonstrant (Arminian) articles reads as follows:

> That they who are united to Christ by faith are thereby furnished with abundant strength and succor sufficient to enable them to triumph over the seductions of Satan, and the allurements of sin; nevertheless they may, by the neglect of these succors, fall from grace, and, dying in such a state, may finally perish. This point was started at first doubtfully, but afterward positively as a settled doctrine.[11]

This is not the place to get into the subject of Christian perfection or "entire sanctification," but this notion, on which Wesley and his followers have insisted, is integrally related to the Wesleyan Arminian understanding of the believer's perseverance. Ironically, Chafer has more in common with Wiley on this point than he does with Calvinism. Chafer denies unconditional election, particular redemption, and irresistible grace. But he also denies the perseverance of the saints and wrongly concludes that "eternal security" is the Calvinistic position. He further maintains that there are two classes of Christians: "carnal" and "spiritual"—a distinction that demonstrates some affinity for at least a Wesleyan separation of justification and sanctification as requiring two distinct acts of faith.

However, full-fledged Arminians (including Wesleyans) have their own proof texts for the possibility of falling from

---

[10]Of the many examples we could cite, Wiley represents this accusation; see ibid., 1:77, 351; 2:383, 396.

[11]Cited in ibid., 2:351.

grace and, consequently, of losing salvation. Why would the psalmist plead with God not to "cast me from your presence or take your Holy Spirit from me" (Ps. 51:11) if such were not possible? Believers are known by their fruit (John 8:31; 15:6; 1 Cor. 15:12; Heb. 3:6–14; James 2:14–26; 2 Peter 1:10; 1 John 3:10). Did Jesus not tell the disciples, "Remain in me, and I will remain in you" (John 15:4)? "If you obey my commands, you will remain in my love, just as I have obeyed my Father's commands and remain in his love.... You are my friends if you do what I command" (15:10–14). Jesus will separate the sheep from the goats on the last day according to their respective responses to caring for the poor (Matt. 25:31–46). There is the familiar warning in 1 Corinthians 3:12–14:

> If any man builds on this foundation using gold, silver, costly stones, wood, hay or straw, his work will be shown for what it is, because the Day will bring it to light. It will be revealed with fire, and the fire will test the quality of each man's work. If what he has built survives, he will receive his reward.

Of all the texts, however, those found in Hebrews appear to be the most supportive of the Arminian position. First, there is Hebrews 6:4–8:

> It is impossible for those who have once been enlightened, who have tasted the heavenly gift, who have shared in the Holy Spirit, who have tasted the goodness of the word of God and the powers of the coming age, if they fall away, to be brought back to repentance, because to their loss they are crucifying the Son of God all over again and subjecting him to public disgrace.
> Land that drinks in the rain often falling on it and that produces a crop useful to those for whom it is farmed receives the blessing of God. But land that produces thorns and thistles is worthless and is in danger of being cursed. In the end, it will be burned.

Hebrews 10:26–29, 36 is as straightforward about the matter:

> If we deliberately keep on sinning after we have received the knowledge of the truth, no sacrifice for sins is left, but only a fearful expectation of judgment and of raging fire that will consume the enemies of God. Any-

one who rejected the law of Moses died without mercy on the testimony of two or three witnesses. How much more severely do you think a man deserves to be punished who has trampled the Son of God under foot, who has treated as an unholy thing the blood of the covenant that sanctified him, and who has insulted the Spirit of grace? . . .

You need to persevere so that when you have done the will of God, you will receive what he has promised.

Calls to perseverance are replete in Scripture and must be taken seriously. In our estimation, many of those who defend "eternal security" do not take these passages seriously enough. For instance, in his discussion of Matthew 24:13 ("but he who stands firm to the end will be saved"), Chafer argues, "The verse refers to those who survive the Tribulation and are rescued by Jesus Christ at His second coming."[12] Warnings about losing divine approval have to do with rewards, fellowship (as opposed to relationship) with God, temporal blessings, and the like, says Chafer.[13] When Paul warns the Galatians that they may have fallen from grace, Chafer concludes, "[Their] fall is from a standard of life, not from a work of salvation."[14]

How then can we do justice to both sets of proof texts? We often hear Christians say, "Well, they have their verses, and we have ours"—as if to suggest that the Scriptures are unclear and indeed contradictory. If it is true that there are "eternal security" verses and "Arminian" verses in the Scriptures, then we can no longer consistently affirm that God's Word tells one story or that it is united by divine authorship. Most readers of this book will probably not want to conclude that Scripture is a collection of merely human reflections on religious experience; thus, we have to do better than leaving the two sets of proof texts out there as two sides of a scale-pan that keep us in balance. We need to discover what Scripture teaches and not attempt to strike our own "balance" between two positions.

In science, a paradigm (or model of incorporating all of the relevant data) lasts only as long as it can account not only for the data that seem explicitly to infer it but for anomalies as well.

---

[12]Chafer, *Major Bible Themes*, 223.
[13]Ibid., 222.
[14]Ibid., 223.

The same is true in theology. A doctrine or system of doctrines must account for the whole range of biblical teaching, even offering a plausible accounting of texts that seem at first blush irreconcilable with the system. Scripture itself offers us this "paradigm" or explanatory grid without our having to impose something from the outside. That paradigm is *the covenant*.

THE COVENANTAL PARADIGM

Covenant theology emphasizes three distinct covenants: the covenant of redemption, the covenant of works, and the covenant of grace. *The covenant of redemption* refers to the everlasting pact made between the persons of the Trinity to elect, redeem, and restore a people for God's glory. Made in eternity past, there is no human partner involved, and the Son has been made the trustee of his people. The Father elected and gave a people to the Son as an inheritance, entrusting the Son with their safekeeping. It is to this covenant that Scripture refers when, for instance, it is said that we were "chosen in him [the Son] ... to be holy and blameless in his sight" (Eph. 1:4), a wisdom "that has been hidden and that God destined for our glory before time began" (1 Cor. 2:7).

It is what Jesus refers to when he declares, "All that the Father gives me will come to me, and whoever comes to me I will never drive away. For I have come down from heaven not to do my will but to do the will of him who sent me. And this is the will of him who sent me, that I shall lose none of all that he has given me, but raise them up at the last day" (John 6:37–39). Notice the close connection between the Son's being sent by the Father and the rescue mission for "all that he has given me." Later in John's Gospel these people are likened to sheep: "I lay down my life for the sheep," he says, telling the religious leaders who interrogated him (10:15, 26–30):

> ... but you do not believe because you are not my sheep. My sheep listen to my voice; I know them, and they follow me. I give them eternal life, and they shall never perish; no one can snatch them out of my hand. My Father, who has given them to me, is greater than all; no one can snatch them out of my Father's hand. I and the Father are one.

Notice here the extent to which the salvation of those given to the Son by the Father is bound up with the intra-Trinitarian solidarity. And in Jesus' prayer in John 17, where he speaks of himself in the third person, we read, "For you granted him authority over all people that he might give eternal life to all those you have given him" (John 17:2). Here again some of the most explicit Trinitarian statements coincide with explicit covenant-of-redemption statements: "I have brought you glory on earth by completing the work you gave me to do. And now, Father, glorify me in your presence with the glory I had with you before the world began" (17:4–5). Furthermore, "I have revealed you to those whom you gave me out of the world. They were yours; you gave them to me and they have obeyed your word.... I pray for them. I am not praying for the world, but for those you have given me, for they are yours. All I have is yours, and all you have is mine" (17:6, 9–10). Lest anyone interpret this as referring only to the apostles, Jesus adds, "My prayer is not for them alone. I pray also for those who will believe in me through their message, that all of them may be one, Father, just as you are in me and I am in you" (17:20–21). Jesus intercedes, not for the world, but for "those whom you have given me," whether from the immediate circle of disciples or "those who will believe in me through their message."

The Holy Spirit applies the benefits of Christ to the elect; this is part of the covenant of redemption as well. So in time, he brings the elect to repentance and faith. It is no wonder, then, that when a number of people received Christ in Antioch, it is reported in the following manner: "... and all who were appointed for eternal life believed" (Acts 13:48). After all, "those [God] predestined, he also called; those he called, he also justified; those he justified, he also glorified.... Who will bring any charge against those whom God has chosen?" (Rom. 8:30, 33). Because of this intra-Trinitarian solidarity, the Redeemer is left at the end of the story announcing upon his royal ascension, in the words of Isaiah's prophecy, "Here am I, and the children God has given me" (Heb. 2:13). It is the reason that Christ's sacrifice is called "the blood of the eternal covenant" (13:20), since those whom the Father gave to the Son were predestined "unto obedience and sprinkling of the blood of Jesus Christ" (1 Peter 1:2, KJV).

Next, there is the *covenant of works*, otherwise known as the covenant of nature (*foedus naturae*) or the covenant of creation. It originates not in eternity but in time, and not simply between the persons of the Trinity but between the triune Godhead and the creature whom God fashioned in his own image. While we do not have the space here to build the case, all of the elements of the ancient Near Eastern covenants or treaties are present in Genesis 2:8–3:24. God relates to Adam not according to grace but according to justice, since this was the original condition in which he was created. Every such covenant had a historical prologue justifying the covenant-maker's authority, a clear set of stipulations, and a list of both rewards and sanctions (blessings and curses) for violating the treaty.

The opening chapters of Genesis follow this pattern closely, with the historical prologue—the justifying narrative of God's authority over his creatures and his desire to incorporate humanity into his own everlasting rest in the seventh day. This is followed by stipulations (viz., not to eat of the Tree of the Knowledge of Good and Evil), the narrative of violation, and the divine invocation of sanctions. The curses are consummated in the act of divine eviction from the common land that God had made his temple-garden of communion with his creation. Had Adam fulfilled the probation in the garden, God would have confirmed him and his descendants in righteousness and ever-lasting life forever (represented by the Tree of Life), so that there could never be a fall. However, Adam's disobedience not only barred him and all of humanity in him from remaining righteous and in communion with God but also aborted his enjoyment of the consummation, entrance into the Holy of Holies—not just the earthly copy in Eden but the heavenly temple itself. He fell short of the pleasures of God's seventh-day rest.

Nevertheless, even in the middle of judgment, God promised another covenant, *the covenant of grace*, which he fore-shadowed not only in word but also in deed, replacing Adam's and Eve's fig leaves with the skins of a sacrifice. Through Seth's descendants, the line of descent for the seed of the woman who would crush the serpent's head came down to Abraham and Sarah. With Abraham, God officially ratified the covenant of grace. As Paul emphasizes in his letter to the Galatians, God did not make this covenant with Abraham and the nation of Israel that would come from his loins but with Abraham and his Seed, meaning Christ (Gal. 3:16).

In fact, through this covenant, all nations would be blessed in Abraham as his offspring. Yet there was a national covenant as well, alongside the covenant of grace. God promised to give Abraham's physical descendants a land, a new Eden, where God would once more descend and tabernacle in the midst of his people. Nevertheless, this was a typological kingdom, not the final rest that was promised to Adam and to Abraham, as the New Testament makes amply clear. As Hebrews 11:13–16 makes plain, these patriarchs

> all died in faith, not having received the promises, but having seen them afar off were assured of them, embraced them and confessed that they were strangers and pilgrims on the earth. For those who say such things declare plainly that they seek a homeland. . . . But now they desire a better, that is, a heavenly country. Therefore God is not ashamed to be called their God, for he has prepared a city for them. (NKJV)

But the typological city was a copy, as Eden was, of God's presence among his people. When God made his covenant with Moses, he did two things in renewing his oath to Abraham: He promised to save all who trusted in his promise, and he promised to give Israel a land. God issued the former as a gracious covenant, dependent solely on his sovereign initiative— the oath he swore to Abraham and his Seed. The latter was to be, like the covenant made with Adam in the garden, a conditional covenant, dependent on the servant's fidelity to the great king.

The distinction between these two covenants, grace and works, running simultaneously side-by-side in the Mosaic economy, becomes more explicit in retrospect, as the pattern of the fall in Eden is repeated in Canaan. Redeemed from Egypt through the separation of waters and led by the pillar of cloud by day and fire by night (the separation of day from night), God's new servant, Israel, was made to see the dry land appear, making a habitable place for communion with God. God descended once more and made his dwelling with his people in an earthly temple that served as a replica or small-scale copy of the heavenly temple.

While individual salvation was assured by faith in the promise (Heb. 4:2), the typological kingdom was conditional. No Israelite could be saved simply because of his or her genealogy, and occasionally outsiders were saved apart from it. But Israel was God's garden as long as obedience was maintained.

We know what happened in this case, as in Adam's. The servant capitulated to the serpent's vain promises of the glory, power, and prosperity of the nations. On that portentous day, God evacuated the temple and exiled his people from his typological land. Ever since, as the apostle Paul reminds us, Jerusalem represents not the glorious liberty of Sarah's sons but the tragic captivity of Hagar's slaves (Gal. 4:21–31). The covenant of works was again violated by the servant, and the servant was cast out as Adam and Hagar had been. The covenant of works and the covenant of grace are in antithesis, as Paul emphasizes for the Galatians who had confused Law and Gospel: "For these are the two covenants: the one from Mount Sinai which gives birth to bondage, which is Hagar ... but the Jerusalem above is free, which is the mother of us all" (Gal. 4:24, 26, NKJV).

At last, the promised Seed of the woman arrives, that Seed to whom (with Abraham) God swore an unchangeable promise. This second Adam and new Israel is also faced with the serpent's enticement to secure his own glorious destiny apart from obedience to the Father's will. Yet this time the Servant sends the serpent away and exposes him to public ridicule by his triumph on the cross. Jesus Christ fulfills the terms of the covenant of works, obeying in the place of those whom the Father had given him. Then by his Spirit he enters into a covenant of grace with his people. It is because the covenant of works has been fully satisfied, not canceled, that the covenant of grace rests on an unshakable foundation. It is not the case that the original creation covenant is left behind but that finally the elect representative endures the probation successfully, absorbs the curse for its violation, and wins for his people at last the right to eat from the Tree of Life in the garden of God (Rev. 22:1–5). In Christ, believers are covenant-keepers, not covenant-breakers.

Still, the covenant of grace requires acceptance. It is an unconditional covenant in the sense that God himself has promised to satisfy his justice and even to give the repentance and faith that are necessary for us to be reconciled to him. But we must respond as the gospel is now proclaimed to us: "Therefore, since the promise of entering his rest still stands, let us be careful that none of you be found to have fallen short of it. For we also have had the gospel preached to us, just as they [those who perished in the desert] did; but the message they heard was of no value to them, because those who heard did not combine it with faith" (Heb. 4:1–2). The promise held out to the true children of Abraham, Jew and Gentile alike, is not only the enjoyment of freedom from the condemnation, power, and presence of sin—a sort of restoration to the original creation—but also the consummation that humanity has never known. Jesus has been repatriated into that Sabbath rest and even now is preparing a place, a true and abiding garden, where we will at last be confirmed in righteousness and blessedness forever.

It is only within this context that the disputed passages seem to come together in one narrative tapestry. First, there are the "eternal security" passages. They are all anchored in the decree issued in the covenant of redemption—that eternal, intra-Trinitarian pact—not in human response. Believers are not secure in Christ because they have made a decision and now God is, in a sense, "stuck" with them regardless of whether they bear fruit and persevere. It is not simply "once saved, always saved," but rather "those he predestined, he also called; those he called, he also justified; those he justified, he also glorified" (Rom. 8:30). In this covenant of grace, there are two sides: "I will be your God, and you will be my people." God graciously gives perseverance in repentance and faith—not just in the first instance, once and for all, but for the rest of our Christian lives in the desert. But we must respond to this word in repentance and faith.

So the warnings that are cited by Arminian theologians are real. Let us look at the Hebrews passages especially for a moment. As we have seen from Hebrews 4, the question posed is not whether those who have entered God's rest can be expelled from it but rather whether those who are in the desert will "fall short of it" (Heb. 4:1). Written primarily to persuade Jewish Christians during the persecution not to return to Judaism to avoid martyrdom, Hebrews labors to show that the old covenant represents the shadows while the new covenant is the reality. Now we are better prepared to understand the warnings.

In Hebrews 6 we read of the impossibility for "those who have once been enlightened, who have tasted the heavenly gift, who have shared in the Holy Spirit, who have tasted the goodness of the word of God and the powers of the coming age" to be renewed to repentance if they fall away, since "they are crucifying the Son of God all over again and subjecting him to public disgrace" (Heb. 6:4–6). The "eternal security" position can explain this only by suggesting that this is a hypothetical warning; that is, it never actually happens that people who enjoy these spiritual benefits fall away and lose them.

But that does not seem to do justice to the text. First, it speaks of the impossibility of their being renewed to repentance. Second, it suggests that they "are crucifying the Son of God all over again." Surely we are dealing with people who not only claim to have been introduced to the realm of God's gracious activity but in fact have experienced the benefits enumerated in verses 4–5. The "eternal security" position falls short of explaining the passage.

On the other hand, the Arminian exegesis apparently fails to place this warning in the context of covenantal history and even within the context of the passage itself. For instance, the warning is immediately followed with: "Dear friends, we are confident of better things in your case—things that accompany salvation" (Heb. 6:9). Why would the writer distinguish the lapsed from his general readership along the lines of "things that accompany salvation" if there is not some sense in which one could enjoy the benefits described in verses 4–5 without necessarily being regenerated and justified?

A covenantal interpretation appears to offer a third alternative that does greater justice to the text. Abraham "received the sign of circumcision, a seal of the righteousness that he had by faith while he was still uncircumcised" (Rom. 4:11). Consequently, according to God's command, Abraham circumcised his children, sealing them in God's covenant of grace. However, this was true not only of Isaac but of Ishmael as well, and not only of Isaac's son Jacob but his son Esau as well. Even during the old administration, the circle of the covenant was larger than the circle of election.

This is Paul's central argument in Romans 9, against the charge that God has failed to keep his promise to Abraham. If we interpret the warnings of being broken off in Romans 9–11 as supporting the notion that those who are genuinely regenerated and justified can lose their salvation, we will miss Paul's point. After all, it is branches that fail to produce fruit that are broken off—that is, members of the covenant who nevertheless fall short of truly embracing the word that is preached. They have a title deed to God's salvation, but they, like Esau, sell it for immediate gratification in this world.

That is why, in Hebrews 6, such people are compared to "land that drinks in the rain often falling on it" but bears thorns instead of fruit (v. 7). It is not that they are regenerated and justified, experiencing sanctification, but then fall away and lose their salvation. Rather, it is that the covenant of grace is that sanctified sphere of the Spirit's work in which a covenant child can experience everything mentioned in verses 4–5. Such a person can be the recipient of the Spirit's sealing in baptism and of the promise of forgiveness in the Supper ("tasting the heavenly gift"), and can in some real sense "share in the Holy Spirit" through word and sacrament, because through these means a member of the covenant, even if he or she does not drink, can "taste . . . the powers of the coming age."

If there is no distinction in being a child of the covenant, although unregenerate and unbelieving, then surely the writer to the Hebrews would not have set his readers apart as those of whom something even better could be said, having experienced the things that accompany salvation itself and not only covenantal incorporation. Covenant theology can integrate both sets of proof texts precisely because it recognizes a third category besides "saved" and "unsaved": the person who belongs to the covenant community and experiences thereby the work of the Spirit through the means of grace, and yet is not regenerate.

So the problem, it seems to me, in a lot of exegesis on this issue is due to the fact that neither the "eternal security" nor the Arminian position appears to have a category for a person who is in the covenant but not personally united by living faith to Jesus Christ. Only with this category can we understand Jesus' warning about abiding in him, as branches in the vine, without surrendering the immutability of God's saving grace. Our covenant children must abide in the Vine, or they will be broken off. Born into the covenant of grace, like all of Abraham's offspring, they must nevertheless be united to Christ through faith. The warnings that Jesus and the writer to the Hebrews issue are challenges not merely to belong to the covenant externally but to embrace the reality that the covenant promises and conveys by the Spirit through the word and sacraments.

And when, in Hebrews 10, the writer warns Jewish believers of falling under a sentence far greater than any under Moses if they willfully "trample the Son of God under foot" (Heb. 10:26–29), this must be seen in this same context. If these professing Christians want to return to the shadows of the law, they are rejecting the reality to which they pointed. They are rejecting any hope of salvation, since they are rejecting the only High Priest who can present them blameless before God's throne. But again, the writer is confident that this will not be the case of his readers:

> Therefore, brothers, since we have confidence to enter the Most Holy Place [access to which was denied under the old covenant] by the blood of Jesus, by a new and living way opened for us through the curtain, that is, his body, and since we have a great priest over the house of God, let us draw near to God with a sincere heart in full assurance of faith, having our hearts sprinkled to cleanse us from a guilty conscience and having our bodies washed with pure water. Let us hold unswervingly to the hope we profess, for he who promised is faithful. (Heb. 10:19–23)

Thus, Jesus' words must be taken at face value: "He who stands firm to the end will be saved" (Mark 13:13). Furthermore, those who abide in Christ will persevere to the end, since it is his everlasting life and righteousness that nourishes them, his strength that upholds them, the sap of his obedience to the Father's will that is not only imputed to them as their righteousness but also imparted to them as living branches of his vine. This is precisely how Paul argues it in Romans 11:11–24.

What good, then, is it to belong to the covenant community, where the Spirit operates in saving rather than in common grace, if many who belong to it evidently fall away? Is there any real benefit? Or, as Paul expresses the question in relation to the old administration in Romans 3:1–4:

> What advantage, then, is there in being a Jew, or what value is there in circumcision? Much in every way! First of all, they have been entrusted with the very words of God. What if some did not have faith? Will their lack of faith nullify God's faithfulness? Not at all! Let God be true, and every man a liar.

Neither the dispensationalist nor the nondispensationalist Arminian has any category for this person who enjoys the benefits of the covenant but falls away from its reality.

A concluding warning should be extended. These very passages that Arminians cite do not focus on the possibility of losing one's salvation by dying in a state of mortal sin, nor on losing one's regeneration (which is identified as an "imperishable seed," 1 Peter 1:23), or being subjected to wrath even after having been justified. Rather, they focus on those who seek to enter God's promised land, not on the basis of his promise but on the basis of their own effort (Rom. 10:1–13; 11:5–10; Heb. 4:10). A covenant of works will present Jesus' parable of the vine and branches as a conditional salvation: "Do this and you shall live." But a covenant of grace will present it, as Jesus did himself, as an unconditional salvation: "Live and you shall do this." After all, he introduces it with these words: "I am the true vine, and my Father is the gardener" (John 15:1). We are in Christ because of the Father's electing will, the Son's redemptive work, and the Spirit's persevering grace:

> He cuts off every branch in me that bears no fruit [even if one is a physical descendant of Abraham], while every branch that does bear fruit he prunes, so that it will be even more fruitful. You are already clean because of the word I have spoken to you.
> . . . You did not choose me, but I chose you and appointed you to go and bear fruit—fruit that will last. Then the Father will give you whatever you ask in my name. (John 15:2–3, 16)

Falling away is a grim reality. There are those who utterly reject the promise that belongs by inheritance to the covenant community. They thereby remove themselves from the covenant of grace and place themselves under the covenant of works. There no longer remains a sacrifice for their sins, but they will stand trial and bear the sentence themselves on the Last Day. The visible church is filled with hypocrites who outwardly have shown signs of faith and repentance but have never been truly united to Christ through faith alone. As illustrated in the parable of the sower and the seed, tough times come and these plants wither. In his time, the gardener will separate the weeds from his garden, but in this age they grow up together and are only distinguishable when the weeds die and are cleared away from the field.

Yet this should not discourage the seed planted by the gardener, since the Son of Man, unlike the Pharisees, does not break off the broken reed but tenderly nurtures it back to health. To those, however, who rest on their physical descent (either from Abraham or from Christian parents), who are confident in their baptism rather than in the promise of which it is the sign and seal, and who are content with a merely external relation to Jesus Christ, all of these warnings we have considered come crashing down around them. Those who boast in their merely external relation to Christ in the new covenant are in no better position than those in the old:

> You will say then, "Branches were broken off that I could be grafted in." Granted. But they were broken off because of unbelief, and you stand by faith. Do not be arrogant, but be afraid. For if God did not spare the natural branches, he will not spare you either.
>
> Consider therefore the kindness and sternness of God: sternness to those who fell, but kindness to you, provided that you continue in his kindness. Otherwise, you also will be cut off. (Rom. 11:19–22)

As a concluding comment, there is something that I would like to offer in the way of a pastoral application. While Reformed Christians do not believe that God's moral law is abrogated or in any way superseded, they have historically shared the Lutheran concern to distinguish Law and Gospel. Everything in Scripture that commands without offering assistance is "Law," and everything in Scripture that promises without threats is "Gospel." Scripture consists of both Law and Gospel running throughout. But the tendency of many Christians today is to seek "balance" by finding some via media between what they regard as extremes. Thus, "Law" passages become watered down with "Gospel," while "Gospel" passages become diluted with "Law." The result is a message that, instead of presenting the seriousness of sin in all of its damning force and the graciousness of the Gospel in all of its overwhelming freeness, ends up proclaiming a single message in which the bad news and good news are mingled. The bad news is not as bad as Scripture represents it, and the good news is not all that good.

When we are considering a subject as essential as this, we should beware of the policy of blending opposites. Instead of taking a middle path between eternal security and Arminianism, we should allow "Law" passages to really be Law and the "Gospel" passages to really be Gospel. Chafer, for instance, regards the warnings as pertaining especially to the loss of rewards. This has led to unnecessary anxiety on the part of those who fear becoming "carnal Christians" who lose their rewards. Charles Stanley similarly explains that Matthew 25:30, warning of being cast into outer darkness "where there will be weeping and gnashing of teeth," actually refers not to hell, but a place

> in the kingdom of God but outside the circle of men and women whose faithfulness on this earth earned them a special rank or position of authority. The kingdom of God will not be the same for all believers.... Some will reign with Christ; others will not (2 Tim.2:12). Some will be rich in the kingdom of God; others will be poor (see Luke 12:21, 33).[15]

So the bad news is not quite as bad: We are talking about a place in heaven, not in hell; but the good news is not quite as good, since one could actually be "saved" (and thus eternally secure) and yet spend eternity in poverty, unhappiness, and indeed suffering.

However, 1 Corinthians 3:12–15 is not talking about either losing salvation or rewards in the sense that Chafer or Stanley has in view. Here again the context is essential. Paul is discussing the ministries of apostles and those commissioned by them. He says, "I laid a foundation ... and someone else is building on it" (1 Cor. 3:10). The apostolic era was foundational, and those who try to lay another foundation—that is, gather their own sectarian

---

[15]Charles Stanley, *Eternal Security: Can You Be Sure?* (Nashville: Thomas Nelson, 1990), 121–29.

following—will watch their ministries "go up in smoke" on the Day of Judgment. This simply cannot be stretched to cover rewards in general.

Whatever in Scripture, then, causes the believer to fear God's wrath should be accepted as God's perpetual verdict on the salvific efficacy of the believer's decisions, habits, and works. But then the believer must turn to the gospel for the solution to this anxiety and not to a greater resolve at satisfying God's commands. The latter, in fact, is the result of turning to the external gospel rather than to inner resources. No longer slaves but sons, believers never have to fear condemnation, not because they have decided to follow Jesus but because Jesus has decided to follow them, keep them, and lead them safely to the land he has prepared for them. Not one of his sheep will be lost—simply because of that eternal covenant that God swore to himself, in the intra-Trinitarian fellowship.

There will be those on the Last Day, Jesus reminded us, who have called him "Lord" but in truth disown him. These are not people who have been regenerated and justified but those who "went out from us, but they did not really belong to us. For if they had belonged to us, they would have remained with us; but their going showed that none of them belonged to us" (1 John 2:19). While it is true that "if we disown him, he will also disown us," it is equally true that "if we are faithless, he will remain faithful, for he cannot disown himself" (2 Tim. 2:12–13). Those who disown the blessings of the covenant of grace will suffer the consequences of being violators of the covenant of works, but those who own Christ and his benefits will be preserved in faith and repentance despite the believer's weakness, half-heartedness, and failures in exercising both.

God cannot cast away those whom he has elected, placed in Christ, redeemed by Christ, and united to Christ without violating his eternal oath. It is not because of the principle of "once saved, always saved," but because of the promise that the God who began the work of salvation will complete it (Phil. 1:6; 2:13). No genuine Christian will revert to being either unregenerate or "carnal." God will see to it that the believer, who is always in this life simultaneously justified and sinful, will persevere, enduring the struggle with sin and suffering, until he or she beholds the Lamb who was slain sitting upon his throne.

A MODERATE CALVINIST RESPONSE TO MICHAEL S. HORTON

Norman L. Geisler

AREAS OF AGREEMENT

There are many points of agreement between the Moderate Calvinism espoused here and the strong Calvinist position. One of the most basic, of course, is our common rejection of the claim that regenerate persons can lose their salvation. Since I have set forth arguments for eternal security completely in my own article, I need not repeat them here, except to emphasize that salvation is a work of God's unconditional grace (Rom. 11:29). Hence, there is nothing any creature can do to void it (8:38–39).

We also agree that doctrine must be based on what the Bible teaches, not on what balances opposite views. On the one hand, theological truth does not result from any Aristotelian golden mean or so-called Hegelian synthesis. Often, on the other hand, extreme digressions from the truth go about equally in opposite directions. Hence, the truth, based on God's revelation, *appears* to be a synthesis of the partial truths in these extreme views. This is indeed the case with Moderate Calvinism, which embraces both of the polar truths of real sovereignty and actual free will. Strong Calvinism emphasizes the former to the neglect of the latter, whereas Arminianism stresses the latter to the neglect of the former.

We also agree with strong Calvinists that Jesus did not intercede for the world in John 17 but only for the elect. For he emphatically stated "*I am not praying for the world*, but for those you have given me, for they are yours" (John 17:9, italics added). Certainly Jesus has a special love for his bride. Of course, unlike the strong Calvinists, Moderate Calvinists hold that Christ desires all to be part of his bride (cf. Matt. 23:37; 1 Tim. 2:4; 2 Peter 3:9) so that they can experience this special love.

We also agree with strong Calvinists that eternal security is based on an intra-Trinitarian act of election. It is not based on our free will (John 1:13), nor on our good works (Eph. 2:8–9), but on God's grace alone (Titus 3:5–7). As Paul declared, "And if by grace, then it is no longer by works; if it were, grace would no longer be grace" (Rom. 11:6). Arminians, by contrast, must in the final analysis deny that the source of salvation is God alone. They hold that God's election is *based on* his foreknowledge of a human being's free choice. But Moderate Calvinism flatly denies this, affirming that it is based on God's grace alone, even though it is *in accordance with* what God foreknows (1 Peter 1:2). For God foreknows what he has elected, since his knowledge and choices are coordinate eternal acts.

We also concur with strong Calvinists when they affirm that we must have "acceptance" of and "respond" to God's grace. God does not transfer grace to humans automatically or mechanically; it is received freely.

Further, many Moderate Calvinists agree with strong Calvinists that God provides the grace to persevere in faith to the end. Unlike the so-called "free grace" position of Zane Hodges, we hold with the strong Calvinists that naturally those who are truly saved will continue to believe until the end, since their faith also results from God's effective grace.

Likewise, we agree that the warnings of Hebrews 6 are real. They are not purely hypothetical, as some strong Calvinists claim. However, we do not see any basis for the claim that the people described in the passage are nonregenerate children of the covenant. This appears to be an ad hoc attempt to solve a knotty problem in covenant theology, which even other strong Calvinists reject. Nevertheless, unlike Arminians, we agree with the strong Calvinists that Hebrews 6 does not teach that we can lose our salvation. The Arminian interpretation ignores the context of the entire book of Hebrews, which speaks of the loss of maturity and rewards, not of salvation.

What is more, unlike Arminians, we agree with strong Calvinists that all the elect will persevere with God's help. Those who do not persevere were professors of salvation but are not true possessors of it, just as John indicated (1 John 2:19).

Finally, we agree that the basis of eternal security is the unconditional promise of God. Unlike Arminians, who make salvation a conditional promise and, hence, dependent on human actions, we believe that salvation is an unconditional gift (Rom. 11:29).

AREAS OF DISAGREEMENT

All these areas of agreement with our fellow Calvinists notwithstanding, we have some important differences. These generally revolve around divergent understandings of the nature of God and of human free choice.

First, we disagree with the strong Calvinist contention that the use of the word "world" in crucial texts on salvation means the world of the elect. Indeed, strong Calvinists are inconsistent in admitting that Jesus prayed for the elect and not for the "world" (in John 17:9). Thus, when the same author uses the same word generically[1] in the same book, there is no reason to take it to mean only the elect. For example, "God so loved the *world* that he gave his one and only Son . . ." (John 3:16). Likewise, "he [Christ] is the atoning sacrifice for our sins, and not only for ours but also for the sins of *the whole world* (1 John 2:2, italics added in both cases).

Further, while Moderate Calvinists agree that God gave Abraham and his physical descendants an unconditional promise, we disagree that the land part of this promise can be wrenched from the rest of it and made conditional. For "God's gifts and his call are irrevocable" (Rom. 11:29). To claim that this land promise to Israel was revoked or will not be fulfilled literally is to say that God reneged on his unconditional promise. But God can no more do this than he can cease being God (2 Tim. 2:13).

What is more, while strong Calvinists admit that we must have "acceptance" of and "respond" to God's grace, they also

---

[1]Strong Calvinists have yet to produce clear instances of a *generic* use of the word "world" (*kosmos*) in the New Testament. Instead, they resort to a *geographical* use of it (cf. John 12:19), which is a different context.

claim that there are no conditions for salvation. But by admitting that salvation must be received, they affirm the Moderate Calvinist view that, while salvation is unconditional from the standpoint of the Giver (God), nevertheless, it is conditional from the perspective of the receiver.

Most strong Calvinists do not take seriously the implications of this claim, since they deny a libertarian concept of free will, namely, the ability to do otherwise. But there is no reason for them to do this, since Calvinists long before them (that is, Augustinians) believed in both predestination and libertarian free will, as we demonstrated in *Chosen But Free*.[2] Thomas Aquinas, heralded by strong Calvinists John Gerstner and R. C. Sproul, held this view. Indeed, even The Westminster Confession of Faith appears to make this same point when it says, "Although in relation to the foreknowledge and decree of God, the first cause, all things come to pass immutably and infallibly, yet by the same providence he ordereth them to fall out, according to the nature of *second causes*, either necessarily, *freely*, or contingently" (3.1).

Furthermore, typically strong Calvinists misrepresent Moderate Calvinists in general and Lewis Sperry Chafer in particular, claiming we "rest" election on God's omniscience, when we do not. Moderate Calvinists hold that election is *according to* but not *based on* foreknowledge.[3] Following in the tradition of Thomas Aquinas, Moderate Calvinists believe, against Molinism, that God's knowledge is identical to his independent being. Hence, all of God's knowledge is independent and not dependent. Nothing causes God to know. Rather, God's knowledge and will (which is identical to his knowledge, since he is a simple being) are the cause of all things.

Further, strong Calvinists are not correct in holding that a Moderate Calvinist's fear of losing rewards generates unnecessary anxiety about *not getting rewards in heaven*. The real fear is generated by the strong Calvinist's claims that people cannot know for sure they are elect until they die. This generates a greater fear of *not even getting to heaven!*

What is more, strong Calvinists wrongly believe they have a franchise on the term "Calvinist," when in fact, as I have

---

[2]Norman L. Geisler, *Chosen But Free* (Minneapolis: Bethany House, 1999), Appendices 1 and 3.

[3]See ibid., 52.

shown in my article, even John Calvin was not a five-point, strong Calvinist, which they assert one must be to lay claim to the term.[4] R. T. Kendall and Robert P. Lightner have shown, as have others, that Calvin did not believe in limited atonement.[5] Calvin said clearly that *"by the sacrifice of his death all the sins of the world have been expiated,"* and *"he suffered and died for the salvation of the human race."* Furthermore, *"it is incontestable that Christ came for the expiation of the sins of the whole world."*[6]

Along with this comes the strong Calvinist's insistence that our Moderate Calvinism is not really Calvinistic when in fact it holds to all five points of Calvinism.[7] In fact, strong Calvinists tend to reduce any view that does not agree with their extreme version of Calvinism to Arminianism or semi-Pelagianism. This is not only false, but it also involves both the logical fallacies of name calling and a false disjunction.

---

[4]Ibid., Appendix 2.

[5]R. T. Kendall, *Calvin and English Calvinism to 1649* (Oxford: Oxford Univ. Press, 1979); Robert P. Lightner, *The Death Christ Died: A Case for Unlimited Atonement*, 2d ed. (Grand Rapids: Kregel, 1998).

[6]See Geisler, *Chosen But Free*, Appendix 2.

[7]See ibid., chs. 4–7.

A REFORMED ARMINIAN RESPONSE TO MICHAEL S. HORTON

Stephen M. Ashby

In his chapter Michael Horton has set out to identify some of the differing approaches that competing theological schools take, including various bodies of biblical texts that are thought to support their individual positions. He identifies one body of texts as the "eternal security" passages, while designating another group of texts as the "Arminian" passages. His purpose in providing this construct is clear-cut. He believes that both those who hold to the "once-saved, always-saved" and "Arminian" positions allow themselves to be satisfied with something less than the whole counsel of God. In fact, he states: "We often hear Christians say, 'Well, they have their verses,' and we have ours—as if to suggest that the Scriptures are unclear and indeed contradictory." Of course, anyone who takes a high view of Scripture should find this sort of attitude as inherently unsatisfying.

Horton is not merely engaging in negative apologetics or polemical attacks when he sets up "eternal security" and "Arminianism" as his two bogeys. He wishes to provide a paradigm that will do justice to "the whole range of biblical teaching." This, he believes, is exactly what the other schools have not done—nor can they do. The triumphalism of his claims rings loud and clear, even though he dresses them in the language of incorrigible phraseology (using such phrases as: "it *seems* to me"; "Arminian exegesis *apparently* fails"; "It is only within this context that the disputed passages *seem to come together*...." and so forth).[1] Hence, we must consider his proposal of the *covenantal paradigm* to see if it alone ties up all loose ends. For, indeed, if that is the case, then it will have won the day. Then, not only all real Calvinists, but even all Arminians who wish to accept the whole counsel of God, will find his argument coercive. The question before us then is this: "Does the grid that Horton sets forth provide us with the best explanation?"

A WORD OF ACKNOWLEDGMENT

Horton has put forth a serious effort at a hermeneutic that will be faithful to the wide scope of biblical teaching. Given the degree of controversy that has swirled around these issues, his paradigm cannot be taken lightly. He calls his view a Classical Calvinist one, and indeed, it is. For the covenantal structure is never far from classical Calvinistic exegesis or systematics. I appreciate his desire not to fall into a proof-texting approach but instead to give an overarching canopy that he believes will account for what many treat as disparate sets of texts. When he says that "calls to perseverance are replete in Scripture and must be taken seriously," I strongly agree. When he continues that "many of those who defend 'eternal security' do not take these passages seriously enough," I again find myself cheering him on.

However, when Horton pits Arminianism against "the Reformed standpoint" and then claims that "Arminian theology regards a full doctrine of justification by Christ's imputed righteousness as 'antinomian,'" he errs! In this regard, he falls into the pattern of so many, who attribute to all "Arminians" a kind of unanimity of thought. Sadly, that which is generally called "Arminian" teaches that which Jacobus Arminius eschewed— indeed, that which he argued against. I look forward to the day when a representative body of scholarship will have clearly delineated the distinctions between a Reformed Arminianism and what I believe to be "Arminianisms" that Arminius himself would have rejected. Then, careful scholars, which I certainly take Michael Horton to be, can avoid reading Wiley or Miley or

---

[1] Italics added.

Wesley or Grotius back into Arminius. For now, I will be content with pointing out an all-too-common mistake.

THE COVENANTAL PARADIGM

Horton rightly points out that covenant theology emphasizes three distinct covenants: the covenant of redemption, the covenant of works, and the covenant of grace. I must admit, however, that I find this approach rather speculative in nature. I would hope that no one would misconstrue my reservations to mean that I question the importance of "covenant" in gaining a right understanding of Scripture. Beginning with God's covenant made with Noah (Gen. 9), we can identify in succession the Palestinian covenant (Josh. 24), the Davidic covenant (2 Sam. 7, 23), and the new covenant (Jer. 31; Ezek. 36; Luke 22); one must therefore acknowledge that a covenantal structure is clearly set forth in Scripture.

My hesitation is not with covenant as the paradigm, but rather with the covenant paradigm that Horton puts forth. In my chapter I dealt with what Robert E. Picirilli calls the "implied covenant of redemption." Even granting that this "covenant of redemption" took place (which is speculative at best), it would stand as a part of God's eternal decrees, within the secret counsel of the Almighty. It seems presumptuous to purport to know, admittedly by inference, but to know nonetheless, the details of the "eternal, intratrinitarian pact."

Not only do I find Horton's presentation of the "covenant of redemption" to be speculative, but even more so the "covenant of works." He rightly adduces the ancient Near Eastern covenants or treaties as a way of informing our understanding of the biblical covenant. Examining the form of the suzerainty-vassal treaty serves to shine great light on the participants within the covenant relationship and their respective status within that relationship. We also learn about the elements that define the relationship: that which serves to define the underlings' proper relationship to the Sovereign. As Horton says, the stipulations clearly set forth "blessings" for those who abide by the terms of the covenant and "cursings" for those who break the terms set forth.

When I view the biblical covenants made with Abraham, Moses, and David, the text informs me that I am viewing covenants that God entered into. Further, I clearly see the elements of the covenant structure. However, when I examine Genesis 2:8–3:24, I do not find the text informing me that I am viewing a covenant that God has entered into. If such a "covenant of works" exists, it is an *implied* covenant. Again, I think, this is speculative at best—unlike the covenants to which I have pointed, which are explicitly declared as such.

I would have to take issue with Horton when he says that "all of the elements of the ancient Near Eastern covenants or treaties are present in Genesis 2:8–3:24." In viewing the passage, it is not difficult to see the *stipulations*. Obviously, God commanded the man and the woman not to eat of the Tree of the Knowledge of Good and Evil (2:17). This stricture was set within the context of manifold freedom—they could freely eat of every other tree in the garden (v. 16). However, if one is expected to view this passage as covenant theology instructs that we should, then it seems to me that the burden of proof should be on them. Rather than simply asserting that all of the elements of the ancient Near Eastern covenants are present, we need demonstration of each element.

We are well aware that ancient Near Eastern treaties attached to the stipulations both blessings and cursings. The case might readily be made that the curses are clearly spelled out ("when you eat of it you will surely die," Gen. 2:17). Yet the careful reader of Scripture can look long and hard and still come up empty when looking for the blessings. Horton takes the approach of others who set this grid on Scripture when he purports a probationary period for Adam. According to this view, had Adam passed the test, then God would have confirmed him and his progeny in righteousness. My response is that this must be *read into* the text; it certainly is not something that a reader naturally gets from the text by normal exegetical methodology. There is a great deal of speculation when the interpreter sets over Scripture a supposed probationary period for an implied covenant that presumably would have confirmed in righteousness those who participated.

Finally, it should be mentioned that if we are indeed looking at a covenant in Genesis 2:8–3:24, it is certainly not a covenant of works. In recognition of the immutability of God, we must give due deference to the principle found in Hebrews

11:6, which states, "Without faith it is impossible to please God." The tempter's *modus operandi* in Genesis 3 was to destroy the woman's faith by undermining God's credibility in her eyes. All of this took place before her eating of the forbidden tree. If this was a covenant, it was a covenant of faith—not of works. Adam and Eve's act of disobedience in eating the fruit was the result of their loss of trust in the goodness and severity of God.[2]

DOES THE PARADIGM MEET ITS BURDEN OF PROOF?

This paradigm of the covenant of redemption, covenant of works, and covenant of grace is what is supposed to make all of the disputed texts related to perseverance make sense. I acknowledged earlier that Classical Calvinism has generally held to this structure. However, many staunch Calvinists do not take this approach. To say that a large body of individuals, that is, the children of the covenant, are included in the covenant of grace through paedobaptism would seem to me to be dismissive of all those Calvinists who do not baptize their infants. While I understand Horton's desire to create a third category between "believers" and "unbelievers," and thus to apply many of the salient passages to that category, I do not believe he has made his case. In fact, I think he will have difficulty even in convincing many of his fellow Calvinists—namely, those who do not baptize their infants—that this is the answer to all their problems.

Nevertheless, I am inclined to ask what would be proven even if the overall paradigm that Horton sets forth were to be granted? Many individuals and groups have held to this sort of covenantal paradigm while at the same time believing that a Christian can forfeit salvation. Wesley and many within Methodism practice paedobaptism. In principle, they would not have a problem with affirming that there are covenantal benefits for those baptized children, even apart from a personal confirmation of individual faith. Yet they take many of those passages concerning perseverance very differently from the way Horton does. The same could be said for many within Lutheranism. In fact, Arminius himself held to a construct very much like Hor-

---

[2] I would like to thank my friend Professor A. B. Brown for stimulating my thinking on this last point.

ton's. He was a paedobaptist and would have had no problem whatever affirming that there are great benefits attached to being a part of that covenant community.

The question I ask is: Does such a paradigm truly satisfy all of the texts that imply a believer might apostatize by abandoning faith in Christ? I do not think it does. When I read such passages as Hebrews 6:4–6; 10:26–29, 35–39; and 2 Peter 2:20–22, it does not seem reasonable to say that all these passages simply refer to "children of the covenant"—that is, those baptized and experiencing the spillover blessings of the redeemed, while they themselves are not justified. We might even listen to the words of Calvin himself as he comments on Hebrews 10:26:

> There is a vast difference between particular fallings and a complete defection of this kind, by which we entirely fall away from the grace of Christ. And as this cannot be the case with any one except he has been already enlightened, he says, *If we sin wilfully, after that we have received the knowledge of the truth*; as though he had said, "If we knowingly and willingly renounce the grace which we had obtained."[3]

He continues on this verse:

> The clause, "after having received the knowledge of the truth," was added for the purpose of aggravating their ingratitude; for he who willingly and *with deliberate impiety extinguishes the light of God kindled in his heart has nothing to allege as an excuse before God. Let us then learn not only to receive with reverence and prompt docility of mind the truth offered to us, but also firmly to persevere in the knowledge of it, so that we may not suffer the terrible punishment of those who despise it.*[4]

Paying careful attention to what Calvin says here, I could almost be convinced that he was a Reformed Arminian. In fact, in commenting on this passage in appendix N2, the editors comment:

> The fathers, such as *Chrysostom, Theophylact,* and *Augustine,* sadly blundered on this passage, because they did

---

[3]John Calvin, *Commentaries on the Epistle of Paul the Apostle to the Hebrews*, trans. and ed. John Owen (Grand Rapids: Eerdmans, 1948), 243 (italics added).

[4]Ibid., 243–44 (italics added).

not understand the sin that is here intended, though it be evidently that of *apostasy* according to the drift of the whole context; and hence they said some strange things about sin after baptism, though baptism is neither mentioned nor alluded to in the whole passage.[5]

When granting to Horton all of the assumptions and preconditions of his position, I can certainly see how one might understand these texts as he has suggested. At the same time, I would encourage interpreters to look to the natural sense of Scripture while avoiding the tendency to allow dogmatics to take precedence over one's exegesis.

[5]Ibid., 393.

A WESLEYAN ARMINIAN RESPONSE TO MICHAEL S. HORTON

J. Steven Harper

Theological response turns on the pivot of its intended purpose. If the purpose is "winning," the response will look more like a debate. If the purpose is "learning," it will be more akin to a dialogue. I hope to write my responses to all three of my colleagues more nearly in the spirit of conversation than controversy. I believe John Calvin, Jacobus Arminius, and John Wesley will all be in heaven. And I would quickly make the same claim for Drs. Horton, Geisler, Ashby—and myself! The point is simply that ours is a discussion among believers, not a diatribe among opponents.

Furthermore, no single system gets it 100 percent correct, at least not in my estimation. When we get to heaven, all of us will be attending "Theology 101," and the risen Christ himself will be the teacher. He alone is the Word, about whom all other words pale into relative insignificance. Our triumphant Lord will lead all of us beyond the systems our finite minds have used to make sense of things. When we no longer see through a glass darkly, none of us will prefer to hold on to our views over against that which he will reveal to be the perfect understanding of all things.

In the meantime, we theologians wrestle somewhere between unspeakable mystery and excessive description. We dare not say too little, but we cannot afford to say too much. So our systems go back and forth between the extremes, sometimes becoming too weak at one end and then later too deficient on the other. With a small amount of humor thrown in at this point, I have to confess that it is our observed shortcomings (i.e., what others see about our theologizing) that provide most of us with jobs! The four of us who have written in this book have been paid to do so precisely because none of our historical champions (much less ourselves) has gotten it right! So we keep having work to do. Part of the theological task is to show where we see differences occurring and why we believe those differences matter—all the while awaiting the time when God will reconcile all things, including our differences.

My work for now is to respond to Dr. Horton, who accepted the assignment to write on the "Classical Calvinist" view. I must begin my response using one word to describe my general reaction to what he has written: *surprise*. I do not have access to what the other two responders will say or how they will begin their critiques. However, I was caught off guard by what I read. Consequently, my critique will be different from what I had anticipated when I knew there would be a "Classical Calvinist" view in the book.

My surprise can be stated in two general comments. First, Horton purports to write the Classical Calvinist view, but he does not make a single reference to Calvin. That surprises me, not only in the sense of amazement, but also in reference to his assigned task. Geisler ends up telling us more about Calvin than Horton does, and I find that both disappointing and defective. We needed a good, solid, and sustained presentation of Calvin—by Calvin—and we did not get it. That makes it difficult for another author to write about "Moderate" Calvinism and leaves me (I will let the others speak for themselves) at something of a loss in knowing how to respond to Horton's chapter.

The second comment is that Horton's unexpected choice to use covenant theology as his frame of reference is one that he leaves us to assume is the way Calvin himself would have approached the matter. Yet he never establishes that fact from a scholarly point of view. The way he has written the chapter leaves the reader only one option: I must believe that what I am reading is what Calvin taught because Horton writes as if it is.

These two comments largely describe my context for responding—namely, that of surprise. I was all set to "have a go" at a strongly argued and finely presented chapter on Classical Calvinism (with all sorts of primary-text references to Calvin's writings) but came to the last page with not a single connect to such. So I must now respond to what I was given.

At the outset, I must say that what Horton wrote was interesting. I would confess that I have not studied covenant theology very much, even to the extent that I did not know it was developed as a means to deal with deficiencies in both "eternal security" and "Arminian" positions. I have to do my homework on his position. If it turns out to be as he has put it, then I am sure I will return to his chapter as a guide to take me farther into the perspective he has described. I will not, however, use it as a guide into Classical Calvinism, given the omissions I have already noted. Geisler's chapter ends up being more helpful in that regard.

Nevertheless, let me enter into dialogue with Horton's point of view, noting some selected places where it is different from the Wesleyan point of view. First, Horton seems to me to state too quickly and easily that "eternal security itself is not a Calvinistic doctrine." I say that not for myself (although I would), but because John Wesley (whose view I am asked to represent) clearly thought and taught that it was. If Wesley was wrong in laying a theology of "eternal security" at Calvin's feet, then it is most interesting that the Calvinists of Wesley's day did not dismiss Mr. Wesley's position by saying in effect, "Sorry, John—you've got the wrong man!" The controversy into which Wesley knowingly entered with his Calvinist counterparts in such writings as *Predestination Calmly Considered* carried significance precisely because *both he and they* believed Calvin's views were at the heart of Reformed teaching.

This does not mean that Wesley believed Calvin invented the doctrine of eternal security (also called by some the perseverance of the saints), but it does mean that he chose Calvin as a dialogue partner because people generally assumed that Calvin's views most specifically and powerfully set forth the doctrine. For Horton to assert (in one sentence and without documentation or defense) that eternal security is not a Calvinistic doctrine is a most unusual way to begin a chapter on the Classical Calvinist view.

Even with that, what Horton does write has "rough edges" from a Wesleyan point of view. It creates what Wesley clearly saw as a "God problem." The covenantal paradigm, according to Horton, "refers to the everlasting pact made between the persons of the Trinity to elect, redeem, and restore *a people* for God's glory."[1] The phrase "a people" is significant, because as we read Horton's explanation of the covenantal paradigm, it is clear that the Trinitarian choice to elect, redeem, and restore is a decision that does not include everyone, but only "a people." I do not have the space in this response to reply to Horton's working out of this fact. Go back and read the chapter, and you will see what I mean. It is clear that those "appointed for eternal life" (Acts 13:48) do not include everyone and that those excluded have been so dealt with in the "intra-Trinitarian solidarity," which sets both the Son and the Spirit on a divine redemption mission *only* for the elect.

Even more confusing is the covenant of works, which, after a long explanation by Horton, ends up asserting that "the circle of the covenant was larger than the circle of election." As far as I know, all Christians would understand God's grace (if, in fact, that is what Horton means by "the circle of the covenant") as being wider than simply *saving* grace. Yet the covenant theology Horton describes ends up creating a third category of people who are essentially "hypocrites" (the term he himself uses to describe them), because they accept the benefits of the covenant without offering their commitment to it. Again, orthodox Christianity recognizes such people, but this lengthy discussion on Horton's part takes us outside the focus of the subject of this book: the perseverance *of the saints*. We have not been asked to write about this third category of persons but rather about whether or not "the saints" (clearly the saved and those going onto perfection) can fall from grace.

In this regard, Horton's third category—even taken on its own terms—fails to deliver precisely because the warnings against falling away cited by him in 1 John and 2 Timothy are warnings given *to believers*, not to hypocrites. Warnings about apostasy given to those who are neither "saved" nor "unsaved" (Horton's way of making room for the third category) do not make sense. Warnings against falling away need only to be given

---

[1]Italics added.

to those who have not done so, and that is what John and Paul are doing when they write as they do. Those who are either "unsaved" or "hypocrites" need to be dealt with in a different way. In the final analysis, I see this as the weakest part of Horton's chapter. By creating the "hypocrites," he takes us wide of the mark of the intended subject.

I come to the end of my response in much the same way as I came to the end of Horton's chapter—interested in what I read but disappointed that what he wrote did not get to the heart of the matter. As a launch chapter for the rest of the book, one could legitimately expect that "Classical Calvinism" would find Calvin somewhere in the picture. Not finding him anywhere in the text leaves us to wonder if the view Horton gives us is as "Classically Calvinistic" as he himself wants us to believe that it is.

Chapter Two

A MODERATE CALVINIST VIEW

Norman L. Geisler

A MODERATE CALVINIST VIEW

Norman L. Geisler

Moderate Calvinism is contrasted with so-called Classical Calvinism, which we call strong[1] Calvinism in terms of the traditional five points of TULIP: Total depravity, Unconditional election, Limited atonement, Irresistible grace, and Perseverance of the saints. Strong Calvinists affirm all of these, and Arminians deny all of them, at least in the sense in which the strong Calvinists hold them.

In between these two poles, moderate Calvinists are typically understood to hold some but not all of these points—minimally at least the P of TULIP, the perseverance of the saints. This is popularly known as eternal security or "once saved, always saved." It is also sometimes called one-point Calvinism. However, we believe the situation is more complicated than this and prefer to slice the theological pie another way by embracing what may be called "Five-Point Moderate Calvinism."

CONTRASTING STRONG AND MODERATE CALVINISM ON THE FIVE POINTS

Using the TULIP acrostic, the moderate Calvinism expressed here holds a moderate view on all five points of traditional

---

[1]This form of Calvinism has been called by several names, such as "classical," "traditional," "strong," and "extreme." A case can be made for each. The editor of this volume prefers the first, and we have made a case for the latter elsewhere (Norman L. Geisler, *Chosen But Free* [Minneapolis: Bethany House, 1999]). However, since "strong" is less controversial and fits better with "Moderate" Calvinism with which it is contrasted here, we have chosen to use it for the purpose of this dialog.

Calvinism. Even strong Calvinists admit that "all the Five Points of Calvinism [as they understand them] hang or fall together."[2] What they often do not say is that there is a moderate way to understand these five points in which they also stand or fall together.[3] So what one believes about eternal security will depend on his or her understanding of the other four points of Calvinism. Thus, an analysis of these is necessary before we focus on eternal security. A more thorough discussion is found in my *Chosen But Free*.[4] Consider this summary of the differences:

The Five Points	Moderate Calvinism	Strong Calvinism
Total Depravity	Extensive (corruptive)	Intensive (destructive)
Unconditional Election	No conditions for God; one for human beings (faith)	No condition for God or for human beings
Limited Atonement	Limited in result (but for all human beings)	Limited in extent (not for all human beings)
Irresistible Grace	In persuasive sense (in accord with the human will)	In coercive sense (against the human will)
Perseverance of the Saints	Not all saints will be faithful to the end	All saints will be faithful to the end

STRONG VERSUS MODERATE CALVINISM ON PERSEVERANCE OF THE SAINTS

Since each point of TULIP stands or falls together, each point is colored by every other point. This is true in particular of the way the other four points color what one means by eternal security. These contrasts form a helpful way to distinguish eternal security as held by a strong Calvinist from that embraced by a moderate Calvinist.

---

[2]Edwin H. Palmer, *The Five Points of Calvinism* (Grand Rapids: Baker, 1972), 69.
[3]This follows the discussion in Geisler, *Chosen But Free*, ch. 7.
[4]Ibid., chs. 4–5.

Total Depravity and Eternal Security

According to strong Calvinism, one cannot receive salvation by his or her own free act of faith, since one is so totally depraved (in an *intensive sense*), being dead in sins, that he or she does not even have the ability to accept the gift of salvation. God must regenerate sinners by irresistible grace before they can believe.

By contrast, the moderate Calvinist, who believes in total depravity in an *extensive sense*, holds that the image of God is not erased in fallen humanity but only effaced. Although individuals cannot initiate or attain salvation by their own acts, nevertheless, they can receive the gift of salvation. Even fallen human beings have the ability to accept or reject God's gift of salvation. For even though salvation does not come from our will (John 1:13), yet it does come "through [our] faith" (Eph. 2:8) by our act of "receiving" Christ (John 1:12).

Unconditional Election and Eternal Security

For the strong Calvinist, salvation is unconditional for both the Giver and the receiver. That is, there are no conditions for a person's *receiving* it, and there are no conditions for God's *giving* it. One receives eternal security apart from any act of faith on his or her part. Indeed, people are incapable of receiving it until God first saves them.

The moderate Calvinist, by contrast, believes election is unconditional from the standpoint of the *Giver* but conditional from the vantage point of the *receiver*. It is an unconditional gift; there are no strings attached. Nonetheless, this unconditional gift must be received. This act of receiving is no more meritorious than it is to give credit to a beggar for taking a handout. The credit should be given to the Giver of the gift rather than to the one who receives it. The same is true of the unconditional gift of salvation (Acts 16:31; Rom. 6:23).

Limited Atonement and Eternal Security

It is well known that strong and moderate Calvinists differ on the extent of the atonement. Strong Calvinists claim that it is limited in its *extent*, insisting that Christ died only for the elect.

Moderate Calvinists hold it is not limited in its extent, since Christ died for all (John 1:29; 2 Cor. 5:15; 1 John 2:2), but they acknowledge that it is limited in its *application* to those who believe. This difference affects the two systems' respective beliefs on eternal security. According to strong Calvinists, God wants only some to have eternal security. Hence, Christ died only for them. By contrast, the moderate Calvinist holds that while only those who believe will be saved, nevertheless, God desires all to be saved (1 Tim. 2:4; 2 Peter 3:9).

Irresistible Grace and Eternal Security

There is also a significant difference between strong Calvinists and moderate Calvinists on how one receives eternal security. For the former, a person receives the gift of salvation against his or her will. All the elect are sinners by nature, dead, and incapable of receiving salvation when God bestowed it on them apart from and against what by nature they really willed.

Moderate Calvinists, by contrast, are convinced that God's irresistible grace is effectual on the *willing* (the elect) but not on the *unwilling*. God works effectually and irresistibly on those who choose to receive it. But on those who do not will to receive divine grace, God refuses to force them against their will. God is love, and love works persuasively but not coercively. Forced love is a moral contradiction (Matt. 23:37). Hence, strong Calvinism and moderate Calvinism differ on the nature and operation of irresistible grace.[5]

Perseverance of the Saints and Eternal Security

The final letter in the Calvinist's TULIP is P for the perseverance of the saints, also known as eternal security. This means all regenerate persons will persevere to the end. That is, they will eventually be in heaven. In popular language, Calvinists of all varieties believe "once saved, always saved," and all Arminians deny it.[6]

---

[5]Moderate Calvinists, along with nearly all major church teachers up to the Reformation (see ibid., appendix 1), held to a more libertarian view of freedom, which involves the power of contrary choice (ibid., ch. 2 and appendices 4, 9).

[6]Many Calvinists hasten to point out, however, that "the perseverance of the saints depends on the perseverance of God." Or, more properly, it depends on "the preservation of God" (see Palmer, *The Five Points of Calvinism*, 69–70).

However, there is a difference between strong and moderate Calvinists here too, as the following chart illustrates:

	Moderate Calvinism on Eternal Security	Strong Calvinism on Eternal Security
T	It is received by a free act.	It cannot be received by a free act.
U	Faith is a condition of receiving it.	Faith is not a condition of receiving it.
L	Christ died so all could have it.	Christ died only so some could have it.
I	It is received in accord with one's will.	It is received against one's will.
P	One need not be faithful to the end to have it.	One must be faithful to the end to have it.

In the words of the Westminster Confession of Faith (17.1), per[sons] whom God hath accepted in his [Belove]d and sanctified by his Spirit, can nei[ther fall] away from the state of grace; but shall [remai]n to the end, and be eternally saved."

RSEVERANCE OF THE SAINTS

[m]isperception, there are other signifi[cant ...] [m]oderate Calvinists, strong Calvinists, [...] security. First, consider the following [...] [moder]ate Calvinists and Arminians:

[Et]ernal Security

[...]m	Arminianism
	No believers have it.
	Any believer can lose it.
	It can be lost by our actions.
[...]nd	God gives assurance but no security.

(handwritten note: ROB HILDEBRANDT (OFF FRIDAYS))

Since most parties on both sides agree to these contrasts, little comment is needed. The most interesting comparison, however, is the next one. Here a threefold comparison is illuminating:

Strong Calvinism	Arminianism	Moderate Calvinism
security, but no assurance[7]	assurance, but no security	security and assurance

Of course, many strong Calvinists insist that assurance is possible before death. However, several factors seriously undermine this claim. First, they admit there is such a thing as "false grace" and "false assurance," whereby one believes he or she is one of the elect when in fact that person is not.[8]

Second, the very word "perseverance" suggests that some who claim to be believers will not persevere to the end and, hence, not be saved.

Third, some strong Calvinists admit the possibility of apparent believers falling away before they die and thus being lost forever. They hold that all true believers will endure in their faithfulness to the end. Those who do not endure in holiness to the end were not true believers. This being the case, there is eternal security for the elect, but the catch is this: *No one can really be sure he or she is one of the elect unless he or she remains faithful to the end.* This is different from the moderate Calvinist view presented here: All believers can be sure they are saved and will continue in their faith to the end. For the presence of "faith" is "evidence" that one is truly saved (Heb. 11:1). Faith is implanted in the heart by the Holy Spirit upon believing the Word of God (Rom. 10:9, 17).

By contrast, strong Calvinists insist that in addition to continuing to have *faith*, individuals must continue to be *faithful* to God to the end as evidence that they are truly saved. Puritan Thomas Brooks affirmed that true perseverance involves perseverance (1) in a holy profession of our faith, (2) in holy and spir-

---

[7]Most strong Calvinists *claim* that full assurance in this life is possible. However, this is inconsistent with their other beliefs that one must maintain a life of faithful works to the end to be sure one is saved and did not really have "false assurance" in one's life and was, therefore, one of the nonelect.

See Thomas Brooks, *Heaven on Earth* (Carlisle, Pa.: Banner of Truth, 1996), 9.

itual principles, (3) by abiding and continuing in the doctrine of Christ, and (4) by continuance in gracious actions.[9]

Fourth, the very things offered as signs of true and enduring assurance make it impossible for people to know for sure that they are saved before they die.[10] But the truth of the matter is that it is practically impossible for anyone to be sure he or she has persevered in all these faithfully before death. Or, to put it another way, anyone who is not doing this up to the time he or she dies cannot be sure he or she is one of the elect.

Another contrast is that moderate Calvinists believe in both temporal assurance on earth and eternal security in heaven for the elect. But some strong Calvinists hold only the latter, since one cannot be really sure that he or she is one of the elect until perseverance to the end occurs. For there is such a thing as "false assurance," and "we may think that we have faith when in fact we have no faith."[11]

A. A. Hodge said, "*Perseverance in holiness*, therefore, in opposition to all weakness and temptations, *is the only sure evidence of* the genuineness of past experience, of the validity of *our confidence as to our future salvation....*" There can be a "temporary withdrawal of restraining grace" while the elect are "allowed to backslide for a time"; nonetheless, "*in every such case* they are graciously restored."[12] This seems to imply that if people backslide and do not return before they meet their Maker, then that is proof that they were not truly saved. If so, then no matter what evidence Christians may have manifested in their lives for many years before this, they cannot have true assurance that they were saved.[13]

---

[9]Ibid., 272–74.

[10]Brooks (ibid., 50–71) offered these as signs of "well-grounded assurance": (1) "Be active in exercising grace." (2) "Assurance is obtained by obedience." (3) "Follow diligently the instructions of the Holy Spirit." (4) "Be diligent in attendance upon [Christ's] ordinances." (5) "Pay particular attention to the scope of God's promises of mercy." (6) "Excel in those choice particular things that may clearly and fully difference and distinguish you, not only from the profane, but also from the highest and most glittering hypocrites in all the world." (7) "Seek to grow and increase more and more in grace."

[11]R. C. Sproul, *Chosen by God* (Wheaton, Ill.: Tyndale, 1986), 165–66.

[12]A. A. Hodge. *Outlines of Theology* (Grand Rapids: Eerdmans, 1949 [1878]), 544–45 (italics added).

[13]To be sure, many strong Calvinists speak about present assurance and evidences of it (see William Ames, *The Marrow of Theology*, trans. and ed. John D. Eusden

In spite of claims to the contrary, strong Calvinists cannot be sure they are saved unless and until they endure to the end. In brief, with regard to the knowledge of one's salvation, the proof of the pudding is in the persevering.

MODERATE CALVINISM VERSUS ARMINIANISM: A DEFENSE OF ETERNAL SECURITY

While significant differences exist between strong Calvinists and moderate Calvinists on eternal security, even stronger ones exist between moderate Calvinists and Arminians. The latter affirm, for example, that individuals can lose their salvation. As Arminian theologian H. Orton Wiley said, Arminians hold that a believer could become *"reprobate"* and *"dying in such a state, may finally perish."*[14] On the contrary, there are many arguments in favor of eternal security, along with present assurance for all believers.

Biblical Arguments in Favor of Eternal Security

The New Testament is replete with verses that teach that salvation can never be lost. What is more, one can be sure of this while one is living. Among them, the following stand out.[15]

Job 19:25–26. *"I know that my Redeemer lives*, and that in the end he will stand upon the earth. And after my skin has been destroyed, yet in my flesh *I will see God."* Job is certain of two things: (1) that his Redeemer lives; (2) that he will see God in his flesh one day (resurrection). That is, Job has present knowledge that he has been redeemed (*"my* Redeemer") and that, in his resurrected body, he will see God in heaven. Such knowledge implies his eternal security.

Ecclesiastes 3:14. Under the inspiration of the Holy Spirit, the wisest man who ever lived said, "I know that *everything God does will endure for ever; nothing can be added to it and nothing taken*

[Durham, N.C.: Labyrinth, 1983], 172; and Sproul, *Chosen by God,* 167–68). However, they then proceed to remind themselves it could be false assurance and that they must endure faithfully to the end to be sure.

[14]H. Orton Wiley, *Christian Theology,* 3 vols. (Kansas City, Mo.: Beacon Hill, 1952), 2:344, 351.

[15]In Scripture references in this chapter, italics have been added.

from it." Applying this principle to salvation, which the Scripture does (Eph. 1:4), results in the doctrine of eternal security. For if what God does is forever, and if salvation is a work of God, then salvation is forever. But if salvation can be lost, then it is not forever. I conclude, therefore, that salvation cannot be lost.

John 3:18. *"Whoever believes in him is not condemned*, but whoever does not believe *stands condemned already* because he has not believed in the name of God's one and only Son." The plain sense of this text is that if one believes *now*, he or she is not condemned (lost) now and will not be later (cf. Rom. 8:1). For John adds that such a person *"will not be condemned; he has crossed over from death to life"* (John 5:24). But if he does not believe now, then he is "already" condemned (lost). In short, a present act of faith assures one of never being condemned, that is, of never being lost. Just as one is condemned already for not believing in Christ, even so one is saved already for believing in him.

John 5:24. "I tell you the truth, whoever hears my word and *believes* him who sent me *has* eternal life and *will not* be condemned; he has crossed over from death to life." That is, those who truly believe *now* can be certain now that they will be in heaven *later*. Eternal life is a present possession the moment people believe, and this assures Christians they will never be condemned.

John 6:37. "All that the Father gives me will come to me, and *whoever comes to me I will never drive away*." Not only is everyone who comes saved, but also everyone who is saved is saved permanently! It is a forever salvation.

John 6:39–40. "And this is the will of him who sent me, that *I shall lose none of all that he has given me*, but raise them up at the last day. For my Father's will is that *everyone who looks to the Son and believes in him shall have eternal life*, and *I will raise him up at the last day*." Jesus said those who *now believe* in him he "will raise up at the last day." That is, they will be saved. Further, he declared emphatically: *"I shall lose none of all that he [God] has given me*." Thus, those who believe are as eternally secure as the promise of Christ. In short, *believe now, be saved forever!*

John 10:27–29. "My sheep listen to my voice; I know them, and they follow me. I give them eternal life, and *they shall never perish*; no one can snatch them out of my hand. My Father, who has given them to me, is greater than all; no one can snatch them out of my Father's hand." What makes our salvation sure is not only God's infinite love, but also the fact that we are held by his omnipotent hand. We are not only saved by his unlimited love, but we are kept by his unlimited power (1 Peter 1:5; cf. Jude 24). "No one," not even ourselves, can pry us out of his hand. Further, Jesus said his sheep (the saved) will *never perish.*" Very plainly, then, if any believer loses his or her salvation, then Jesus is wrong! But if Jesus is the Son of God, then this is impossible. Hence, our salvation is as eternally secure as the words of Jesus. As Jesus said, "Heaven and earth will pass away, but my words will never pass away" (Matt. 24:35).

John 17:9–24. "I pray for them. I am not praying for the world, but for those you have given me, for they are yours. . . . Holy Father, protect them by the power of your name—the name you gave me—so that they may be one as we are one. . . . I pray also for those who will believe in me through their message. . . . Father, I want those you have given me to be with me where I am, and to see my glory, the glory you have given me because you loved me before the creation of the world." It is noteworthy that Jesus' prayer also includes believers not yet born (see v. 20). Jesus' prayer assures us that all true believers will be saved, for he said *"none of them is lost"* (v. 12). Only those, like Judas (v. 12), doomed to destruction by their own unwillingness to repent, will be lost (cf. 2 Peter 3:9). Since Jesus' prayer for us as our high priest is efficacious (Heb. 7:25), as is his advocacy for us in heaven (1 John 2:1), it is impossible that any of his children will be lost. If they are, then God has failed to answer his Son's prayer as high priest when the Bible informs us that God was pleased with what Jesus did for us (Heb. 7:25–27; 1 John 2:1).

Romans 4:5–6. "However, to the man who does not work but trusts God who justifies the wicked, his faith is *credited [imputed] as righteousness.* David says the same thing when he speaks of the blessedness of the man to whom God *credits [imputes] righteousness* apart from works." The doctrine of divine imputation, asserted here and elsewhere in Scripture (Gen. 15:6; Rom. 4:11, 22–24; 5:13–21; 2 Cor. 5:21; Phil. 3:9), argues strongly for eternal security. For if we are already accounted as perfectly righteous because of Christ's righteousness imputed to us, then there is no sin that can keep us out of heaven. We have been dressed in Christ's righteousness (2 Cor. 5:21), and this is more than sufficient to get anyone into heaven. Indeed, in view of his righteousness imputed to us, there is literally nothing that can keep us out of heaven.

Romans 8:29–30. "For *those* God foreknew he also predestined. . . . And *those* he predestined, he also called; *those* he called, he also justified; *those* he justified, he also *glorified*." This golden chain is unbroken. The same persons who are predestined are called, justified, and eventually glorified (make it to heaven). In order to avoid eternal security, one would have to insert the word "some" into the text, but it is not there. All who are justified will eventually be glorified.[16]

Romans 8:33. "*Who will bring any charge against those whom God has chosen? It is God who justifies.*" Charles Ryrie's comment is to the point: "It makes no difference who in all the universe may try to charge us with whatever. It makes no difference as long as it is not God who charges us. And God does not." For God "*has already announced the verdict in all instances when we are and will be charged. And that verdict is 'not guilty.'*"[17]

Romans 8:35, 37–39. "*Who shall separate us from the love of Christ?* Shall trouble or hardship or persecution or famine or nakedness or danger or sword? . . . No, in all these things we are more than conquerors through him who loved us. For *I am convinced that neither death nor life, neither angels nor demons*, neither the present nor the future, nor any powers, neither height nor depth, *nor anything else in all creation, will be able to separate us from the love of God that is in Christ Jesus our Lord*." This passage needs little comment, merely contemplation. There is literally nothing "in all creation" that can separate a believer from Christ! Because of his unconditional love, the Creator will not do it, and no creature can do it.[18]

Romans 11:29. "*For God's gifts and his call are irrevocable.*" Salvation involves both the gift (6:23) and calling (8:30) of God.

---

[16]Unlike strong Calvinists, this does not prove atonement is limited in its extent but only in its application. The "call" here refers to the effectual call of the elect, not the general call, offer, or command for all to be saved (Acts 17:30; 2 Peter 3:9).

[17]Charles Ryrie, *So Great Salvation* (Chicago: Moody, 1997), 127.

[18]Of course, God still loves people who are in hell, but they are *separated from that love*. Like a cup turned upside down under Niagara Falls, they have refused the love being poured over them.

And Paul here declares emphatically that God's gifts are "irrevocable." Hence, the gift of salvation can never be revoked.

1 Corinthians 12:13. "For *we were all baptized by one Spirit into one body*—whether Jews or Greeks, slave or free—and we were all given the one Spirit to drink" (cf. Eph. 1:22–23; 4:4). As Charles Ryrie keenly observes, "at conversion the believer is joined to the body of Christ by the baptism of the Holy Spirit. If salvation can be lost, then one would have to be severed from the body, and the body of Christ would then be dismembered."[19]

2 Corinthians 5:17, 21. "Therefore, *if anyone is in Christ, he is a new creation*; the old has gone, the new has come! . . . God made him who had no sin to be sin for us, so that in him *we might become the righteousness of God*." According to this text, we are already a new creation; this guarantees us a place in heaven. Indeed, we have been robed in "the righteousness of God." Thus, in God's eyes we are as perfect as we can be—not because of our merits but because of Christ's work. In turn, our sins were laid on Christ. Since our sins have been imputed to him and his righteousness to us, if anyone is to be kept out of heaven for any of our sins, it must be Christ. And if anyone gets into heaven because of Christ's righteousness, it must be us.

Ephesians 1:4–5. "*For he chose us in him before the creation of the world* to be holy and blameless in his sight. *In love he predestined us to be adopted as his sons* through Jesus Christ, in accordance with his pleasure and will." Believers were predestined to be adopted into God's family before the world began. God knew in advance everything that we would do, even after we had been saved, including all our sins. Yet there is nothing that can undo an eternal decree of God (Rom. 11:29). Hence, those who are adopted into his family are eternally secure. There is no such thing in Scripture as being unadopted. He adopted us because he wanted us, even though he knew everything about us in advance.

Ephesians 1:13b–14. "Having believed, *you were marked in him with a seal, the promised Holy Spirit, who is a deposit guaranteeing our inheritance until the redemption* of those who are God's possession—to the praise of his glory" (cf. 4:30). Elsewhere Paul said that all who have the Holy Spirit belong to Christ (Rom. 8:9). However, according to this text, having the Holy Spirit is a

---

[19]Ryrie, *So Great Salvation*, 129.

guarantee of one's ultimate redemption. Hence, to argue that persons can lose their salvation is tantamount to saying that God's guarantee that believers will reach the ultimate day of redemption is not good! Put in the vernacular, God has put money on the fact that every believer is going to make it. He has guaranteed it with the presence of his own Holy Spirit in our lives, who "himself testifies with our spirit that we are God's children" (8:16).

Ephesians 2:5–6. Paul declared that *God has "made us alive with Christ even when we were dead in transgressions—it is by grace you have been saved. And God raised us up with Christ and seated us with him in the heavenly realms in Christ Jesus."* According to this passage, the saved are already in heaven positionally. And we are there, not because we put ourselves there, but because God put us there. He "raised us up" there. Thus, our position in heaven is as secure as that of Christ. We can no more be kicked out of our heavenly position than Christ can. What we do practically should and will to some degree reflect this heavenly position, but it in no way negates it. Otherwise our works after salvation would be necessary to obtain salvation.

Philippians 1:6. *"Being confident of this, that he [God] who began a good work in you will carry it on to completion until the day of Christ Jesus."* Paul expresses confidence that the God who initiated the saving process in our lives will finish it. That is, all the regenerate will make it to heaven. God finishes what he starts. To deny this is a slur on the divine character.

Philippians 4:3. "Yes, and I ask you, loyal yokefellow, help these women who have contended at my side in the cause of the gospel, along with Clement and the rest of my fellow workers, *whose names are in the book of life."* Clearly Paul teaches that believers can know here and now whether they are on their way to heaven. Furthermore, since names in the book of life have been there from eternity (Rev. 13:8), it is evident that God knows they are eternally secure. Indeed, John reveals that once one's name is in this book, it will never be taken out (3:5). Thus, both present assurance of salvation and eternal security are found in these passages.

2 Timothy 1:12. Paul proclaims: *"I know whom I have believed, and am convinced that he is able to guard what I have entrusted to him* *for that day.*" Since our salvation does not depend on our faithfulness but on God's (2:13), our perseverance is assured by him. Hence, we can "know" now that we will later be saved when he returns.

2 Timothy 4:18. The apostle Paul expresses confidence that "the Lord will rescue me from every evil attack and *will bring me safely to his heavenly kingdom.*" This assurance would not be possible if believers could lose their salvation. How else could Paul have such present confidence that he will eventually be saved? Scripture promises that God will do this for all believers (Phil. 1:6; 1 Peter 1:5).

Hebrews 10:14. "By one sacrifice *he has made perfect forever* those who are being made holy." According to this passage, the one sacrifice of Christ on the cross secures forever the salvation of the elect. Since this was secured at the cross before we were ever born, it follows that true believers can be assured now that they will be in heaven later. They are as perfect now, dressed in Christ's righteousness (2 Cor. 5:21), as they will ever be or need to be to enter heaven.

Hebrews 12:2. "Let us fix our eyes on Jesus, *the author and perfecter of our faith*, who for the joy set before him endured the cross, scorning its shame, and sat down at the right hand of the throne of God." God is both the author and "perfecter" or "finisher" (KJV) of our faith. He begins it, and he completes it (Phil. 1:6). Indeed, the author of Hebrews calls it "eternal redemption" (Heb. 9:12). It certainly cannot be eternal salvation if it lasts only for a short time and if one can lose it. And this eternal salvation was procured "once for all" some two thousand years before we were born.

1 Peter 1:5. Peter speaks of those "who through faith are *shielded by God's power* until the coming of the salvation that is *ready to be revealed in the last time.*" Once people place their faith in Christ, they are protected by God's power until they reach heaven. Since God is all-powerful, it follows that nothing can penetrate this divine shield. Of course, this is accomplished "through faith," which is strengthened by God's grace and assured in advance by his foreknowledge that it will come to pass (1 Peter 1:2).

1 John 3:9. "No one who is born of God will continue to sin, because *God's seed remains in him; he cannot go on sinning, because* *he has been born of God.*" Here is a confirmation of the moderate Calvinist view of eternal security. First, anyone truly born of God cannot go on sinning. If such a person does, then he or she is not born of God. That is, one's perseverance in avoiding continual sin is a proof of one's salvation. Second, the word "cannot" indicates that a true believer has a divine nature that guarantees ultimate salvation. God has planted a "seed" in each believer at conversion that will grow to fruition (cf. Phil. 1:6).

Jude 24–25. "To *him who is able to keep you from falling* and *to present you before his glorious presence without fault* and with great joy—to the only God our Savior be glory, majesty, power and authority, through Jesus Christ our Lord, before all ages, now and for evermore!" Whatever warnings the Bible may give about our falling,[20] we are assured that a true believer will experience no fall that will involve the loss of heaven. For an all-powerful God is able "to keep us from falling."

Biblical Arguments in Favor of Present Assurance

Eternal security is an objective matter. Present assurance of that eternal security is a subjective matter. As the Puritan writer Thomas Brooks noted, "Being in a state of grace will yield a man a heaven hereafter, but seeing of himself in this state will yield him both a heaven here and a heaven hereafter." For "it is one thing for me to have faith, and another thing for me to know that I have faith. Now assurance flows from a clear, certain, evident knowledge that I have grace, and that I do believe."[21]

Both strong Calvinists and Arminians claim that present assurance is not a guarantee of ultimate salvation. Strong Calvinists cannot be certain because they may have "false assurance" of permanent salvation. Arminians cannot be sure of their ultimate salvation because they have true assurance only of temporary salvation. Arminian theologian Richard Watson believed he had "established" and "proved from Scripture" that "*true believers may*

---

[20]Calvinists of various varieties interpret the warning passages differently. Some, following Calvin, take them as hypothetical, not actual. Others, like the author, consider them to be actual but to be warnings about losing our rewards (1 Cor. 3:15), not losing our salvation. See Jodie Dillow, *The Reign of the Servant King* (Hayesville, S.C.: Schoettle, 1992), for a treatment of loss of rewards.

[21]Brooks, *Heaven on Earth*, 14.

'turn back unto perdition,' and be 'cast away,' and fall into a state in which it were better for them 'never to have known the way of righteousness'"; thus, *"the number of the elect may be diminished."*[22]

On the contrary, the moderate Calvinist can have true assurance of eternal salvation. Indeed, the Bible exhorts believers to gain assurance. Paul urges the Corinthians: *"Examine yourselves to see whether you are in the faith;* test yourselves. Do you not realize that Christ Jesus is in you—unless, of course, you fail the test?"* (2 Cor. 13:5).[23] Peter urges: "My brothers, *be all the more eager to make your calling and election sure.* For if you do these things, you will never fall" (2 Peter 1:10). Jude adds, *"Keep yourselves in God's love* as you wait for the mercy of our Lord Jesus Christ to bring you to eternal life" (Jude 21).

Just what provides the basis of our assurance that we are in the faith? As Paul says, "For everything that was written in the past was written to teach us, so that *through endurance and the encouragement of the Scriptures we might have hope"* (Rom. 15:4). John declares: *"I write these things* to you who believe in the name of the Son of God so *that you may know* that you have eternal life" (1 John 5:13). It behooves us, then, to look at the Scriptures for an answer to the question of assurance of salvation.

Job 19:25–26. *"I know that my Redeemer lives,* and that in the end he will stand upon the earth. And after my skin has been destroyed, yet in my flesh *I will see God."* This text not only implies eternal security (see above) but also entails present assurance. Job says, in effect: "I *know now* that I *will later be* in heaven ['I will see God']."

Romans 8:16. Paul writes: *"The Spirit himself testifies with our spirit that we are God's children."* This is a present witness of our ultimate state. We know now that we are God's children. And being God's children means being saved (John 1:12). If Arminians are right and one can lose his or her salvation, then the testimony of the Holy Spirit might be wrong. But this is impossible,

---

[22]Richard Watson, *Christian Institutes; or A View of the Evidences, Doctrines, Morals, and Institutions of Christianity* (New York: T. Mason & G. Lane, 1836), 340 (italics added).

[23]Some Moderate Calvinists take these passages to refer to confirmation of one's election to outsiders (see Hodges, *Absolutely Free,* 174–75, 200). Be that as it may, this only makes the confirmation indirect. Further, given the many passages about false believers (cf. Matt. 7:22), every confessed believer is well advised to know what genuine saving faith is and whether he or she has exercised it.

since God cannot lie (Rom. 3:4; Titus 1:2; Heb. 6:18). Hence, believers can have present assurance of their ultimate salvation.

2 Corinthians 5:1–2. *"Now we know* that if the earthly tent we live in is destroyed, *we have a building from God, an eternal house in heaven,* not built by human hands."* Paul says he not only knew he was destined for heaven, but he knows it *"now"*; that is, he has present assurance of his future place "in heaven." Such assurance is possible for all believers.

2 Corinthians 5:5–8. "Now it is God who has made us for this very purpose and has given us the Spirit as a deposit, *guaranteeing what is to come.* Therefore *we are always confident and know* that as long as we are at home in the body we are away from the Lord.... *We are confident,* I say, and would prefer to be away from the body and at home with the Lord." Here Paul expresses his *"confidence"* that, were he to die, he would be with Christ. This is an emphatic expression of his present assurance of his future in heaven. Further, he declares that God has given him a *present "guarantee"* of *"what is to come,"* namely, the Holy Spirit (see Eph. 4:30). To deny either the present assurance or the eternal security of the believer is to say that God's guarantee is no good.

Philippians 1:6. *"Being confident* of this, that *he [God] who began a good work in you will carry it on to completion until the day of Christ Jesus."* This text not only teaches the eternal security of believers but also that they can be "confident" that they are among the elect.

1 Thessalonians 1:4–5. "For *we know,* brothers loved by God, that *he has chosen you,* because our gospel came to you not simply with words, but also with power, with the Holy Spirit and with *deep conviction."* Here again, as in Romans 8:16, one's deep conviction that one is a member of the elect (a "chosen" one) is a result of the powerful work of the Holy Spirit; the Thessalonians had this assurance immediately upon conversion.

2 Timothy 4:18. "The Lord will rescue me from every evil attack and *will bring me safely to his heavenly kingdom.* To him be glory for ever and ever." Paul is sure that God will preserve him to the end. His present confidence is that his future in heaven is assured. This indicates not only present assurance but also eternal security.

Hebrews 10:22–23. "Let us draw near to God with a sincere heart *in full assurance of faith,* having our hearts sprinkled to cleanse us from a guilty conscience and having our bodies washed with pure water. *Let us hold unswervingly to the hope we profess,* for he who promised is faithful." According to this passage, believers can have "full assurance" and "hold unswervingly" to their confident expectation (hope) based on the fact that God is "faithful" (cf. 2 Tim. 2:13).

1 John 5:13. John declares: "I write these things to you who believe in the name of the Son of God so *that you may know that you have eternal life.*"

Other evidences of salvation. Throughout his first letter John lists ways we can "know" now that we are one of God's elect, namely, if we keep his commandments (1 John 2:3); keep his word (2:4); walk as he did (2:5); love the brethren (3:14); love in deed, not just word (3:19); have the Holy Spirit within us (3:24); love one another (4:13); and do not continue in sin (5:18 cf. 3:9). In short, if we manifest the fruit of the Spirit, then we have the presence of the Spirit in our hearts and manifest his fruit in our lives (cf. Gal. 5:22–23). Then we can be assured we are of the elect. We do not have to wait until we meet Christ to know that we belong to him. The first fruit of the Spirit is agapic love. Paul informs us what its unmistakable characteristics are (1 Cor. 13).[24]

Theological Arguments in Favor of Eternal Security

In addition to the above specific verses supporting eternal security, many other Bible-based theological truths ground this teaching. Let us examine some of the more important ones.

Salvation is of the Lord. Jonah summarizes the teaching about salvation in Scripture: "Salvation comes from the LORD" (Jonah 2:9). Salvation does not derive from the human will but from God's will. The saved are "children born not of natural descent, nor of human decision or a husband's will, *but born of God*" (John 1:13). As Paul said, "*It does not, therefore, depend on man's desire or effort,* but on God's mercy" (Rom. 9:16). If the source and end of salvation does not depend on our effort but only on God, then our security is as eternal as God is.

God cannot deny himself. The apostle declares: "*If we are faithless, he will remain faithful, for he cannot deny himself*" (2 Tim.

---

[24]Robert Gromacki has a similar list in *Salvation Is Forever* (Schaumburg, Ill.: Regular Baptist Press, 1996), 177–83.

2:13, NKJV). This is a particularly powerful text for eternal security. It addresses the Arminian challenge directly, since it declares that even if our faith falters, God's faithfulness does not. Because salvation comes from God, in order for us to lose our salvation, God would have to "deny himself," which is impossible. So we can no more lose our salvation than God can cease being God.

Election is from eternity. Salvation was not decided in time, and it cannot be dissolved in time. "For *he [God] chose us in him before the creation of the world* to be holy and blameless in his sight" (Eph. 1:4). Christ is the "Lamb that was slain from the creation of the world" (Rev. 13:8). Further, "*This grace was given us in Christ Jesus before the beginning of time*" (2 Tim. 1:9). In short, our salvation has not been gained in time, and it cannot be lost in time. It was effected in eternity and is for eternity.

God has infallible foreknowledge. Both Calvinists and traditional Arminians agree that God has infallible foreknowledge (Isa. 46:10). If so, then it seems unreasonable to assume that God regenerates people he knows will not persevere. Indeed, this is precisely what Paul implies when he writes: "For *those* God foreknew he also predestined. . . . And *those* he predestined, he also called; *those* he called, he also justified; *those* he justified, he also glorified" (Rom. 8:29–30). To claim that God begins but does not complete our salvation is to say that he does not finish what he starts. But this is contrary to his character and practice. Note Paul's words, "being confident of this, that *he who began a good work in you will carry it on to completion until the day of Christ Jesus*" (Phil. 1:6).

Salvation was completed by Christ. What the song writer says is strongly supported by Scripture: "Jesus paid it all"! Jesus said on the cross: "*It is finished*" (John 19:30). Looking forward to the cross, he declared to the Father: "*I have brought you glory on earth by completing the work you gave me to do*" (John 17:4). The writer of Hebrews says of Jesus' work on the cross, "By one sacrifice *he has made perfect forever* those who are being made holy" (Heb. 10:14). According to this passage, the one sacrifice of Christ on the cross secures forever the forgiveness of our sins.

From God's perspective the work of the cross is an accomplished fact from all eternity (Eph. 1:4; Rev. 13:8). This means that in God's eyes, which see with infallible foreknowledge, all our sins—past, present, and future—were already taken care of before we were ever born. This being the case, then even the sins Arminians deem worthy of losing one's salvation were paid for by Christ on the cross before we were ever born. So the loss of one's salvation would have to effect a loss in God's omniscient foreknowledge that we would receive the gift of salvation. Contrary to Arminian claims, never does the Bible qualify the "all sins" for which Christ died by asserting that it is only "all sins *up to the time they were justified.*" And it is not wise to add to the Scriptures.

Salvation is an irrevocable gift. Paul states emphatically that "God's gifts and his call are irrevocable" (Rom. 11:29). He also says, however, that salvation is "a gift of God" (Rom. 6:23; Eph. 2:8). God can never take back the gift of salvation. He is bound by his own unconditional promise to be faithful, even if we are faithless, for he cannot deny himself (2 Tim. 2:13).

Salvation is an unconditional promise. God makes promises that cannot be broken. *Salvation is an unconditional promise.* Hebrews declares: "Because God wanted to make *the unchanging nature of his purpose* very clear to the heirs of what was promised, he confirmed it with an oath. God did this so that, by *two unchangeable things* in which *it is impossible for God to lie,* we who have fled to take hold of the hope offered to us may be greatly encouraged" (Heb. 6:17–18). Salvation is an unconditional gift (Rom. 11:29; Eph. 2:9). Hence, God cannot take back his unconditional promise of salvation.

Salvation cannot be gained or lost by our efforts. We cannot gain salvation by good works, and we cannot lose it by bad works. "For it is by grace you have been saved, through faith— and this not from yourselves, it is the gift of God—*not by works,* so that no one can boast (Eph. 2:8–9). For "he saved us, *not because of righteous things we had done,* but because of his mercy. He saved us through the washing of rebirth and renewal by the Holy Spirit" (Titus 3:5). If we do not gain salvation by our works, then how can we lose it by our works? Bad behavior, even the kind Arminians claim is sufficient to cause loss of salvation, can no more cause individuals to lose their salvation than good behavior can help them gain it.

To the objection that salvation is received by our free choice and can be lost by our free choice, we note that salvation is an unconditional gift (Rom. 11:29) and as such cannot be taken back by God. Like the gift of physical life itself, once eternal life is received, it cannot be given back or given away. Only God can take it back, and his character guarantees that he will never renege on his promise. Further, some acts of freedom are one way. We can choose to get into situations that we cannot choose to get out of (e.g., suicide).

Likewise, just because salvation is received by faith does not mean it can be lost by faith. As noted above, receiving the gift of salvation is not dependent on a continual act of faith. The initial act of faith is the means through which salvation comes to us (cf. Rom. 13:11). Thus, the gift of salvation (Rom. 6:23) is a present possession (John 5:24), and God's gifts are irrevocable (Rom. 11:29).

Salvation is by grace alone. Closely associated with the previous point is the fact that if believers are not eternally secure but can lose their salvation by bad actions, then Arminianism is a tacit form of works salvation. Indeed, Arminian theologian H. Orton Wiley admits so when he says, "Arminians deny the merit of good works but insist upon them as a condition of salvation." He even notes: "Mr. Wesley's formula was, 'works, not as a merit, but as a condition.'"[25] Why are works a condition? Because, according to the Arminian view, one must maintain good works in order to keep one's salvation. In order to guarantee their ultimate salvation, believers must not perform the kind of bad actions that precipitate the loss of salvation after they are saved.

In fact, the Arminian view is similar to the Roman Catholic view,[26] which demands that once one receives initial justification by grace alone, then one must not commit a mortal sin or else one will lose his or her salvation. But if works are necessary for the maintenance of my salvation, then how can I avoid the conclusion that I am saved by my good works?

A RESPONSE TO THEOLOGICAL ARGUMENTS USED BY ARMINIANS

Arminians use certain texts and arguments to show that individuals can lose their salvation. Moderate Calvinists must

---

[25]Wiley, *Christian Theology*, 2:373.

[26]See Norman L. Geisler and Ralph MacKenzie, *Roman Catholics and Evangelicals: Agreements and Differences* (Grand Rapids: Baker, 1995), ch. 12.

respond to these. At the heart of the Arminian argument is the contention that all the salvation passages are conditional, either implicitly or explicitly.

The Promise of Salvation Is Conditional

Noted Arminian Robert Shank has argued that there are at least eighty-five "NT Passages Establishing the Doctrine of Conditional Security."[27] He stressed texts that speak of "continuing," "abiding," "holding fast," and so forth. Colossians 1:23 is often used in this connection: *"if you continue in your faith,* established and firm, not moved from the hope held out in the gospel." Likewise, 1 Corinthians 15:2 says: "By this gospel you are saved, *if you hold firmly* to the word I preached to you." Hebrews 3:12–14 affirms: "See to it, brothers, that none of you has a sinful, unbelieving heart that turns away from the living God. But encourage one another daily, as long as it is called Today, so that none of you may be hardened by sin's deceitfulness. *We have come to share in Christ if we hold firmly till the end the confidence we had at first."*

However, moderate Calvinists affirm that these texts do not assert that true believers will ever lose their salvation. Moreover, the context indicates that the author of Hebrews is speaking about practical and progressive holiness, not our positional and perfect holiness in Christ, though the former is to flow from the latter (cf. Eph. 1:4; Heb. 10:14). For he speaks of being "presented blameless, and irreproachable"—phrases reminiscent of those used in Ephesians where Paul writes: "Christ loved the church and gave himself up for her *to make her holy,* cleansing her *by the washing with water through the word,* and to present her to himself as a radiant church, without stain or wrinkle or any other blemish, but holy and blameless" (Eph. 5:25–27).

Further, to "continue in the faith" (in Col. 1:23) does not mean simply to continue believing but to continue *to live* the Christian faith. Paul here also speaks of being "established and firm"—images that he uses elsewhere for a fruitful Christian life. For example, he tells the Corinthians to "stand firm. Let nothing move you. Always give yourselves fully to *the work of the Lord,* because you know that *your labor in the Lord* is not in vain" (1 Cor. 15:58). Since these figures of speech refer to working for

---

[27]Robert Shank, *Life in the Son* (Minneapolis: Bethany House, 1989), 334–37.

the Lord and since we are not saved by works (Eph. 2:8–9), the reference to continuing steadfastly in the faith in Colossians 1:23 is best taken as implying that, if we so continue walking in the Christian faith, we will be rewarded by Christ when we are presented before his judgment seat (1 Cor. 3:11–12; 2 Cor. 5:10).

Other passages dealing with continued faithfulness in the Christian life also refer to faithfulness that yields a reward for service, not the gift of salvation. For example, Jesus says, "*Be faithful*, even to the point of death, and *I will give you the crown of life*" (Rev. 2:10).

Finally, there is a difference in *having faith to the end* and *being faithful to the end*. Perseverance in faith naturally involves the former but not necessarily the latter (see below). That is, if one is a true believer, then he or she will *continue to believe in Christ to the end*. Jesus places those who "believe for a while" among those who are not saved like the one who continues to believe (cf. Luke 8:13; cf. v. 15). Hence, *continuance in the faith* is a *demonstration* of who is saved, not a *condition* of being saved. But continuance in faithfulness to Christ is not a demonstration of salvation or a condition for getting it.

Belief Is a Continual Process

Arminians argue that the Bible uses the term *belief* in the present tense, not as a once-for-all, completed act when we were first saved. For example, they assert that the participles in John's Gospel that promise eternal life for believing speak of belief in the present tense, namely, as a continual process. Hence, they translate, for example: "For God so loved the world that he gave his one and only Son, that *whoever continues to believe in him* shall not perish but have eternal life" (John 3:16).

In response to this, moderate Calvinists point out several important things. (1) The present participle does not necessarily mean perpetual action, only current action.[28]

(2) Jesus' use of the present participle in John 4:13 of drinking physical water is an obvious example of an initial act that does not go on forever. For no one who is continuously drinking gets thirsty again, as John 4:13 says he or she will.

---

[28]See Charles Stanley, *Eternal Security: Can You Be Sure?* (Nashville: Thomas Nelson, 1990), ch. 9, on this point.

(3) The present participle is sometimes used of a one-time event, such as the incarnation of Christ (cf. John 6:33; note 6:38 and 42, which use the perfect indicative, and 6:41, which uses an aorist participle). The present participle is often used of actions that have stopped (cf. Matt. 2:20; John 9:8; Gal. 1:23).[29] Thus, the act of faith that is the condition for receiving the gift of salvation can be a moment of decision. It simply means that one begins to believe in the present.

(4) If an initial act of belief were not sufficient for salvation but required a continual process, then there is no way Scripture could pronounce that one has already received the gift of eternal life as a present possession, which it does (e.g., John 5:24). Continual faith after one first receives the gift of salvation is not a condition for *retaining* salvation, it is simply a natural *manifestation of it.* As Wiley noted, "The initial act becomes the permanent attitude of the regenerate man."[30] For God is able to keep us in a continual state of belief by his power (1 Peter 1:5; cf. Phil. 1:6).

(5) Not all references to belief that brings salvation are in the present tense. Some are in the aorist tense and indicate a completed action (e.g., John 4:39–41). Romans 13:11 declares: "The hour has come for you to wake up from your slumber, because our salvation is nearer now than *when we first believed.*" Indeed, the famous passage in Acts 16:31 is not in the present tense but in the aorist (which indicates a decisive kind of action, not the duration of the action). Paul said, "*Believe* [aorist] in the Lord Jesus, and you will be saved" (Acts 16:31).

(6) Since salvation is in three stages, it should come as no surprise that the Bible stresses belief in the present. We *were saved* in the past from the penalty of sin (justification); we *are being saved* in the present from the power of sin (sanctification); we *will be saved* from the presence of sin in the future (glorification). But even though we must "work out [our] salvation" in the present (Phil. 2:12), it is God "who works in" us, both "to will and to act according to his good purpose" (2:12–13). As the apostle put it, "I worked harder than all of them—yet not I, but *the grace of God that was with me*" (1 Cor. 15:10).

---

[29]See Hodges, *Absolutely Free*, 210–11.
[30]Wiley, *Christian Theology*, 2:375.

(7) Finally, nowhere does Scripture say that those who once truly believed might eventually lose their salvation. It only says that those who believe should continue to work out this salvation they already have (Phil. 2:13).

Symmetrical Nature of Belief and Unbelief

Arminians also argue that if we can exercise faith to get "in Christ," then we can use the same faith to "get out" of Christ. Just as we can get on and off something at will, we can exercise our free choice to get off the "bus" of salvation anywhere along the way. Not to be able to do this would mean that once we get saved, we are no longer free. Freedom is symmetrical; if you have it to get saved, then you also have it to get lost again.

In response to this argument, it is important to observe a few things. (1) As has been shown above, it is not biblically based; it is *speculative* and should be treated as such. (2) It is not necessary to accept this reasoning, even on a purely rational basis. Some decisions in life are one way, with no possibility of reversing them—suicide, for example. Saying "oops" after jumping off a cliff will not reverse the decision. (3) By this same logic Arminians would have to argue that we can be lost even after we get to heaven. Otherwise, they would have to deny that we are free in heaven. But if we are still free in heaven and yet cannot be lost, then why is it logically impossible for us to be free on earth and yet never be able to lose our salvation? In both cases the answer is that if we freely submit to God by saving faith, then his omnipotent power is able to keep us from falling—in accordance with our free choice (Jude 24).

A RESPONSE TO BIBLICAL ARGUMENTS USED BY ARMINIANS

Arminians use many verses to show that believers can lose their salvation. Space does not permit a detailed explanation of all of them,[31] but they all fall into two broad categories.

---

[31]See Augustus Hopkins Strong, *Systematic Theology* (Philadelphia: Judson, 1907), 882–86, for a complete listing of such verses. Also consult Stanley, *Eternal Security*, for a discussion of the most important verses Arminians use to claim we can lose our salvation.

Professing But Not Possessing Believers

First, there is a group of verses that deals with professing believers who never really had saving faith to begin with.

Matthew 7:22–23. Jesus says, "Many will say to me on that day, 'Lord, Lord, did we not prophesy in your name, and in your name drive out demons and perform many miracles?' Then I will tell them plainly, *'I never knew you.* Away from me, you evil-doers!'" In spite of the profession of these people and even signs done in Jesus' name, it is clear from the words "*I never knew you*" that they were never saved.

Matthew 10:1, 5–8. "He [Jesus] called *his twelve disciples* to him *and gave them* authority to drive out evil spirits and to heal every disease and sickness. . . . These *twelve* Jesus sent out with the following instructions: '. . . Go rather to the lost sheep of Israel. As you go, *preach this message:* "The kingdom of heaven is near." *Heal the sick, raise the dead,* cleanse those who have leprosy, *drive out demons.*'" It seems evident from this passage that these gifts were given to all the disciples, including Judas (v. 4), and that he too "preached" the message of Jesus. Indeed, we know from other Scripture that Judas was Jesus' treasurer (John 13:29). Moreover, after he betrayed Christ, we read that he was lost, being called "the one doomed to destruction [damnation]" (John 17:12). This phrase is used of the Antichrist (2 Thess. 2:3). Further, Jesus said it would have been better if Judas had never been born (Matt. 26:24) and Luke writes that, after hanging himself, Judas went "where he belongs" (Acts 1:25). Judas, therefore, seems clearly a professed follower of Christ. Yet he ended in perdition (hell). Is this not an example of someone who was saved but then lost his salvation by betraying Christ?

Strangely enough, the answer is No. Rather, Judas was only a professing believer, a sheep in wolf's clothing. Jesus called him a "devil" (John 6:70), who was eventually indwelt by Satan himself (13:27). The word used of his so-called "sorry" after he betrayed Christ reveals that he was not a true believer. The Greek word used is *metamelomai*, which denotes regret, not repentance (Gk., *metanoeo*). Indeed, in his great high priestly prayer, Jesus excluded Judas from those who were truly his own (17:12).

Matthew 24:13. *"But he who stands firm to the end will be saved."* Matthew 10:22 says the same thing: "All men will hate you because of me, *but he who stands firm to the end will be saved*." Some scholars take this to be speaking of the perseverance of the saints. If so, it does not disprove eternal security. Rather, it merely affirms that the elect will persevere, since they are God's chosen ones. Again, their perseverance is a *sign* of their salvation, not a *condition* of it. However, in context it would appear that this passage does not refer to losing either salvation or rewards. It is probably speaking about the believers who live through the "tribulation" period to come at the "end of the age" (cf. 24:3, 29). If so, then it means that only those who live through the Tribulation will go into the millennial reign of Christ (Rev. 20:4–5).

Luke 8:13–15. "Those on the rock are the ones who receive the word with joy when they hear it, but they have no root. *They believe for a while*, but in the time of testing *they fall away*." On the face of it, this passage seems to favor the Arminian view, since the persons described here were "believers for a while" and then they "fell away." However, there are two kinds of belief: nominal (nonsaving) belief and saving belief. The former is mere belief *that* something is so; the latter is belief *in* it.[32]

James in James 2:14–26 stresses that nominal belief does not lead to good works and is not saving faith. Zane Hodges argues that James is not speaking of salvation from hell but from death, not justification but sanctification. He believes the "dead" faith is that of a believer who lacks vitality and that "works" are necessary for God's blessing on one's life. So he sees "justification" in James 2 as meaning justification *before people*, not justification in the eyes of God, as Paul used it in Romans 3–4.[33] Even if this is so, James clearly says, "You see that his [Abraham's] faith and his actions were working together, and his faith was made complete by what he did" (James 2:22).

James goes on to connect this with the same faith that alone justified Abraham. Where Hodges goes wrong is to assume that

---

[32]Hodges recognizes that true faith involves "trust" (*Absolutely Free*, 32, 60). But what we really trust we naturally act upon. Further, true faith involves repentance and obedience (see Acts 20:21; Rom. 16:26). Hodges also acknowledges that true faith "appropriates" Christ (p. 40). This implies that there is a kind of faith that does not. So regardless of his rejection of the belief *in* and belief *that* distinction, he does recognize that there is a difference between a "dead" faith and one that is operative. This amounts to the same thing as the "belief in" vs. "belief that" distinction is getting at, namely, a dead faith does not bring justification while an operative one does.

[33]Hodges, *Absolutely Free*, 74–75.

we are justified by faith alone without works (which is true), but we are sanctified by faith plus works (which is false).[34] This is neither the biblical position nor that of the Reformers. Contrary to Hodges, faith—the same faith that alone justifies us—inevitably produces good works. We are justified by faith alone, but the faith that justifies us is not alone; good works flow naturally and inevitably from it. We are not saved by works but by a faith that works (see below).

As Peter said, true believers *"through faith* are shielded by God's power until the coming of the salvation that is ready to be revealed in the last time"* (1 Peter 1:5). Further, it is evident from this passage that only the faith that takes "root" and produces "fruit" (Luke 8:13, 15) is true saving faith. Seed that does not take root in a heart of true belief is no better than the seed that falls by the wayside, of which it is said, "the devil comes and takes away the word from their hearts, *so that they may not believe and be saved"* (v. 12).

2 Thessalonians 2:3. Paul warns of a great apostasy from the faith, saying, "Don't let anyone deceive you in any way, for *that day will not come until the rebellion [apostasy] occurs and the man of lawlessness is revealed, the man doomed to destruction"* (cf. v. 8). It appears from the context that apostasy leading to ultimate doom and destruction (hell) not only can but will occur. However, those who make up this group are not true believers from the beginning, for this deception will take place among *"those who are perishing.* They perish because *they refused to love the truth and so be saved"* (v. 10).

1 Timothy 4:1–2. "The Spirit clearly says that in later times *some will abandon the faith* and follow deceiving spirits and things taught by demons. Such teachings come through hypocritical liars, whose consciences have been seared as with a hot iron." Arminians point out that such people must have once had the

---

[34]The whole point of Galatians is that progressive sanctification, like initial justification, is by faith and not by works. The emphasized and bracketed words help bring out the proper meaning in its context. Paul said: *"Did you receive the Spirit [initial act of justification] by observing the law, or by believing what you heard? Are you so foolish? After beginning with the Spirit [by faith], are you now trying to attain your goal [of progressive sanctification] by human effort? ... Does God give you his Spirit and work miracles among you because you observe the law, or because you believe what you heard? ... All who rely on observing the law are under a curse.... 'The righteous will live [the life of sanctification as well as initial act of justification] by faith'"* (Gal. 3:2–11).

faith or they could not have later departed from it. In response, the phrase "the faith" is used by Paul in the Pastoral Letters (see 1 Tim. 3:9; 2 Tim. 2:18; Titus 1:13) and elsewhere (1 Cor. 16:13; Eph. 4:13; Phil. 1:27; Col. 2:7); as well as in Acts (see Acts 6:7; 13:8; 14:22), as equivalent to "the Christian faith" with all its essential doctrines (1 Tim. 3:9; 4:6) and ethics (1 Tim. 6:10). One may give mental assent to "*the* faith" without really making it *one's own personal* faith.

Further, the New Testament speaks of persons who have "wandered" from the faith (1 Tim. 6:10), "denied" it (5:8), "destroyed" it in some (2 Tim. 2:18), "turned from" it (Acts 13:8), "opposed" it (2 Tim. 3:8), and "departed" from it (1 Tim. 4:1). It is difficult not to believe that at least some of these phrases, if not all, describe people who are truly lost. The phrase "the faith" here means "the Christian faith," so that one can depart from *the* faith without its ever being *one's own* faith.

We need only ask whether there is any indisputable evidence that the Bible affirms that any of these people were true believers to begin with. An examination of these texts yields a negative answer. These are people who indeed professed the doctrines of the Christian faith, but the passages describe none of them as having once been true believers. Like Simon the sorcerer, they may have "believed" and been "baptized" (Acts 8:13). However, the subsequent action of Simon in trying to buy the power of the Holy Spirit and Peter's condemnation of him reveal that his faith was only nominal and not saving faith. Note Peter's comments: "May your money *perish with you*, because you thought you could buy the gift of God with money! *You have no part or share in this ministry*, because *your heart is not right before God*" (8:20–21). Thus, like all unsaved people (cf. Acts 17:30), he needed to "*repent of this wickedness* and pray to the Lord. . . . For I see that *you are full of bitterness and captive to sin*" (8:22–23). This is scarcely a description of a saved person.

Hebrews 12:14. "Make every effort to live in peace with all men and to be holy; *without holiness no one will see the Lord.*" If this is so, then how can one avoid the Arminian conclusion that living a holy life is necessary for one to make it to heaven? There are several problems with taking this as a passage that teaches individuals can lose their salvation. How holy does one have to be? Whose holiness is it speaking about? All Christians are dressed in Christ's righteousness and thus are as holy as one can be (2 Cor. 5:21). Indeed, Paul said to a presently unholy church at Corinth that they were already "sanctified in Christ Jesus" (1 Cor. 1:2). And Hebrews speaks of those who, in spite of presently "being sanctified," are nevertheless "perfected forever" (Heb. 10:14). If the passage is speaking of our righteousness, then they are as filthy rags in the eyes of God (Isa. 64:6).

What then is Hebrews 12:14 speaking about? It seems certain that it does not mean that all believers must attain perfect, practical holiness before they can be saved. Few, if any, have ever done this, despite some claims to the contrary. Further, this would be a kind of works salvation, which is repeatedly condemned in the Bible. Perhaps there is help in the word *"pursue"* as opposed to *attain*. We should pursue practical holiness, even if we do not attain it perfectly. Even if this is not in view here, surely the idea that we should pursue practically what only Christ has achieved positionally for us is a biblical one. One thing seems certain: Nowhere does this text affirm that believers will lose their salvation if they do not live perfect lives of holiness.

2 Peter 2:1–22. Peter speaks of *those who denied "the sovereign Lord who bought them"* (v. 1) but *who had "known the way of righteousness"* (v. 21). This seems to indicate, so Arminians argue, that they were at one time truly saved. But the rest of the chapter indicates that their present denial has led to their ultimate doom, since the "blackest darkness is reserved for them" (cf. v. 17). They are "dogs" (a figure used of unbelievers), not lambs (see v. 22). Also, they are called "slaves of depravity" (v. 19). In brief, they are not a "new creation" (2 Cor. 5:17) of God. However, a closer look at the context reveals that the persons who are "denying the sovereign Lord" (2 Peter 2:1) were never true believers but were "false teachers" and "false prophets" (v. 1). Hence, their "knowledge" of the Lord (v. 20) was obviously one of mental assent, not heart commitment. They knew Christ merely as the "Lord and Savior" (v. 20), not as *their* Lord and Savior. They were wolves in sheep's clothing (Matt. 7:15).

True Believers Losing Rewards, and so on, but Not Salvation

The second group of verses Arminians use to show that believers can lose their salvation refers instead to those who are truly saved but are only losing their rewards (fellowship, maturity, or physical life). Below are several sample texts.

Psalm 51:1–12. David prays after his terrible sins of murder and adultery: *"Against you [God], you only, have I sinned and done what is evil in your sight,* so that you are proved right when you speak and justified when you judge.... Hide your face from my sins and blot out all my iniquity. *Create in me a pure heart, O God, and renew a steadfast spirit within me. Do not cast me from your presence or take your Holy Spirit from me. Restore to me the joy of your salvation* and grant me a willing spirit, to sustain me" (Ps. 51:4–12). Some argue that when David committed adultery and murder, he feared the loss of his salvation. However, the wording of his prayer is very important. Even in these gross sins, he does not worry about losing his salvation but the *joy* of it. He prays only: "Restore to me the *joy* of your salvation and grant me a willing spirit, to sustain me" (51:12). Believers living in sin are not happy. They are children of the Lord, but they are under his discipline (Heb. 12:5–11; cf. 1 Cor. 11:28–32).

Psalm 69:27–28. "Charge them with crime upon crime; *do not let them share in your salvation. May they be blotted out of the book of life* and not be listed with the righteous." Some believe this is referring to the book of eternal life, namely, the Lamb's "book of life" (Rev. 13:8), which records the names of all the saved (cf. 3:5; 20:15). If this is the case, then David is presumably praying that the people to whom he is referring will lose their salvation.

This, however, is unlikely. First, these people are God's "enemies" (Ps. 69:4, 18, 19), who do not "share in ... [God's] salvation" (v. 27). Thus, they are unbelievers, whose names never were in the Lamb's book of life.

Moreover, the Old Testament refers to many "books," none of which are the book of salvation in which the names of the elect are recorded (Rev. 21:27). There is the book that counts all the living (Ps. 87:6), the book that recounts the events of our lives (56:8), the book that keeps track of the days of our lives (139:15–16), and the book that records the deeds of our lives (51:1). None of these is the Lamb's book of life, the book of eternal life that records from all eternity who is saved. These "books" are in fact probably all figures of speech describing God's omniscience about things in this life.

Finally, Psalm 69 cannot be referring to the Lamb's book of life since no name can be blotted out of that book. Jesus said: "*I will never blot out his name from the book of life*, but will acknowledge his name before my Father and his angels" (Rev. 3:5, see discussion of this verse below), and all the names of the elect have been in it for eternity (17:8; cf. 13:8). Since God knows the end from the beginning (Isa. 46:10), why would he have put their names there to begin with if he knew he would eventually have to erase them?

Thus, it seems best to understand Psalm 69 in its Old Testament context of a book recording those who are alive. Since God is in control of life (Deut. 32:39; Job 1:21), David is referring to God's book of physical life, not eternal life. Charles Stanley puts the reasons for this succinctly:

> First of all, the other things David asks God to do to his enemies are physical in nature (see vs. 22–26). . . . Second, to interpret "book of life" as the Lamb's book of life implies that David's enemies were believers. . . . Third, in the previous verse, David asks that his enemies "not come into God's righteousness" (see Ps. 69:27). If their names were in the Lamb's book of life, they would have already come into His righteousness.[35]

Matthew 10:33. "But *whosoever shall deny me before men, him will I also deny before my Father which is in heaven*" (KJV). Many Arminians believe this is proof that one can lose his or her salvation by denying Christ. However, there are other ways to understand this text that fit better with the immediate context and with the rest of the New Testament.

The NIV translates "deny" (Gk. *arneomai*) as "disown," but this is too strong, since this same word is used in 2 Timothy 2:12 for believers whom God will not disown because of his faithfulness (see above). Also, a related term is also used of Peter's denial (Matt. 26:34–36, *aparneo*). However, he did not lose his salvation as a result of his denials. He was restored to fellowship with God, but his relationship with God had never ceased. He was still "wheat" (a symbol of believers) as opposed to "weeds" (a symbol of unbelievers, 13:25), and he retained his "faith" in Christ (see Luke 22:31–32) even when he denied that he knew Christ (vv. 47–62).

---

[35]Stanley, *Eternal Security*, 189.

It should also be observed that these individuals are "in heaven" (Matt. 10:33); they are only being denied special recognition by the Father, not a place in his family. They will receive no "Well done, good and faithful servant" (25:23) approbation from their Father, but they will be in his heaven.

Matthew 12:31–32. Jesus affirms the reality of an unpardonable sin: "And so I tell you, every sin and blasphemy will be forgiven men, *but the blasphemy against the Spirit will not be forgiven*. Anyone who speaks a word against the Son of Man will be forgiven, but *anyone who speaks against the Holy Spirit will not be forgiven, either in this age or in the age to come.*" Of the many things this passage has been taken to mean, nothing in it supports the Arminian position.

(1) Arminians believe that one can regain his or her salvation after losing it, but it is clear that this is not possible with the unpardonable sin. (2) There is no indication here that believers can commit this sin. The context shows that the passage is referring to hard-hearted unbelievers, who attributed the work of the Holy Spirit through Christ to the devil (see Mark 3:30). (3) It is possible that this sin is not one that can be committed today but only when Jesus was personally present on earth and the Holy Spirit was working through him. (4) Jesus died for all our sins (John 1:29; 1 John 2:2). Hence, if any so-called unpardonable sin exists, it must be the sin of not accepting Christ's forgiveness. But believers have accepted it, and Jesus has promised them that they will "never perish" (John 10:28).

1 Corinthians 3:11–15. "For no one can lay any foundation other than the one already laid, which is Jesus Christ. If any man builds on this foundation using gold, silver, costly stones, wood, hay or straw, his work will be shown for what it is, because the Day will bring it to light. It will be revealed with fire, and the fire will test the quality of each man's work. If what he has built survives, he will receive his reward. If it is burned up, *he will suffer loss.*" This text scarcely needs comment. True believers can lose their "reward," not their salvation. Further, a believer's "works" are never the grounds for salvation (Eph. 2:8–9). Finally, this passage emphatically declares that *"he himself will be saved,* but only as one escaping through the flames."

1 Corinthians 8:11. "So this weak brother, for whom Christ died, is *destroyed* by your knowledge." Also, "if your brother is distressed because of what you eat, you are no longer acting in love. Do not by your eating *destroy* your brother for whom Christ died" (Rom. 14:15). The Greek word *apollymi*, translated "destroy" or "perish" (KJV), is sometimes used of hell (Matt. 10:28). From this, a careless interpreter might conclude that such a one has lost his or her salvation. However, this is not the case. The word "destroy" most often simply means to "lose" something temporally, such as the loss of one's physical life (Matt. 26:52) or conveniences (10:39). Sometimes it is used of the loss of one's "reward" (10:42) but not one's salvation.

Further, the context in 1 Corinthians 8 (and Romans 14) has to do with offending a weaker "brother" (v. 11) by eating meat that had been offered to idols. Yet this can scarcely refer to the loss of salvation. (1) It speaks only of "wound[ing] their weak conscience" (v. 12), not sending them to hell. (2) Surely a trivial act of offense would not precipitate such a soul-damning sin. (3) The description of the weaker "brother" indicates a "stumbling block" in his life, not the eternal condemnation of his soul. By it the brother is merely caused to "stumble" (v. 13) in his Christian life, not to go to hell. (4) The parallel passage in Romans simply speaks of the offended brother as being "made weak" in his faith, not as losing it altogether (v. 22). (5) Whatever the situation causes the weaker brother to do, he is still a "brother" in Christ. It does not turn him from a brother into a nonbrother.

1 Corinthians 9:27. "I beat my body and make it my slave so that after I have preached to others, *I myself will not be disqualified for the prize.*" Paul is speaking here of loss of reward, not of salvation (cf. 1 Cor. 3:15; cf. 2 Cor. 5:10). For he speaks of it as a "prize" to be won, not a "gift" to be received (Rom. 6:23). In any event, warnings to persevere are not inconsistent with an assurance of salvation, any more than exhortations to "work out [our] salvation" (Phil. 2:12) are contradictory to "God who works in [us]" (v. 13) to accomplish it (cf. 1 Cor. 15:10).

Galatians 5:4. "You who are trying to be justified by law have been alienated from Christ; *you have fallen away from grace.*" Many Arminians insist that this means they had lost their salvation. However, a careful examination of the context reveals the contrary. For one thing, the people referred to are called "brothers" (6:1), who have placed their "faith" in Christ (3:2) for their "justification" (3:24). These are clear indicators that they are already saved. Moreover, they have "begun in the Spirit" (3:3) but are now "fallen from grace" (5:4) as a means of their sanctification and have gone back to the bondage of keeping the law (3:5, 10). They have not lost their salvation but only their true sanctification, since they are attempting to work *for* sanctifying grace, not working *from* grace. Hence, they have fallen from grace as a means of living a sanctified (holy) life. Finally, if falling from grace means the loss of salvation, why does Paul not refer to hell? The only threat mentioned is that of eventuating in the "yoke of slavery" (5:1), not in eternal torment (Rev. 20:10, 15).

1 Timothy 5:15. The apostle states: *"Some have in fact already turned away to follow Satan."* This text does not support the Arminian view of loss of salvation for a number of reasons. For one thing, the writer is speaking of believing widows in the context (vv. 5, 8). For another, "to follow Satan" is not a phrase that means the person is lost. Anyone who falls into sin, as all believers can (1 John 1:8), is following Satan's temptations (2 Cor. 2:11). Jesus said to Peter, "Get behind me, Satan," for a sin far short of apostasy (Matt. 16:23).

2 Timothy 2:12. "If we endure, we shall also reign with Him. *If we deny Him, He also will deny us"* (NKJV). Some Arminians take this to mean that these believers will be denied heaven. However, there is a better way to understand this. The immediate context reveals that Paul is speaking about a denial of *reward*, not of salvation, since the phrase just before he said, "If we endure, we will also reign with him." But reigning is part of a believer's reward (cf. Rev. 20:6; 22:12), not part of salvation, which one receives even if one loses his or her reward (cf. 1 Cor. 3:15). Further, the next verse makes it clear that we cannot lose our salvation, for it declares, *"If we are faithless, he will remain faithful, for he cannot disown himself"* (2 Tim. 2:13).

2 Timothy 2:17–18. "Their teaching will spread like gangrene. Among them are Hymenaeus and Philetus, who have wandered away from the truth. They say that the resurrection has already taken place, and *they destroy the faith of some.*" There are several reasons why this text does not point to a loss of salvation. (1) Only a few verses earlier is one of the strongest verses on eternal security: "If we are faithless, he will remain faithful, for he cannot disown himself" (v. 13). (2) The context focuses on belief in the resurrection. Hence, it may refer only to loss of belief in the resurrection as a future event (see v. 18). (3) Even if the text refers to the loss of faith in general, it is not a genuine faith (1 Tim. 1:5) that endures but a formal faith (2 Tim. 3:5)—one that even demons have (James 2:19). Such a faith is not sufficient for salvation (cf. 2:14–15).

2 Timothy 4:7. "I have fought the good fight, *I have finished the race, I have kept the faith.*" This seems to imply that there may be those who do not keep the faith and, hence, will be lost. However, while Paul speaks of keeping the faith, he does not say that those who do not keep the faith will not be saved. Further, he says in the next verse that the result of his keeping the faith is not salvation but a reward—a *"crown* of righteousness" (v. 8). Those who are not faithful will not receive such a crown. "He will suffer loss; *he himself will be saved*, but only as one escaping through the flames" (1 Cor. 3:15). God also awards other "crowns" for faithfulness (Rev. 2:10). This does not imply that those who are faithless get no salvation but only that they get no crown. John expresses this idea when he says: "They went out from us, but *they did not really belong to us*. For if they had belonged to us, they would have remained with us; but their going showed that none of them belonged to us" (1 John 2:19).

Hebrews 2:1. "We must pay more careful attention, therefore, to what we have heard, so *that we do not drift away*." Like the other warnings in Hebrews (see 6:4–7; 10:26–29), the context indicates that these believers are warned about losing their rewards, not their salvation, which is an "eternal redemption." The context calls them "those who will inherit salvation" (1:14) and "brothers" (2:17). The use of "we" (2:1) also points to other believers along with the author. Further, to "drift away" is not a figure of speech indicating a loss of salvation. Later warnings to the same audience indicate that the author is speaking of a loss of "maturity" (6:1; cf. 5:13–14).

Hebrews 6:4–6. "*It is impossible* for those who have once been enlightened, who have tasted the heavenly gift, who have shared in the Holy Spirit, who have tasted the goodness of the word of God and the powers of the coming age, *if they fall away, to be brought back to repentance*, because to their loss they are crucifying the Son of God all over again and subjecting him to public disgrace." There are several problems with taking this to refer to unbelievers. First of all, the passage declares emphatically that "it is impossible . . . to renew them again to repentance" (Heb. 6:4, 6). Few Arminians believe that, once a person has backslidden, it is impossible for him or her to be saved again.

Further, while the description of their spiritual status differs from other ways of expressing it in the New Testament, some of the phrases are difficult to take any other way than that the person was saved. For example, (1) those spoken of had experienced "repentance" (Heb. 6:6), which is the condition of salvation (Acts 17:30). (2) They were "enlightened . . . [and had] tasted the heavenly gift" (Heb. 6:4). (3) They "shared in the Holy Spirit" (v. 4). (4) In addition, they had "tasted the goodness of the word of God" (v. 5). (5) They had tasted the "powers of the coming age" (v. 5). None of these are phrases befitting unbelievers.

Of course, if they were believers, then the question arises as to their status after they "fall away" (v. 6). In response, it should be noted that the word for "fall away" (*parapipto*) does not indicate a one-way action. Rather, it is the word for "drift," indicating that the status of the individual is not hopeless. That it is "impossible" for them to repent again indicates the once-for-all nature of repentance. In other words, they do not need to repent again, since they did it once, and that is all that is necessary for "eternal redemption" (9:12). Further, this text seems to indicate that there is no more need for "drifters" (backsliders) to repent again and get saved all over any more than there is for Christ to die again on the Cross (6:6).

Finally, the writer of Hebrews calls those he is warning "beloved" (NIV "dear friends," 6:9), a term hardly appropriate for unbelievers. Thus, there is no loss of salvation here. Rather, it is a loss of "maturity" (6:1) and growth (5:13–14), which is precisely the context of the discussion.

Hebrews 10:26–29. "*If we deliberately keep on sinning after we have received the knowledge of the truth, no sacrifice for sins is left, but only a fearful expectation of judgment and of raging fire that will consume the enemies of God. Anyone who rejected the law of Moses died without mercy on the testimony of two or three witnesses. How much more severely do you think a man deserves to be punished who has trampled the Son of God under foot,* who has treated as an unholy thing the blood of the covenant that sanctified him, and who has insulted the Spirit of grace?"

As strong as this sounds, like the other warning passages in Hebrews (see comments on Heb. 6:4–6), this too is not a warning about loss of salvation but about loss of rewards. This is evidenced by many facts.

- The persons involved are described clearly as *"brothers"* (v. 19), *"his [God's] people"* (v. 30), and believers who have "a great priest" (Christ, v. 21) and a "hope we profess" (v. 23).

- The passage is not speaking of salvation of these people but of their being *"richly rewarded"* (10:35).

- The people being referred to already have "a better and lasting possession" in heaven (v. 34).

- They have "received the light" from God and possess the "knowledge of the truth" (vv. 26, 32), phrases that fit with believers.

- They have suffered with and had compassion for the author of the book as believers (vv. 33–34).

- They are described as those who can do "the will of God" (v. 36), something only believers can do (John 9:31).

- The reference to those who "insulted the Spirit of grace" (v. 29) implies these people were believers who had that Spirit to insult.

- The illustration used of those who died under the law of Moses (v. 28) speaks of physical death for disobedience, not of eternal death of separation from God. Paul speaks of physical death of believers for sin in 1 Corinthians 11:30 (cf. 1 John 5:16).

- The "fearful expectation of judgment" (v. 27) fits the description of the believers coming before the judgment seat of Christ (2 Cor. 5:10), where their works will be tried by fire and they will suffer loss of reward (see 1 Cor. 3:13–14 and the comments above).

- The passage in question does not support the Arminian view, since it says those who commit this sin cannot be restored again, for *"no sacrifice for sins is left"* (Heb. 10:26).

- This chapter ends with the writer affirming with confidence that believers will not be lost: "But *we are not of those who shrink back and are destroyed*, but of *those who believe and are saved*" (10:39).

2 Peter 3:17. "Therefore, dear friends, since you already know this, *be on your guard so that you may not be carried away by the error of lawless men and fall from your secure position.*" To fall from a secure position sounds very much like falling from one's salvation, which is a secure position. However, upon examining the text, the fall proves to be a fall from a position of maturity. This is indicated by the fact that the people Peter is addressing are called "dear friends" (3:14, 17), who are spiritual brothers of the apostle Paul (3:15). Further, the text says explicitly that the fall is from "steadfastness" (v. 17, an alternate translation of *sterigmos*, which the NIV translates as "secure position"), not from salvation. Finally, their failure is a loss of being able to "grow," not a lack of being saved (v. 18).

2 John 1:8. John wrote to believers called spiritual "children" (see v. 1), saying: "Watch out that you do not lose what you have *worked for*, but that you may be *rewarded* fully." This verse is not speaking of loss of salvation but loss of rewards, as the italicized words indicate. What these people are being warned about losing is what they have "worked for," but salvation is not a result of our works (Rom. 4:5; Eph. 2:8–9; Titus 3:5–6).

Revelation 3:5. "He who overcomes will, like them, be dressed in white. *I will never blot out his name from the book of life*, but will acknowledge his name before my Father and his angels." There are four other passages referring to the "book of life" (not counting 22:19 [see below], which may be rendered "tree of life").

- *Rev. 13:8.* "All inhabitants of the earth will worship the beast—all *whose names have not been written in the book of life belonging to the Lamb that was slain from the creation of the world.*"
- *Rev. 17:8.* "The inhabitants of the earth whose names have not been written in the book of life from the creation of the world will be astonished when they see the beast, because he once was, now is not, and yet will come."
- *Rev. 20:12, 15.* "And I saw the dead, great and small, standing before the throne, and books were opened. *Another book was opened, which is the book of life.* The dead were judged according to what they had done as recorded in the books. . . . *If anyone's name was not found written in the book of life, he was thrown into the lake of fire.*"

- *Rev. 21:27.* "Nothing impure will ever enter it, nor will anyone who does what is shameful or deceitful, but *only those whose names are written in the Lamb's book of life.*"

Several things are noteworthy about these texts. (1) John affirms that anyone's name, once in the book of life, will never be erased. Jesus said, "*I will never blot out his name from the book of life*" (3:5). Thus, no believer need fear losing salvation once he or she gets it.

(2) The names of the saved have been written there from eternity (13:8). Thus, there is literally eternal security for the elect. And once they know their name is there (namely, have personal assurance), they can be certain that they will never lose that salvation.

(3) God wrote the names of the elect in the book of life (and will never erase them) long before any of them ever did anything either to gain or lose salvation. Moreover, he knows the end from the beginning (Isa. 46:10). Hence, in his omniscient foreknowledge, he knew about any sins (even big ones) that the elect would commit after they were saved. Yet he made them eternally secure anyway. He knew they would persevere in their faith through everything.

Hence, rather than deny eternal security, these passages are strong affirmations of it. Only the names of the elect are in the book of life (20:15). They have been there forever (13:8), and God will never erase them (3:5)! What could be better?

Revelation 3:15–16. "I know your deeds, that you are neither cold nor hot. I wish you were either one or the other! So, because you are lukewarm—neither hot nor cold—*I am about to spit you out of my mouth.*" This, it would seem, supports the Arminian view that God rejects those who reject him. This appears to be confirmed by the fact this threat is given "to the churches" (v. 22) and that it refers to God's warning to "discipline" (v. 19) any who do not repent of their sins. However, even if true believers are in view, to "spit [them] out" is not a phrase that speaks of hell. More likely it is addressed to those believers who have turned "lukewarm" in their walk with God and need their fellowship restored. Notice the church is asked by Christ to "dine" (i.e., have fellowship) with him (v. 20).

This is reminiscent of the figure of speech in John 15:4, in which believers who are not abiding in Christ are said to wither on the vine. Hence, they become useless to God. Of them Jesus said: "If anyone does not remain in me, he is like a branch that is thrown away and withers; such branches are picked up, thrown into the fire and burned" (15:6). Notice, the passage does not say they are thrown by angels into the "eternal fire" (hell), but by human beings into a temporal fire. Paul spoke of such as "castaways" (1 Cor. 9:27, KJV). They are like Paul's "castaways" (cracked vases), which are put on the shelf because they have become useless in the service of the Master.

Revelation 22:19. "And if anyone takes words away from this book of prophecy, *God will take away from him his share in the tree of life*[36] and in the holy city, which are described in this book." Some believe this warning is to unbelievers, not believers, since the text says they are "outside" the heavenly gates (v. 15) and are described as those who "do wrong" (v. 11). Others argue that the whole book of Revelation is to "the churches" (1:4), a word repeated in this chapter (22:16). Moreover, those to whom it is addressed are not "outside" as the unbelievers are (22:15). In either case, there is no reason to take it as a reference to a true believer losing his or her salvation.

FAITH AND WORKS IN MODERATE CALVINISM

True Believers Manifest Their Faith in Good Works

There are crucial differences between the proponents of various views on eternal security with regard to the relation of faith and works. Strong Calvinists often hold that, moved by God's grace, saving faith *automatically* produces good works. Moderate Calvinists hold that works flow *naturally*,[37] but not automatically,

---

[36]The rendering "book of life" (KJV) does not follow the best manuscript tradition. Even so, it possesses no insurmountable problem for eternal security. It could be another way to designate unbelievers by noting that they have no place in the book of life.

[37]The word "inevitable," since it is weaker than "automatic," seems to imply there is no free choice involved, but there is. Yet, it is stronger than "accompany," a word that does not imply any direct connection between the works and the faith from which they spring, which the Bible entails. So, perhaps "natural" is a better word, denoting the essential connection without guaranteeing a necessary product. For example, love for children comes natural to mothers; however, some mothers abuse their children. When this happens, however, they are not doing what comes naturally. Something else has influenced them to choose to act in this unnatural way.

from saving faith. Some free grace proponents claim that works always *accompany* saving faith, even though they are not the direct result of it. Others insist that works are not automatic and *not necessary* at all.

Why Works Do Not Flow Automatically from Faith

There are many reasons for rejecting the strong Calvinist view that works flow automatically from saving faith.

- Sanctification is a process involving obedience, and obedience is not automatic but is an act of the will (Rom. 6:16; Eph. 6:5; 1 John 2:3, 22, 24).
- Sanctification is a manifestation of our love for God, but love is not an automatic act but a free one (Matt. 22:37–39; John 15:10; 1 John 5:3).
- Even strong Calvinists admit that sanctification involves cooperative grace and is a synergistic act that involves the cooperation of our free choice.
- Romans 6:16 describes sanctification as a free act in which you *"offer yourselves."*
- Other acts of good works are described as free and not coerced but *"entirely on their own"* (2 Cor. 8:3)—*"spontaneous and not forced"* (Philem. 14; cf. 1 Cor. 7:37, 39).
- Sanctification is a duty, but every responsibility implies the ability to respond, if not in our own strength, then by God's grace.[38]
- We are rewarded for good works (1 Cor. 3:11–14; Rev. 22:12). But it makes no sense to reward someone for actions that come automatically.
- We suffer loss of rewards for bad actions (1 Cor. 3:11–15). But it is senseless to punish someone for what he or she cannot avoid doing, since it comes automatically.

---

[38]In response to the strong Calvinist claim that synergistic acts by which we are saved are free acts, we note that according to Calvinism, they are not free in the libertarian sense that one could have done otherwise. They flow from a God-given desire that one cannot resist. Hence, it is meaningless to call them free when they resulted ultimately from irresistible grace on the unwilling (see Geisler, *Chosen But Free*, chs. 2, 6; appendices 1, 4, 5, 9).

Why Works Flow Naturally from Saving Faith

While works do not flow *automatically* from saving faith, they do flow *naturally*, just as buds come naturally from a live bush. As Charles Ryrie correctly observed, "every *Christian will bear fruit; otherwise he or she is not a true believer.*" For "*fruit, then, furnishes evidence of saving faith.* The evidence may be strong or weak, erratic or regular, visible or not. But *a saving faith works.*"[39] Certain circumstances, however, may put it into a dormant state for a while. But even in this condition, one can find signs of life. So it is with a true believer. Like other kinds of life, spiritual life cannot hide completely or long. It just naturally buds forth. Of course, to be fruitful it needs to be cultivated (2 Peter 3:18). Many lines of evidence from the Scriptures support this view.

- Saving faith is likened to a seed that grows naturally in good soil (Luke 8:11–18; cf. 1 Peter 1:23).
- Activity follows naturally from one's nature, and a true believer receives a new nature (2 Cor. 5:17; Col. 3:10).
- Believers are "born again" (John 3:3, 7) and as such manifest both life and a desire to grow by their hunger for food.[40]
- The close connection between faith and works in Scripture indicates that works flow naturally from faith (cf. Eph. 2:8–10; Phil. 2:12–13; Titus 2:11–13; 3:5–8; James 1:26–27; 2:12–13; 2 Peter 1:5–8; 1 John 3:16–18).
- It is widely acknowledged, even by free grace proponents, that saving faith involves trust,[41] and trust in someone leads naturally to good actions toward them.
- True repentance is involved in saving faith (Acts 17:30; 20:21; cf. 19:4),[42] and true repentance will lead to good

---

[39]Ryrie, *So Great Salvation*, 42–43 (italics added).

[40]Of course, new life can be stunted if it is not cultivated (cf. Heb. 5:12–6:1). Hence, the Bible urges us to encourage this natural desire for growth (1 Peter 2:2).

[41]Hodges wrote: "Yet the faith that receives so great a salvation has the utter directness of childlike *trust*" (*Absolutely Free*, 60, italics added). He also said of Abraham's act of saving faith that "this act of *trust* was put down to his account as righteousness" (32).

[42]The precise connection between faith and repentance is debated, but Ryrie seems to explain all the biblical data best when he notes that repentance as such does not save, since it only means to change one's mind (about anything). Thus, "the only kind of repentance that saves is a change of mind about Jesus Christ."

(Footnote continues on following page.)

works, as Scripture clearly indicates (Matt. 3:8; Acts 26:20).[43]

- The fact that true faith involves love for God (Matt. 22:37; 1 John 4:7) reveals that it will result in actions. True love naturally expresses itself (1 Cor. 13:1–2).
- True faith is not mere mental assent. It involves the mind, emotions, and will.[44] If so, the actions would tend to flow from such an act of faith of the whole person.
- That true faith involves obedience shows that belief naturally expresses itself in works (Acts 5:32; 2 Thess. 1:8; cf. Rom. 15:18; Heb. 5:9; 1 Peter 4:7).
- James said explicitly: "What good is it, my brothers, *if a man claims to have faith but has no deeds? Can such faith save him? [No]. . . . In the same way, faith by itself, if it is not accompanied by action, is dead. . . .* You see that *his [Abraham's] faith and his actions were working together, and his faith was made complete by what he did*" (James 2:14–22).
- We are sanctified the same way we are saved, namely, by faith (see Gal. 3:4, 11), but sanctification is conditioned on our "obedience, which leads to righteousness" (Rom. 6:16, cf. Eph. 6:5; 1 John 2:3, 22, 24).

Speaking of verses like Luke 24:46–47 and Acts 2:38; 17:30–31, which make repentance necessary for salvation, Ryrie says, "If repentance is not a synonym for faith in these verses, then the verses do not state the Gospel. If repentance is only part of conversion (faith being the other part), then these verses state only a half Gospel" (*So Great Salvation*, 88).

As to Acts 20:21, which appears to separate faith and repentance, Ryrie notes that "the two words, *repentance* and *faith*, are joined by one article which indicates that the two are inseparable, though each focuses on a facet of the single requirement for salvation" (ibid., 88).

Repentance and faith appear to be related as the two sides of one act. If someone says, "Come here," he or she cannot do it without leaving there. Faith is like the "coming here" and repentance like the "leaving there." As directed toward Christ, they both happen simultaneously and in the same act.

[43]Hodges's attempt to make repentance refer to the believer after conversion (*Absolutely Free*, ch. 12) is without foundation, as is indicated by (1) the order of the words (repentance first and then faith) in Acts 20:21), (2) the fact that true faith involves a change of mind, and (3) the fact that unbelievers are called upon to do both as a condition for salvation (cf. Acts 16:31; 17:30; 20:21). See Ryrie, *So Great Salvation*, 82–90, for a more balanced view.

[44]Ryrie, *So Great Salvation*, 110–11.

Some have objected that if good works flowed naturally from faith, then the Bible would not exhort us to good works as it does. Paul said, "so that those who have trusted in God *may be careful to devote themselves to doing what is good*" (Titus 3:8). However, while good works come naturally from saving faith, they do not flow automatically. Further, *some* works come naturally, but *more* fruit comes by hard work of cultivating, fertilizing, watering, and pruning (John 15:2). Finally, spiritual life is naturally present in true believers, but without works it can be dormant and stunted.

Similarly, some have argued that grace is said to be a teacher of godliness (Titus 2:11–12). Yet if godliness followed naturally from saving faith, one would not need grace to teach believers to do good works. However, teaching helps to produce better fruit (John 15:2). Further, nature will produce some fruit naturally, but not as much as if it is properly cultivated (1 Cor. 3:6; 2 Peter 3:18). As Ryrie put it, "*Saving faith is a working faith*, and those works justify believers in the courtroom on earth," and an "unproductive faith is a spurious faith."[45]

True Believers Can Fall into Sin

All of this is not to say that true believers cannot be "faithless" (Jer. 3:14) or be "caught in a sin" (Gal. 6:1) or "sin" (1 John 1:8–9). They indeed can fall into sin. David did (2 Sam. 11), and he paid for it dearly (2 Sam. 12). Lot was saved, but he was living in Sodom and lost everything. The Bible calls him "a righteous man" (2 Peter 2:7), but he fell into great sin, as did Noah, who was a great man of faith (Gen. 9). Likewise, Abraham, "the father of the faithful," was beset by sins of lying and unbelief in God (Gen. 20–21).

In the New Testament John the Baptist had his doubts (Luke 7:19), but Jesus said he would be in the kingdom of God (Matt. 11:11). Even Peter, who denied the Lord three times, did not lose his salvation (cf. Matt. 26:34–35; see Luke 22:31–32). Paul speaks of "worldly" believers (1 Cor. 3:1, 3). Indeed, the church at Corinth as a whole was living in various kinds of sin, yet Paul addressed them as "saints" (1 Cor. 1:2). Even the believer who committed incest was "saved" (5:5). Of course, not

---

[45]Ibid., 121.

all believers will receive rewards in heaven (3:12–14). Some will be *saved "as through fire"* (v. 15, NKJV). These texts plainly pronounce that one does not have to be a faithful Christian to get into heaven.

True Believers Are Disciplined When They Sin

Arminians often charge that eternal security leads to carnality, but this is not true for one simple reason: God disciplines his children. Hebrews tells us that *"the Lord disciplines those he loves, and he punishes everyone he accepts as a son"* (Heb. 12:6). God spanks all his wayward children. Thus, "for what son is not disciplined by his father? *If you are not disciplined (and everyone undergoes discipline), then you are illegitimate children and not true sons"* (12:7–8).

Paul writes in 2 Timothy 2:19: "'The Lord knows those who are his,' and, *'Everyone who confesses the name of the Lord must turn away from wickedness.'"* In short, when believers fall into sin, God disciplines them. If a believer goes too far, God will even take his or her physical life so as to save that person's name from further dishonor. Paul tells the Corinthians that their abuse at the Lord's table has resulted in the fact that *"a number of you have fallen asleep [died]"* (1 Cor. 11:30; cf. 15:20). This may be what John is speaking about when he says, *"There is a sin that leads to death. I am not saying that he should pray about that"* (1 John 5:16).[46] Perhaps this believer has gone so far that God will no longer entertain prayer to save his life. This also may be what James is warning about when he writes, "Whoever turns a sinner from the error of his way will *save him from death* and cover over a multitude of sins" (James 5:20).[47]

Speaking of a gross sin in the church at Corinth, Paul instructs believers there to "deliver such a one unto Satan for the *destruction of the flesh, that the spirit may be saved in the day of the Lord Jesus"* (1 Cor. 5:5, KJV). Two things are evident here: First, in spite of this believer's great sin, he will be ultimately saved; moreover, he will receive severe discipline for his sin (cf. 11:30–32).

---

[46]Since there is no indefinite article "a" in Greek, this might better be translated "There is sin that leads to death."

[47]They are called "my brothers" (James 5:19), and the context here is about believers who sin (v. 16) and "wander from the truth" (v. 19).

Paul writes these words to believers: "Do not be deceived: God cannot be mocked. *A man reaps what he sows*" (Gal. 6:7; cf. v. 8).

In brief, no believer can get away with sin. "For *we must all appear before the judgment seat of Christ*, that each one may receive what is due to him for the things done while in the body, whether good or bad" (2 Cor. 5:10). At this judgment seat, the believer's "work will be shown for what it is, because the Day will bring it to light. It will be revealed with fire, and *the fire will test the quality of each man's work*. If what he has built survives, he will receive his reward. If it is burned up, *he will suffer loss*; he himself will be saved, but only as one escaping through the flames" (1 Cor. 3:13–15).

In this life, all true believers are disciplined for their sin. Those who do not respond properly may be taken home to face their Master before whose presence they will suffer loss of rewards and will be saved "only as one escaping through the flames." Nonetheless, everyone once saved will always be saved. God does not renege on his promises (Rom. 11:29), nor does he begin a project he does not complete (Phil. 1:6).

Can True Believers Ever Lose Their Faith Completely?

One question not specifically addressed yet, which divides even moderate Calvinists, is whether continual faith in Christ throughout one's life is a necessary indication that one is truly saved. Or, put negatively, can a believer lose his or her faith and still be saved?

Continued belief is not a condition for keeping one's salvation. Two related questions here must be distinguished. The first one is whether continual belief throughout one's life is a necessary condition for keeping one's salvation. In distinction from Arminians, the answer is negative. There are no conditions of any kind for God giving or for our keeping salvation. Salvation is an unconditional gift (Rom. 11:29). Continued faith and its fruit in good works is a *manifestation* of true faith, but it is not a *condition* of it. If it were, then works (that result from saving faith) would be a condition of keeping one's salvation.

Continued faith is a manifestation that one is saved. Following Zane Hodges,[48] Charles Stanley and others claim that

---

[48]See Hodges, *Absolutely Free*, 105–6, 112.

continued faith is not a necessary sign of the elect. Stanley affirms that "God does not require a *constant attitude* of faith in order to be saved—only an *act* of faith."[49] With this we agree, but that is not the question. More precisely, the question is whether or not it is natural for one to exercise continual belief in Christ throughout his or her life in order to be shown that he or she is one of the elect. This is another question to which Zane Hodges and Charles Stanley give the answer No. Stanley writes: "[Hodges] argues convincingly that *Satan can completely shipwreck a believer's faith but that this in no way affects the believer's security.*"[50] He adds, "The Bible clearly teaches that God's love for His people is of such magnitude that *even those who walk away from the faith have not the slightest chance of slipping from His hand.*"[51]

Nevertheless, Scripture does not support the view that a true believer can totally lose his or her faith.

(1) As shown above, continued works are the natural result of saving faith.

(2) True faith is the kind that produces good works. James says explicitly that true faith manifests itself in works, for faith without works is dead (see James 2:14–22).

(3) As Jesus said in the parable of the soils, saving faith is not in those "who believe for a while," but such faith bears fruit (Luke 8:13, 15). Faith is not a work, but true faith continues to work.

(4) True faith will persevere to the end because it is *"through faith"* that we *"are shielded by God's power until the coming of the salvation that is ready to be revealed in the last time"* (1 Peter 1:5; cf. Phil. 1:6).

(5) Those who do give up their faith were not true believers in the first place (1 John 2:19). Peter denied he knew Christ to a few persons, but he never stopped believing in Christ (Luke 22:32). John the Baptist had questions about whether Jesus was the Messiah (Matt. 11:1–4), but he never denied it. Rather, he sent his disciples to ask Jesus his question and to have his wavering faith confirmed.

(6) The Bible declares that *"no one who is born of God will continue to sin,* because God's seed remains in him; he cannot go on

---

[49]Stanley, *Eternal Security*, 80.

[50]Ibid., 91 n. 2 (italics added).

[51]Ibid., 74.

sinning, because he has been born of God" (1 John 3:9). But to avoid continual sin one must be in continual faith, for faith is the victory that overcomes the world (5:4).

(7) Those who depart from the faith were not really in it to begin with. John said, "*They went out from us, but they did not really belong to us. For if they had belonged to us, they would have remained with us*" (1 John 2:19).

True Believers Are Not Always Faithful

To continue in faith and to continue in faithfulness are not the same. One can continue to believe in Christ and manifest a modicum of good works springing from it without being a faithful and fruitful Christian. True believers are not always faithful. But when they are unfaithful to the Lord, they do not lose their salvation, for "if we are not faithful, he will remain faithful, for he cannot deny himself" (2 Tim. 2:13 NRSV).

Abraham, Lot, David, John the Baptist, and Peter are only a few examples. Most of these were great saints, yet they sinned without losing their salvation. None of them, however, renounced faith in God. They were unfaithful to one or more of God's commandments, but none of them were without faith in the God of these commandments. *There is not a single undisputed example of anyone anywhere in Scripture who was known to be saved and who then completely gave up his or her faith in God.* As discussed earlier, all the examples of people who denied the faith were only professing, not possessing, Christians. That is, they were never saved. They fall into the category of whom Jesus spoke when he said, "I *never* knew you" (Matt. 7:23).

CONCLUSION

In contrast to Arminianism, moderate Calvinism is convinced there is strong biblical and theological support for the doctrine of eternal security. In distinction from the implication of strong Calvinism, moderate Calvinism asserts that believers can have real assurance that they are God's elect, apart from whether they are faithful to the end. Moderate Calvinists reject the view that there is security for the elect but no assurance that one is elect unless he or she endures faithfully to the end.

In this regard, it is ironic that Arminians are more Calvinistic than strong Calvinists. For Arminianism holds that one can have assurance that one is now saved,[52] even if that person does not have security that he or she will ultimately be saved. *Moderate Calvinism, on the contrary, holds that one can have both present assurance and eternal security—the best of both worlds.*

---

[52]Wiley notes, however, that "the assurance is the fruit, and not the essence of faith" (*Christian Theology*, 2:375–76).

A CLASSICAL CALVINIST RESPONSE TO NORMAN L. GEISLER

Michael S. Horton

It is somewhat difficult to know precisely how to assess Norman Geisler's chapter, since his entire paradigm, to my mind, rests on a remarkably ill-informed understanding of both Calvinism and Arminianism. Furthermore, the exegetical section seems to substitute rapid-fire proof-texting for serious wrestling with key texts. For his most controversial descriptions, Geisler does not cite traditional Reformed or Arminian authorities. This may explain why the view he labels "strong Calvinism" is alien to any respectable presentation of that position and why the view he defends as "moderate Calvinism" is in fact semi-Pelagianism. This is a strong charge, so let me try to attend closely to the author's line of argument.

First, Geisler (like many who identify themselves as "Calminians") sets his position up as the golden mean between the twin excesses of Calvinism and Arminianism.[1] "In between these two poles, moderate Calvinists are typically understood to hold some but not all of these points—minimally at least the P of TULIP, the perseverance of the saints," he writes. However, as I

---

[1]Historically, "Moderate Calvinism" has referred to the seventeenth-century Amyraldian position within the Reformed churches. Soon rejected by those churches, this Moderate Calvinism rejected particular redemption ("limited atonement") and held to mediate imputation. Geisler's position is much further from Calvinism than Amyraldianism—in some respects, even beyond Arminianism.

have argued in my chapter, the doctrine of "eternal security," at least as presented by those of Geisler's theological persuasion, is not the same as the Augustinian-Reformed doctrine of perseverance. If that is the case, Professor Geisler is not a one-point Calvinist but a no-point Calvinist, who nevertheless describes his position as moderate Calvinism.

Next, the author compares and contrasts allegedly moderate and strong Calvinism by creating a caricature of the latter. While the former view regards total depravity as "extensive (corruptive)," the latter sees it as "intensive (destructive)." This contrast is followed through the so-called "TULIP": Election has no conditions for God, but one for humans (faith) versus its having no condition for God or humans; the atonement is limited in result but for all versus limited in extent and not for all; the divine call "in [a] persuasive sense (in accord with the human will)" versus "in [a] coercive sense (against the human will)"; a view of perseverance in which "not all saints will be faithful to the end" versus "all saints will be faithful to the end."

A cursory consultation of Reformed systematic theologies would have corrected the author's misunderstanding. Geisler does not clearly define his terms, and many of those pertaining to Calvinism are used pejoratively. I can respond only briefly to each "petal" of the TULIP. First, regarding total depravity, Geisler charges: "According to strong Calvinism, one cannot receive salvation by his or her own free act of faith. . . . By contrast, the moderate Calvinist, who believes in total depravity in an *extensive sense*, holds that the image of God is not erased in fallen humanity but only effaced." The very language of "effaced, not erased" I learned from reading Reformed systems, beginning with Calvin's *Institutes*: The divine image "was not totally annihilated and destroyed in him."[2] Thus, non-Christians are capable of creating reasonably just governments and culture:

> Whenever we come upon these matters in secular writers, let that admirable light of truth shining in them teach us that the mind of man, though fallen and perverted from its wholeness, is nevertheless clothed and ornamented with God's excellent gifts. . . . Those men whom Scripture calls "natural men" were, indeed, sharp and

---

[2]John Calvin, *Institutes of the Christian Religion*, ed. John T. McNeill, trans. F. L. Battles (Philadelphia: Westminster, 1960), 1.15.4.

penetrating in their investigation of earthly things. Let us, accordingly, learn by their example how many gifts the Lord left to human nature even after it was despoiled of its true good.[3]

In contrast to Lutheran theology, which regarded the divine image as lost in sinners until the new birth, Reformed teaching has insisted on the endurance of God's image in all people. This is strengthened by the Reformed emphasis on "common grace." Berkhof explains, "Common grace enables man to perform what is generally called *iustitia civilis*, that is, that which is right in civil or natural affairs, in distinction from that which is right in religious matters...."[4] "The doctrine of man's inability, therefore," says Charles Hodge, "does not assume that man has ceased to be a free moral agent. He is free because he determines his own acts.... He is a moral agent because he has the consciousness of moral obligation, and whenever he sins he acts freely against the convictions of conscience or the precepts of the moral law."[5]

The Westminster Confession similarly distinguishes between a natural and a moral ability according to which human beings even after the Fall are naturally free to choose whatever they prefer. However, because of the seriousness of the Fall and their own participation in it, they only prefer rejection of God apart from his grace. "God hath endued the will of man with that natural liberty, that it is neither forced, nor by any absolute necessity of nature determined to good or evil." While the natural person is able to choose whatever one desires, one is not free to desire that from which one's soul recoils. Therefore, one "is not able, by his own strength, to convert himself, or prepare himself thereto."[6]

Of course, one's view of total depravity controls one's understanding of God's effectual calling of sinners to Christ. So, if it is permissible, I would like to transgress the proper order of the TULIP and treat Geisler's account of "irresistible grace." For moderate Calvinists grace is persuasive, while for strong Calvinists it

[3]Ibid., 2.2.15.

[4]Louis Berkhof, *Systematic Theology* (Grand Rapids: Eerdmans, 1941), 443.

[5]Charles Hodge, *Systematic Theology*, 3 vols. (Grand Rapids: Eerdmans, 1946, from the Charles Scribner ed., 1871), 2:260–61.

[6]The Westminster Confession of Faith, in *The Book of Confessions* (Louisville: PCUSA General Assembly, 1991), 6.059–61.

is coercive. If Geisler wanted to argue that, despite its stated position, Calvinism seems to imply coercion, and then make that case, how could one object in principle? Instead, however, he caricatures Calvinism as holding a position that it explicitly rejects. Just beneath the reference cited above, the Westminster Confession holds: "When God converteth a sinner and translateth him into the state of grace, he freeth him from his natural bondage under sin, and, by his grace alone, enableth him freely to will and to do that which is spiritually good ... yet so as they come most freely, being made willing by his grace."[7]

The failure to distinguish natural and moral ability leads many Arminians to conclude that Calvinism is deterministic, but this is far too general a criticism. Surely everyone involved in this conversation can agree that human actions are determined by something other than the actions themselves. We all do things for a reason, whether we recognize that reason explicitly or not. The reasons are themselves dependent on the dispositions or loves of the moral agent. When saints are eventually glorified, they will no longer be able to sin—this much has received the widest consent of Christian churches. Does that mean that they will no longer be free moral agents? Certainly not, but rather they will be released from the conflict of competing loves and will be liberated finally to enjoy their true end in a perfect degree.

To count as a free moral agent, one must have liberty merely to do what one chooses, without coercion. Regardless of whether critics think that Calvinists provide a successful account of how this can be, it is in fact the stated position. Therefore, it should at least be treated as such and then criticized on that basis rather than on the basis of a blatant misstatement of the position.

No standard Reformed treatment maintains that human beings are unable to make choices before and after conversion. What we are eager to affirm is that, while our decisions are not coerced by an external entity (even God), they are determined by our moral condition. We sin because we are sinners rather than vice versa; that is, our fallen condition precedes our sinful actions. We do evil things because our hearts are wicked. In conversion, God turns the heart of stone to a heart of flesh, graciously and

---

[7]Ibid.

effectively persuading sinners, on the basis of their prior regenerating work, to turn from themselves to Christ for everlasting
life. It is therefore not an issue of persuasion versus coercion but
of effective persuasion versus ineffective persuasion.

When God makes the dead to live, the blind to see, and the
deaf to hear, they are not free to be dead, blind, and deaf—not
because they are coerced, but because they now freely love and
embrace their liberation from sin and death. By analogy, did
Jesus' resurrection of Lazarus bring the latter to a point of being
able freely to choose resurrection or death? Rather, Jesus' word
raised Lazarus. Having been raised, Lazarus exulted in his liberation from the grave. This is an apt analogy, given the
prophecy of Ezekiel 37. Of course, the regenerate remain saint
and sinner simultaneously, and the Christian life, as Romans 7
indicates, involves a lifelong struggle. There are neither "victo-
rious Christians" nor "carnal Christians," but only Christians
who struggle with their sin and look to Christ and his ultimate
victory over it.

In this situation, believers are, for the first time, able to
choose that which pleases God as well as that which displeases
him. Decisions and acts, therefore, are not free; moral agents are.
The former are the effects of preferences, which are in turn the
fruit of conditions. Those who are spiritually dead cannot please
God, nor do they desire to do so (1 Cor. 2:14), for even when
their actions appear to other people to be righteous, they are not
done in faith and are therefore unacceptable. They are free moral
agents in the sense of deciding their actions without external
compulsion. Yet they are not morally free in the sense that they
can choose what they abhor. Far from coercion, the Calvinist
understanding of regeneration affirms the truest freedom: The
Holy Spirit frees unbelievers to embrace God as he is revealed
in Christ for their redemption. Otherwise, no one would ever
come to Christ (John 6:44; Rom. 3:11).

Furthermore, Geisler confuses the Calvinist *ordo salutis*
(order of salvation). First, he speaks of "salvation" as apparently
equivalent to regeneration, while Reformed theology regards
regeneration or the new birth as simply one step in a divine
series of acts. So salvation, according to Geisler comes "'through
[our] faith' (Eph. 2:8) by our act of 'receiving' Christ (John 1:12)."
He nowhere observes that Paul includes in the Ephesians

passages, "and this not from yourselves," referring not only to faith but to the entire package of salvation.

Geisler states that "election is unconditional from the standpoint of the *Giver* but conditional from the vantage point of the *receiver....* One receives eternal security apart from any act of faith on his or her part." This assertion is pure caricature, but he repeats it throughout: "Faith is not a condition of receiving it.... It is received against one's will."

Any standard Reformed account insists that while the eternal covenant of redemption (the intra-Trinitarian pact to save the elect) is unconditional, the historical execution of that decree in the covenant of grace establishes the conditions of repentance and faith. But Geisler and Calvinists understand "conditions" quite differently. For us, since the covenant of grace rests on the unconditional pact made only between the members of the Trinity, "condition" simply means that God will not grant X apart from our doing Y. But since it is God alone who gives us repentance and faith, he receives the glory for it. The suggestion that Calvinists deny the necessity even of faith for security in Christ is pure caricature, which may explain why Geisler does not footnote his accusation.

In Reformed theology, the elect must believe and must persevere in this faith until the end (in view of the covenant of grace). Yet they will do so by God's preserving grace (in view of the covenant of redemption). Not all professing believers, however, are elect. So some do "fall away"—losing their membership in the visible church, not in the invisible church. The biblical support for this scheme was laid out in my chapter.

By contrast, in Geisler's view, salvation is "conditional" in relation to the receiver. Nevertheless, "it is an unconditional gift; there are no strings attached." Not only has he erroneously criticized the Calvinist for holding an "unconditional" view; he also represents his own view as simultaneously "unconditional" and "conditional." But even with respect to God, it cannot be unconditional, since Geisler argues for conditional election. All of this leaves at least this reader confused.

In any case, Geisler is wrong to say that in Calvinism one receives the gift of salvation "against one's will." Geisler himself seems (as Stephen Ashby's chapter observes) to defend not an Arminian but a semi-Pelagian view, which sees the unregenerate in a neutral condition, able to accept or reject salvation even apart from prevenient grace. "God works effectually and irresistibly on those who choose to receive it," says Geisler. But what does this really mean? Apparently, no more than that those who save themselves by choosing subsequently become candidates for grace. This is beyond anything that Arminius advocated.

Finally, with respect to perseverance, Geisler says that "Calvinists of all varieties believe 'once saved, always saved.'" However, this phrase is foreign to the Reformed tradition, and the more one learns of the teaching itself, the greater the cleavage appears to be. Since I have outlined these differences in my chapter, I will move on to the next point. It is remarkable that Geisler contrasts the Calvinist view with his own in terms of the former being unconditional, while he urges, "One need not be faithful to the end to have it." God's action in regeneration is dependent entirely on human decision, and yet human choice has no role in whether one remains a Christian. This seems contradictory.

A few other points require response. Geisler labors the alleged contrast between strong Calvinism's view of assurance and his own: The former offers "security but no assurance," while the latter maintains "security and assurance." First, Geisler appears to be unaware of the difference between the Reformed churches (subscribing to the Belgic Confession, Heidelberg Catechism, and Canons of Dort) and the Presbyterian churches (subscribing to the Westminster Standards). The former affirm that assurance is of the essence of faith: To believe is to be assured. The latter affirm that faith and assurance are distinct: One may truly believe and yet struggle with assurance. However, in neither confession is the possibility of assurance denied. According to the Heidelberg Catechism,

> True faith is not only a knowledge and conviction that everything God reveals in his Word is true; it is also a deep-rooted assurance, created in me by the Holy Spirit, through the gospel, that out of sheer grace earned for us by Christ, not only others, but I too, have had my sins forgiven, have been made forever right with God, and have been granted salvation.[8]

---

[8]The Heidelberg Catechism, Lord's Day 7, Q. 21, in *Ecumenical Creeds and Reformed Confessions* (Grand Rapids: CRC Publications, 1988), 19.

The Westminster Confession affirms that believers

> may in this life be certainly assured that they are in a state of grace, and may rejoice in the hope of the glory of God: which hope shall never make them ashamed. This certainty is not a bare conjectural and probably persuasion, grounded upon a fallible hope; but an infallible assurance of faith, founded upon the divine truth of the promises of salvation, the inward evidence of those graces unto which these promises are made, the testimony of the Spirit of adoption witnessing with our spirits that we are the children of God; which Spirit is the earnest of our inheritance, whereby we are sealed to the day of redemption.[9]

Space does not permit a response to the theological and exegetical arguments alleged in favor of Geisler's view; I will have to allow my chapter to stand in that place. I will only briefly repeat my concern, accentuated by Geisler's exegesis, that the relegation of classic warnings against falling away to rewards rather than to salvation appears arbitrary. Notice how many times the author cites 1 Corinthians 3. However, this passage itself, taken in context, has reference not to believers in general, but to the apostles and their unique ministry. No other foundation can be laid than that foundation-laying ministry of the apostles, Paul says. It is the work of these coworkers with the apostles that will be tested on the last day, and their church plants will be tested by the refiner's fire.

When John writes, "Be faithful, even to the point of death, and I will give you the crown of life" (Rev. 2:10), does he really mean, as Geisler suggests, that this "crown of life" is something other than salvation? Similar criticisms can be lodged against Geisler's exegesis elsewhere, and his appeal to the aorist tense seems rather strained. One must already accept his dispensationalist eschatology (on rewards distinct from eternal life, on the Tribulation, and so forth) in order to accept his particular interpretations of the texts. Some Christians, for instance, will apparently reign while others barely but successfully make it into heaven and will not reign. A subtle form of works-righteousness, therefore, enters into the heavenly state.

While he eschews the peculiar views of Zane Hodges and Charles Stanley, Geisler nevertheless holds that a momentary act

---

[9]Westminster Confession of Faith, 6.097–98.

of repentance and faith secures a person who subsequently turns back to unbelief. Believers may go into a "dormant state," and yet "even in this condition, one can find signs of life ... spiritual life cannot hide completely or long" (which then makes one wonder what "dormant" implies).

Hebrews 6, Geisler insists, can only describe genuine believers and refers merely to losing a reward, not salvation. However, as I have argued in my chapter, the covenantal view that is explicit throughout Hebrews makes it much easier to understand how the writer could be referring to those who have been baptized, regularly received communion, and heard the saving Word of God (which is always accompanied by the Holy Spirit), and who nevertheless are not regenerate. They are, he says, like well-watered ground that never bears fruit. They are not regenerate (v. 9), but they do "fall away" (v. 6). Like the church in the Old Testament, the readers of this letter belonged to the covenant and benefited from its external administration, but, like their fathers in the old covenant, "those who heard did not combine it [the gospel] with faith" (4:2). But Geisler has already determined what such texts cannot say to the extent that the reader can easily gain the impression that he does not treat them seriously.

To conclude, Geisler argues a classic semi-Pelagian (not even Arminian) position with respect to human depravity and ability. His chapter, both in its content and harsh (if unfounded) criticism, seems at least in some respects further removed from the two Arminian contributions that follow. He takes up the Pelagian-Kantian rule, "ought implies can": "Every responsibility implies the ability to respond, if not in our own strength, then by God's grace." Tacking on this latter phrase qualifies his use of this rule in the direction of semi-Pelagianism. And yet, the one "work" performed by the unregenerate prior to divine grace secures their salvation even apart from God's preservation of their faith and lifelong repentance.

Having been raised in that theological world, I can better understand now the confusion that I felt in trying to understand how salvation could be entirely of grace while the "condition" on which everything depended was entirely self-determined. Surely it is better news to hear that not only at the last, but in the first instance and throughout the Christian life, "it does not ... depend on man's desire or effort, but on God's mercy" (Rom. 9:16).

A REFORMED ARMINIAN RESPONSE TO NORMAN L. GEISLER

Stephen M. Ashby

Norman L. Geisler has long been the dean of evangelical apologists. His tireless efforts and prolific production have given to the church a corpus of scholarly writings that is scarcely to be matched over the last quarter of a century. I am sure that I stand as one among many who feels a personal debt of gratitude for the excellent work he has done in helping to provide a credible intellectual framework for those who wish to maintain a high view of Scripture and defensible Christian world and life view. Even when I have disagreed with him, Dr. Geisler has often been instrumental in framing the issues that have helped me to hone my own positions. Thus, I count it a particular pleasure to be included in a volume in which his views are also represented.

THE MEANING OF MODERATE CALVINISM

Geisler wastes no time in carving out his space for the view he calls moderate Calvinism. In distinguishing his view from "strong Calvinism," or what Michael Horton calls "Classical Calvinism," Geisler compares the five points of the TULIP. It has become popular among those holding the "once saved, always saved" position to call themselves Calvinists. However, their rejection of the heart of Calvinistic belief would seem to mitigate their right to that ascription. Changing the meaning of four of the five points while still wishing to maintain the name seems somewhat less than credible to me. Of course, Calvinists (in the historical sense of the term) do not need me to fight their battles for them. For additional brief details in this regard, see my chapter in this book. As I stated there, I believe Geisler to be a one-point Calvinist. Perhaps he might consider a name change for his position.

Far more interesting to me is Geisler's contrast of moderate Calvinism and Arminianism. Sadly, he has done what is typically done when characterizing Arminians: He has treated them as a homogeneous whole. In so doing, he makes the comment: "Since most parties on both sides agree to these contrasts, little comment is needed." I must respectfully demur. His characterization of Arminianism within his chart early in his essay in no way represents the Reformed Arminian view. I will leave it to other types of Arminians to decide whether the chart fairly represents them. Reformed Arminians would likely not choose to make the comparison revolve around "eternal security," since that is not a biblical term. Of course, given the title of the book, I understand why Geisler has chosen to do so. I would prefer to make the comparison based on either "justification" or "eternal life." In using either of these biblical terms, the following would hold true for Reformed Arminians:

All believers have it.
No believer, while he remains a believer, can lose it.
It can only be lost by apostasy, and that without remedy.
God gives assurance and security, but only to those "in Christ" by faith.

BENEFITS OF SALVATION NOT ABSTRACT POSSESSIONS

Though I have sought just above to reformulate Geisler's chart with reference to Reformed Arminian beliefs, I do so with serious reservation. Even though I mention either "justification" or "eternal life" as posing better terms for comparison, I find myself—given Geisler's rubric—falling into a trap. In my view, the Bible teaches that all the benefits of salvation inhere *in Christ* alone. No one possesses any of the benefits of salvation in abstraction. Geisler's chart, and even my rewriting of the chart, would seem to treat the benefits of salvation as entities that individuals simply *possess*.

Yet this notion is foreign to Scripture. No matter which of the benefits of salvation I may be talking about, I should never refer to them as though they are mine by right. I am elect "in Christ" (Eph. 1:4). My deliverance from condemnation is "in Christ" (Rom. 8:1). Christ *is* our wisdom, righteousness, and sanctification (1 Cor. 1:30). I receive the benefits of the crucifixion, resurrection, and ascension all because I am a participant in or sharer together with Christ (Eph. 2:5–6). Eternal life is in the Son (1 John 5:11–13). What I have in salvation is not simply an *it* that is mine to possess. I must refrain from speaking as though the benefits of salvation are objects that God has given to me, which I now possess as my own. Everything I possess is mine only because I have been forensically joined in union with Christ. Were Geisler to pay more careful attention to this construct, I believe that he would find it easier to avoid some of the difficulties to which his position falls prey.

Just two passages will have to suffice out of the many proof texts Geisler gives in his "Biblical Arguments in Favor of Eternal Security" section. Concerning 2 Corinthians 5:17, 21, he states: "According to this text, we are already a new creation; this guarantees us a place in heaven." This sort of abstracting of the benefit is perilous, for the text says anyone *in Christ* is a new creation. In his quotation of this passage he writes: "God made him who had no sin to be sin for us, so that in him *we might become the righteousness of God*." The italicizing of what we might become seems to highlight that this is ours by right. It is only ours as we are *in him*. I chose this text from among the twenty-seven proof texts Geisler deals with in this section because his explanation here comes nearer to what I am commending than any of the others. Yet even in the exposition of this passage, the tendency to treat the benefit as an abstract entity peeks through.

The other passage from this section that I mention is Romans 4:5–6. Geisler's explanation is dealing with the doctrine of the imputation of Christ's perfect obedience to believers. He writes that "we are already accounted as perfectly righteous." However, it is not *we*, but *we in Christ* who are accounted as perfectly righteous. In other words, we are forensically in union with Christ. This imputed righteousness of Christ is not something we possess in abstraction, given to us as a gift as though imparted, infused, or inherent. We have it accounted to us solely because we are "in Christ," and that by faith.

I think that Geisler believes everything that I have been saying here. However, his tendency, along with others who hold the "once saved, always saved" position, to talk about eternal security as "a gift" that God gives me, thus making it mine, leads to poor applications and misunderstanding. Note his comments that "salvation is an irrevocable gift." Moreover, he claims that God's "character guarantees that he will never renege on his promise." And again, "salvation is an unconditional gift (Rom. 11:29) and as such cannot be taken back by God." The danger I wish to point out here is in treating the "spiritual blessings" of salvation (Eph. 1:3) as though they are simply mine by right. They are mine only as I am found "in Christ Jesus," whose they are by right.

IS CONTINUANCE IN FAITH NECESSARY?

Geisler seems to be internally conflicted at this point when considering whether continued faith is a condition of salvation. He makes clear that anyone who receives salvation does so on the condition of faith. However, once one is saved, the nature of that salvation evidently changes. For he says, "There are no conditions of any kind for God giving or for our keeping salvation." It is heartening to see that Geisler is distancing himself from the claims of Zane Hodges and Charles Stanley, who argue that "those who walk away from the faith have not the slightest chance of slipping from His hand." Nevertheless, the distinction he draws when he says that continued faith is a *manifestation* and not a *condition* of true faith is a rather odd one.

The fact that at the beginning salvation was conditioned on faith tells us something about the nature of salvation. The fact that one must actually exercise this faith in order to receive God's gift tells us something about the nature of human beings. Yet Geisler is never quite clear concerning what changes the nature of salvation from that of having a condition to that of having no condition. Likewise, he never is quite clear concerning what changes the nature of human beings from needing to exercise faith to not needing to exercise faith.

While Geisler wants to avoid the pitfalls inherent in Hodges and Stanley, he is still drawn toward their view that saving faith is "only an act of faith" rather than "a constant attitude." He wishes to part ways with them, however, when they work out the logical implications of that view.[1] For Geisler, this seems incommensurate with what the Bible teaches. Indeed, he says, "Scripture does not support the view that a true believer can totally lose his or her faith." Obviously, Geisler is having trouble reconciling the notion of *saved unbelievers*, which is certainly what Stanley and Hodges are asserting.

Still, Geisler immediately finds himself going to 2 Timothy 2:13. Again, he is in tension at this point. In his book *Chosen But Free*, he quotes this verse six times.[2] Each time he does so, he uses the exact same wording: "*If we are faithless, he will remain faithful, for he cannot deny Himself.*" He even renders the text that way early on in his chapter in the present book. Why, then, does he choose to render this verse differently toward the end of his article? He writes, "If we are *not faithful*, he will remain faithful, for he cannot deny himself." Given his desire to distinguish himself from Hodges and Stanley on this point, the word "faithless" just will not do. I believe that Geisler along with Stanley fails to take into account the context found in 2 Timothy 2:11–13. I will not repeat here what I believe is a far better treatment of the passage (see my chapter). Geisler would do well to ask himself about this internal conflict.

RELATIONSHIP OF WORKS TO SALVATION

I affirm almost everything that Geisler says about the relationship of works to salvation. I completely agree that "salvation cannot be gained or lost by our efforts." Nevertheless, he moves immediately from that premise toward painting all Arminians with a broad brush. I am reminded of the passage I quoted by R. C. Sproul in my chapter, who said, "As a Calvinist I frequently hear criticism of Calvinistic thought that I would heartily agree with if indeed it represented Calvinism. So I am

---

[1]In this connection, consult my chapter, where I note how Stanley likens salvation to getting a tattoo, which one may detest the moment after receiving it, yet its permanence is assured regardless of that person's attitude toward it.

[2]See Geisler, *Chosen But Free*, 108, 120, 128, 139, 143, 179.

sure the disciples of Arminius suffer the same fate and become equally frustrated."

The problem that I see here is that Geisler's characterization is all too true of many Arminians. When he says that "Arminianism is a tacit form of works salvation," he rightly points out what many bearing the name Arminian believe. When he refers to the view held by H. Orton Wiley and John Wesley, wherein "good works [are] a condition of salvation," we should be reminded of how far such a notion is from the Reformed essentials of *sola fide, sola gratia*. When he notes the similarity of such a view to the Roman Catholic view, even using the term "mortal sin" to describe it, he points to a concept that Steve Harper adduces out of Wesley's thought (see his chapter). In the "Introductory Comment" to Wesley's sermon "On Sin in Believers," it is noted that "[Wesley's] distinction already had a history in Catholic moral theory ('mortal' versus 'venial')."[3] So, I find broad agreement with what Geisler is saying about the relationship of works to salvation.

Where I become frustrated, to use Sproul's term, is in the attribution of Wiley's and Wesley's understanding to all Arminians. Repeatedly Geisler writes "Arminians claim ..." or "according to the Arminian view...." Yet he never quotes Arminius—and he certainly is not presenting the Reformed Arminian view with the statements he is making with a broad stroke. Indeed, even in reference to the question of perseverance, Geisler is implicitly committing the fallacy of composition by making the view of some "Arminians" to be that of all. For in commenting on Hebrews 10:26–29, he says that "[the passage] does not support the Arminian view, since it says those who commit this sin cannot be restored again." However, the irremediability of apostasy is exactly the view that Reformed Arminians believe. Even as Paul said, "They are not all Israel, which are of Israel" (Rom. 9:6, KJV), I would say, "Not all 'Arminians' are of Arminius."

LOSS OF REWARDS OR LOSS OF SALVATION?

As I have mentioned elsewhere concerning Geisler's position, he is partially correct and partially incorrect on the issue of

---

[3]*The Works of John Wesley*, ed. Thomas Jackson, 14 vols. (London: Wesley Methodist Book Room, 1872; repr., Grand Rapids: Baker, 1986), 1:315.

loss of rewards versus loss of salvation. There can be no question but that believers can lose rewards, as Geisler rightly notes concerning 1 Corinthians 3:11–15; 2 Corinthians 5:10; 2 Timothy 4:7–8; 2 John 8. On the other hand, his attempt at a one-size-fits-all category, wherein he includes such passages as Matthew 12:31–32; 1 Corinthians 9:27; 2 Timothy 2:12, 17–18; Hebrews 6:4–6; 10:26–29 as referring merely to "loss of reward" will not withstand the scrutiny of credible exegesis. In my chapter in this book I address several of these passages along with some others.

I feel the need at this point to emphasize again what I have noted in my chapter, which must not be overlooked by anyone who is considering this issue. When looking at many of the proof texts used to support the "once saved, always saved" view, Reformed Arminians, believing as they do that salvation is conditional from beginning to end, are able to read those texts (John 3:15–16; 5:24; 10:27–28) and add the *Amen* without further comment. This simply cannot be said for eternal securitists regarding texts that appear to teach that true believers can lose their salvation by abandoning their faith in Christ.

Since I have dealt with several of the passages in my chapter—chief among them John 15:1–6; 2 Timothy 2:12; the warnings of Hebrews; 2 Peter 2:20–22—I will here address only a couple of other verses that Geisler uses. Concerning Matthew 12:31–32, Geisler again mischaracterizes Reformed Arminians. I do not believe, as he claims, that a Christian who has apostatized by rejecting faith in Christ can regain salvation. My entire argument militates against his claim. I agree with Geisler that "there is no indication here that believers can commit this sin." However, to assume that the context must explicitly say "believers can commit this sin," otherwise I am justified in saying that believers cannot commit this sin, is to commit the fallacy of "appealing to ignorance"—sometimes called an "argument from silence."

My position insists that believers are *still persons*, able to do both good and bad. When the passage says that this form of blasphemy shall not be forgiven unto *men* (KJV), I would think that believers are still a part of the generic category called "men." When it says that *whosoever* does this shall not be forgiven, neither in this world nor in the world to come, I have to think that if a Christian commits this sin there is no forgiveness for it. So when Geisler says the passage refers to "hard-hearted unbelief," I would agree. But following on his logic, "there is no indication here that believers can [not] commit this sin."

Geisler's treatment of Paul's statement in 1 Corinthians 9:27 is certainly a common one. Further, given the imagery of the athletic competition in the context, it is easy to see how one might make his case (being disqualified [*adokimos*] from receiving the prize-rewards). However, the word Paul uses to describe what he wishes to avoid is an extremely strong term. Except for its use in Hebrews 6:8, it is only to be found in Paul's writings. It is instructive to see how the apostle uses this word elsewhere.

- Romans 1:28: "And even as they did not like to retain God in their knowledge, God gave them over to a reprobate [*adokimos*] mind ..." (KJV).
- 2 Corinthians 13:5: "Examine yourselves, whether ye be in the faith; prove your own selves. Know ye not your own selves how that Jesus Christ is in you, except ye be reprobates [*adokimoi*]?" (KJV).
- 2 Timothy 3:8: "Now as Janes and Jambres withstood Moses, so do these also resist the truth: men of corrupt minds, reprobate [*adokimoi*] concerning the faith" (KJV).
- Titus 1:16: "They profess that they know God; but in works they deny him, being abominable, and disobedient, and unto every good work reprobate [*adokimoi*]" (KJV).

In examining particularly Paul's use of *adokimos* we find that "human existence stands under the divine testing in which it must prove itself ... the attestation which God seeks in the judgment is to be found only in those who believe in Christ, and ... there is no such attestation outside this faith."[4] In 1 Corinthians 9:27, Paul uses *adokimos*, which time and again he uses to refer to rejection by God or reprobation. And the apostle says that he wants to take every precaution, lest even he himself become *adokimos*.

[4]W. Grundmann, "δόκιμος," *Theological Dictionary of the New Testament*, trans. G. W. Bromiley (Grand Rapids: Eerdmans, 1964), 2:257–59.

A WESLEYAN ARMINIAN RESPONSE TO NORMAN L. GEISLER

J. Steven Harper

Norman Geisler writes with the eclectic spirit necessary to capture the reality of theological inquiry and formulation. He ends his chapter with the phrase, "the best of both worlds," believing that moderate Calvinism finds the preferable blend between Classical Calvinism and Arminianism. While I will comment on that assertion in the course of this response, I want at least to acknowledge with appreciation that Dr. Geisler recognizes that theology can get "better" as it interfaces with more than one point of view. As you will see in my chapter, this is one of the key points I make in commending Wesley as an example of beneficial eclecticism—an approach that makes Christian doctrine stronger than if only one perspective were considered.

I also appreciate the clear way Geisler compares Classical and moderate Calvinism through the oft-cited TULIP summary. If this is your first time to compare and contrast the five traditional elements in Reformed theology, you will likely find this part of his chapter to be both helpful and memorable. Also, by using the TULIP configuration, Geisler reveals (as I do in my chapter) the wholistic nature of theology. TULIP is his way of not chopping theology into disconnected doctrinal pieces, and I appreciate that approach.

Finally, one cannot but be impressed with Geisler's commitment to the formulation of doctrine through a clear and comprehensive appeal to Scripture. The two sections in his chapter in which he cites one passage after another evince his belief that all doctrine must conform to the Bible. I could not read his listings without thinking of Wesley's similar approach in *Predestination Calmly Considered*. I will have more to say about this in this response, but I mention it now as a way of respecting Geisler's desire to connect biblical revelation and theological interpretation.

As a means of transitioning into the "critique" portion of my response, let me simply say that I am at a loss to respond adequately to Geisler's chapter precisely because he has packed so much into it. Compared to Horton, who left me wanting more, I wish Geisler had given me less—by less I mean, fewer targets worthy of being aimed at in a brief response. There is simply too much that merits a response/critique. I must mention in passing that I could have wished for more "primary Calvin" in Geisler's chapter, as with Horton's. However, at least the former has given a wealth of interpretive material from which to select my responses.

With these comments in place, I will now move into his chapter per se and comment on selected items wherein the Wesleyan Arminian view is different and/or wherein his description of the Wesleyan Arminian view is deficient. In his chapter there are surely places where both relationships can be noted. Given the organized and orderly arrangement of his chapter, I can take a similar view in my response.

First, there is a problem in Geisler's definition of "irresistible grace." He states that it is "effectual on the *willing* (the elect) but not on the *unwilling*." But what kind of irresistibility is that? The logic (or illogic) of the sentence ends up defining irresistible grace away—at least as it is used in traditional theological discussions. If anyone can resist grace, it is not irresistible. To draw a distinction between the *willing* and the *unwilling* (Geisler uses the italics) is finally meaningless. Furthermore, it uses words that are typically outside the preference of Reformed theology (willing and/or unwilling). What I am saying is that his chapter gets off on a bad footing through a confusing definition of grace—confusing because it uses a term (irresistible) while at the same time limiting it in a way that undoes the definition.

Second, despite the fact that I generally like his comparison charts, Geisler really sets up a false comparison in his alignment of strong Calvinism, Arminianism, and moderate Calvinism. His goal, of course, is to show that moderate Calvinism has "the best of both worlds" (both security and assurance). Yet in order to make that conclusion, he caricatures strong Calvinism and Arminianism. To say, for example, that Arminianism has *no security* is simply not true. All orthodox Christian theology posits Christ as our security, even if nuanced differently. I could excuse (even understand) the limitations of a one-sentence comparison of the three views, except for the fact that Geisler uses the three-fold distinction to expand his ideas. On that I can only say that a faulty interpretation at the start makes difficult a faultless conclusion at the end. This section must be read carefully, because Geisler sets up a scenario that hangs together only if one accepts the simple distinctions that he makes.

Third, I am personally troubled by what I would call a "quantification motif" in his voluminous reference to Bible passages. I will give him the benefit of the doubt in hoping that this approach means he wants to show that what moderate Calvinism believes can be seen repeatedly throughout Scripture. The problem is that in giving us so many references without much else, we are again forced to accept his arrangement not ultimately on the texts themselves but because he presents them to the reader as evidence to support his views.

Furthermore, as Geisler himself surely knows, some of the passages he cites as *evidence* are interpreted differently by other theological traditions. But by largely giving only a catalogue listing of texts, he gives the reader the false impression that these texts irrefutably teach the moderate Calvinist view. He leaves no room for us to realize that other Christians read these texts differently. There is no time for that kind of thinking because we have to move on to the next passage. Again, I would urge the reader to read his two large Bible-citation sections with appreciation, but not to the point of thinking that his view on every text is the only legitimate way to read that passage.

Fourth, we eventually come to an oft-stated maxim in Reformed theology, "God can never take back the gift of salvation," with textual support from Romans 11:29. From the Wesleyan Arminian point of view, this both belabors the obvious and begs the question that this book is all about. I do not know of any serious, orthodox theology that believes *God* "takes back" the gift of salvation. God has done everything possible to save the human race, and God is not in the business of "withdrawing" that gift. But that begs the question as to whether or not *we* can do anything to lose the gift of that salvation. We do not have to say (as if it might not be true) that God "cannot deny himself." We know that! But what can (or must) we say about our denying him? This line of reasoning, so often found in Calvinistic theological interpretation, misses the point of the subject at hand. The issue is the perseverance of the saints, not the reliability of God.

Fifth, I cannot overlook a caricaturing of "good works" as another way of attempting to make his position win the day. If Wesley denied anything (as my chapter shows), it is that his views were a form of works righteousness. Yet Geisler and other Reformed theologians persist in trying to set up that scenario, so that they can then turn around and knock it down. Let us say it once and be done: Wesleyan Arminianism does not teach works righteousness, as the phrase typically means. Works are not "necessary" in the sense of maintaining one's salvation. They are "necessary" only in the way Jesus meant when he said, "A good tree cannot bear bad fruit" (Matt. 7:18). Works have evidential value, not causative value, and can only be called "necessary" in the first sense.

Finally, Geisler leaves the matter dangling when he writes, "Moderate Calvinism asserts that believers can have real assurance that they are God's elect, apart from whether they are faithful to the end." Building on examples of Peter and John the Baptist, he shows how significant vacillation did not eliminate final victory. This is doubtless the case, but do the examples verify the assertion? Or to say it another way, Geisler does not address the question, "How *unfaithful* can you be and not put your salvation in any sort of jeopardy?" Peter and John the Baptist do not illustrate the assertion, simply because in both cases they came back from their denials and doubts. All Geisler can do at the end of this line of thought is to revert to another oft-used maxim of Reformed theology: "Those who depart from the faith were not really in it to begin with." That is much too short and sweet to sound the depths of the issue being considered. From a Wesleyan Arminian point of view, that last maxim raises at least as many questions as it tries to answer.

In my opinion, Geisler comes closer than does Horton in recognizing and addressing the key issues that have given rise to this book. He also acknowledges that, to arrive at truth, one must do some theological integration. I left his chapter wishing that the general term "Arminianism" did not hold such immediate and widespread negativity for those of a Reformed persuasion. I think Geisler would come out even better in the end. The two chapters by Stephen Ashby and myself will try to show that as Reformed Arminianism and Wesleyan Arminianism are given their time at the podium.

Chapter Three

A REFORMED
ARMINIAN VIEW

Stephen M. Ashby

A REFORMED ARMINIAN VIEW

Stephen M. Ashby

A couple of years ago I had a conversation with a Presbyterian pastor in the city where I work. Upon hearing that I had graduated from a Calvinist seminary, he waited for the appropriate moment and said, "So you are one of those rare birds who was educated in Reformed thought ... but just didn't get it." My response was, "Oh, I'm very Reformed; in fact, I call myself a Reformed Arminian." To which he laughed incredulously and said, "That's the first time I've ever heard of that."

No doubt, many people who might pick up this book will ask themselves, "What is Reformed Arminianism?" The answer to that question is simple: It is the view of Jacobus Arminius himself. Arminius always considered himself to be Reformed, right up until his death. And there were many within the Dutch Reformed movement who held his approach to theology. Of course, given the popular usage of the term *Reformed* today— which makes it interchangeable with *Calvinist*—it is probably not surprising that my Presbyterian friend reacted so strongly to the thought of Reformed Arminianism. However, if we get beneath the surface of handy and well-worn labels and compare the actual substance of the views held by those within my community with views typically thought to be Reformed, it will become clear that this is not a contradiction of terms but an accurate ascription.

The brand of Arminianism that I am proposing will not be immediately recognizable either by those regularly acknowledged as being *Reformed* or by those who otherwise carry the label *Arminian*. Within this volume Michael Horton is presenting a Reformed Calvinistic position, while Steve Harper represents a Wesleyan Arminian perspective. I fully expect that I will find myself betwixt and between these two views. R. C. Sproul, in a chapter devoted to Arminius, made a fine statement:

> In the perennial debate between so-called Calvinism and Arminianism, the estranged parties have frequently misrepresented each other. They construct straw men, then brandish the swords of polemics against caricatures, not unlike collective Don Quixotes tilting at windmills. As a Calvinist I frequently hear criticisms of Calvinistic thought that I would heartily agree with if indeed they represented Calvinism. So, I am sure, the disciples of Arminius suffer the same fate and become equally frustrated.[1]

Sproul is certainly correct. Followers of Arminius do feel unduly maligned and misrepresented. Without question, my view will be criticized, as indeed each of the views represented here will be and should be. Nevertheless, I appreciate the opportunity to present the Reformed Arminian position. And I trust that a greater degree of the criticism that is to come in the future will be on point with respect to the actual views held by those of this perspective.

REFORMED ARMINIANISM'S
SIMILARITIES WITH CALVINISM

The Reformed Arminian view was forged in the context of Dutch Reformed thought. Hence, it bears many of the identifying characteristics of that movement. Many interpreters have incorrectly read later Arminian theology into Arminius. Yet up to the time of his death, Arminius believed himself to be Reformed. Unlike most later Arminians, who broke more completely from Reformed categories, he retained key Reformed concepts.

Among the important theological constructs that Arminius held in common with other Reformed thinkers was his view of human depravity. Without equivocation, he claimed that the human will in its fallenness cannot achieve *any* spiritual good, except as it is assisted and enabled by divine grace. It is hard to

---

[1] R. C. Sproul, *Willing to Believe* (Grand Rapids: Baker, 1997), 125–26.

imagine any Reformer, or any Reformed thinker, before or after him who could state the doctrine of total depravity in more categorical terms:

> In this state [man's fallen condition], the Free Will of man toward the True Good is not only wounded, maimed, infirm, bent, and weakened; but it is also imprisoned, destroyed, and lost: And its powers are not only debilitated and useless unless they be assisted by grace, but it has no powers whatever except such as are excited by Divine grace: For Christ has said, "Without me ye can do nothing."[2]

Fallen humanity is devoid of any ability to effect even the least spiritual good. To wit, Arminius approvingly quotes Augustine, who wrote:

> Christ does not say, Without me ye can do *but little*; neither does He say, Without me ye cannot do *any arduous thing*; nor Without me ye can do it with difficulty: But He says, Without me ye can do *nothing*! Nor does he say, Without me ye cannot *complete* anything; but Without me ye can do *nothing*![3]

This view of total depravity is Reformed to the core. Arminius explains it as affecting every part of the human being: *The mind* is "darkened," "incapable of those things which belong to the Spirit of God," "vain," and "foolish" (see 1 Cor. 2:14; Rom. 1:21–22; Eph. 4:17–18; Titus 3:3). *The affections of the heart* are "perverse," "deceitful," "hard and stony," and "they love and pursue what is evil" (see Jer. 13:10; 17:9; Ezek. 36:26; Matt. 15:19; Rom. 8:7). And in exact correspondence "to this Darkness of the Mind, and Perverseness of the Heart, is *the utter Weakness of all the Powers* to perform that which is truly good" (see Matt. 7:18; 12:34; John 6:44; Rom. 7:5; 6:20; 2 Tim. 2:26).[4] In this regard Arminius always wished to maintain "the greatest possible distance from Pelagianism."[5]

---

[2]Disputation 11, "On the Free Will of Man and its Powers," in *The Works of James Arminius*, London ed., trans. James Nichols and William Nichols, 3 vols. (London: Longerman, Hurst, Rees, Orme, Brown, & Green, 1825–75; repr., Grand Rapids: Baker, 1996), 2:192 (hereafter cited as *Works of Arminius*).

[3]Ibid. (italics added).

[4]Ibid., 2:192–94.

[5]Ibid., 1:764.

Another crucial concept on which Arminius agreed with the Reformers was the meaning of Christ's atoning work. Christ's atonement was not merely a passion play or an exhibition, either to show how loving God is or to display his displeasure toward sin. Christ's death was not intended merely to exert a "moral influence" on humankind or to "uphold the public justice" by affirming the moral order.[6] Rather, following the Reformers, whose views have precursors in the thought of Anselm, Arminius asserted a *penal satisfaction* view of the atonement. He invoked the image of God as a judge, and he argued that justification for the sinner could be effected in one of only two ways: either by fully keeping the law or by the righteousness of another being accounted to the sinner as his or her own.[7]

The reason these are the only ways that justification could come about rests in the character of the One who is the Judge. God is holy and just. Thus, he must judge sin. His character demands no less. The term *satisfaction* expresses that internal aspect of God's nature that cannot overlook sin or wink at sin. His holiness cannot be satisfied with anything less than payment for sin. The notion of payment brings us to the "penal" aspect of the term. The penalty for sin cannot be simply "set aside" or declared by fiat no longer to adhere. Indeed the penalty must be paid.

In Public Disputation 19, "On the Justification of Man Before God," Arminius articulated his conviction that

> justification, when used for the act of a Judge, is either purely the imputation of righteousness through mercy from the throne of grace in Christ the propitiation made to a sinner, but who is a believer (Rom 1:16–17; Gal 3:6–7), or that man is justified before God of debt according to the rigour of justice without any forgiveness (Rom 3, 4).[8]

Arminius allowed for only two possible ways in which the sinner might be justified: (1) by our absolute and perfect adherence to the law, or (2) purely by God's imputation of Christ's righ-

---

[6]For these views see H. Orton Wiley, *Christian Theology*, 3 vols. (Kansas City, Mo: Beacon Hill, 1952), 2:252–68.

[7]This was the view of John Calvin. See John Calvin, *Institutes of the Christian Religion*, ed. John T. McNeill, trans. Ford Lewis Battles, 2 vols. (Philadelphia: Westminster, 1960), 1:532–34.

[8]*Works of Arminius*, 2:256–57.

teousness to the sinner through faith. Allowing for no other possibilities, he clearly positioned himself with the second view.

The term *imputation* was an important term for Arminius and other Reformed thinkers. A major issue that had spawned the Reformation was Luther's delving into the question of how one attains justification. Rome had taught that Christ's righteousness was "infused" into believers through the sacraments, giving them an "inherent" righteousness.[9] Reformation thought reacted against this notion, holding instead that the righteousness of Christ is "imputed" to the believer, that is, it is credited to the believer or placed on the believer's account. Hence, the righteousness whereby God the Judge declares sinners justified is the righteousness of Christ alone. Arminius defined justification in this Reformed sense when he wrote:

> It is a Justification by which a man, who is a sinner, *yet a believer*, being placed before the throne of grace which is erected in Christ Jesus the Propitiation, *is accounted* and pronounced by God, the just and merciful Judge, righteous and worthy of the reward of righteousness *not in himself* but *in Christ*, of grace, according to the Gospel, to the praise of the righteousness and grace of God, and to the salvation of the justified person himself (Rom 3:24–26; 4:3, 4, 5, 9, 10, 11).[10]

This is a forensic definition, and Arminius held it tenaciously throughout his works. Again, to show that he held to this view of justification, he spoke of the term *imputed* as referring to "that which is righteousness in *God's gracious account*, since it does not merit this name according to the rigour of justice or of the law,—or as being *the righteousness of another*, that is of Christ, which is made ours by God's gracious imputation."[11]

---

[9]See "Creeds of Modern Roman Catholicism" in *Creeds of the Churches*, ed. John H. Leith (Atlanta: John Knox, 1963), relating the teachings of the Council of Trent. Particular attention should be given to item 5 of the Fifth Session regarding baptism; Canon 29 of the Canons Concerning Justification; also Canon 11 on the imputation of Christ's righteousness. All of this should be viewed in light of Chapter VII of the Sixth Session, wherein "reputed" righteousness in justification is denigrated, preferring instead a righteousness that "inheres" in the justified one because it has been "infused" into that person.

[10]*Works of Arminius*, 2:256 (italics added).

[11]Ibid., 2:257 (italics added).

It should be clear from the foregoing discussion that Arminius did not hold to any sort of "works righteousness." Indeed, he was Reformed in declaring what the essence of redemption is, what it means to be in a state of grace, and how that works itself out in the Christian life. For Reformed Arminians, to be in a state of grace means to be found *in Christ*. Of course, this characteristically Pauline designation has certain existential or subjective elements to it. But it is not first and foremost related to one's subjective experience. It is above everything else objective in nature.

Certain redemptive events have taken place in real, timespace history *in Christ*. Jesus lived a sinless life (1 Peter 2:22; 1 John 3:5). He died a substitutionary death (Rom. 5:6–8). He rose the third day (1 Cor. 15:4). He ascended back to the Father, where he abides forever to make intercession for us (Acts 1:9; 7:56; Heb. 7:24–25). These are objective, redemptive events of history.[12] They have occurred in Christ, and they are objective and redemptive, irrespective of my subjective response to them. For "God was reconciling the world to himself in Christ" (2 Cor. 5:19).

The way Paul typically uses the phrase "in Christ" has to do with the believer's union with Christ. Christ paid the penalty due for sin. In order to do that, the sins of humanity were imputed to him so that his righteousness (both active obedience—i.e., his sinless life—and passive obedience—i.e., his substitutionary death) might be imputed to those who are *in him*. "God made him who had no sin to be sin for us, so that in him we might become the righteousness of God" (2 Cor. 5:21). This is above all a legal or a forensic designation. Accounting terms are used often in this regard, such as *counted for, reckoned, imputed*. What takes place with the believer's being in Christ or

---

[12]For a brief but excellent discussion of *Heilsgeschichte* (i.e., "redemptive history"), see George Eldon Ladd, *A Theology of the New Testament* (Grand Rapids: Eerdmans, 1993), 25–32. Cf. Geerhardus Vos, *Redemptive History and Biblical Interpretation*, ed. Richard B. Gaffin Jr. (Phillipsburg, N.J.: Presbyterian & Reformed, 2001), 5–7. D. A. Carson, in speaking about assurance of salvation, makes a salient point that is equally applicable to the matters presently being considered: "Some of the lines of the debate are seriously askew because they too quickly press toward temporal dogmatic questions without pausing adequately to reflect on redemptive-historical matters lodged in Scripture itself" (D. A. Carson, "Reflections on Assurance," in *Still Sovereign: Contemporary Perspectives on Election, Foreknowledge, and Grace*, ed. Thomas R. Schreiner and Bruce A. Ware [Grand Rapids: Baker, 2000], 254).

in union with Christ has to do with a transfer of what was on the sinner's account over to the account of Christ and vice versa.

So what was on the account of each? The sinner's account is filled with debits, demerits, a sinful nature, as well as sinful attitudes and actions against a holy God. Christ's account, by contrast, boasts a life of perfect righteousness; no guile was found in his mouth; he came and fulfilled the law; and he was obedient unto death—even the death of the cross. Of him, God said, "This is my Son, whom I love; with him I am well pleased" (Matt. 3:17). The accounts could not look any more different.

However, in God's great plan of redemption, a transferring of accounts has occurred. Christ did not become a sinner at the crucifixion. Rather, the sins of humankind were placed on his account so that he took responsibility for them. Likewise, those who are in Christ do not metamorphose into ontologically righteous and perfect individuals. Instead, Christ's righteousness and his death are placed on their accounts. Thus, God's estimation of them is according to Christ's accomplishments.

REFORMED ARMINIANISM'S DIFFERENCES WITH CALVINISM

Now the question clearly becomes: How can one be found *in Christ*? What effects this imputation? Is it by a particularistic understanding of God's unalterable decree, which is grounded in nothing else but God's good pleasure? If so, then Calvinists are correct in asserting their views of unconditional election, irresistible grace, and the necessary perseverance of the saints. This view, however, presupposes particularism in setting forth the *ordo salutis* (order of salvation). Louis Berkhof states that the covenant of grace is "a particular and not a universal covenant," that God intended redemption to be only for particular individuals. He decries both the notion of universal salvation held by classical universalists as well as the idea of "Pelagians, Arminians, and Lutherans" that the offer of the covenant comes to all.[13]

In other words, in eternity past, for reasons known only to him, God has set his affections on particular individuals. This is often seen in terms of an eternal covenant that the three persons of the Godhead have made among themselves. David N. Steele

---

[13]Louis Berkhof, *Systematic Theology* (Grand Rapids: Eerdmans, 1941), 278.

and Curtis C. Thomas explain that in this covenant, the Father elects a definite number of individuals for himself. The Son does what is necessary to save those the Father has given him. The Spirit then applies that salvation to the elect.[14]

Certain passages of Scripture (e.g., John 5:30, 43; 6:38–40; 17:4–12) are thought to imply this "covenant of redemption," wherein a certain number of elect are given by God to his Son. Robert E. Picirilli is correct when he says that

> such discussion of a covenant between the Father and the Son ought to proceed, if at all, with great hesitation. Nowhere is there direct indication that such a covenant was made, and even more important is the fact that the terms of such a covenant are not revealed—especially not whether those promises were or were not conditional. Calvinists generally take the lead in insisting that the secret things belong to God, that His eternal counsels are not directly revealed. If there was such a covenant of redemption (and I do not object to the idea in principle), the *only* way we have of "reading" its terms respecting salvation is by reading in the New Testament how salvation is actually effected and applied. If, then, the New Testament makes clear that salvation really is *conditional*, then we *dare not "read" the unrevealed terms of an implied covenant of redemption in such a way as to destroy that conditionality.*[15]

Picirilli has truly caught the essence of the point here. In order to assert the Calvinistic understanding of salvation, one must assume a priori particularism and an unconditional notion of salvation. Once that is assumed, it is clear to see how one might read many biblical texts in light of that assumption.

However, the pressing question should be: Do the scriptural texts concerning salvation require particularism and unconditional election? I do not think they do. I believe, in fact, that the exact opposite is seen: Christ's atonement was for "all," indeed for the whole world, and God's salvation is conditional—that condition being faith in Christ. Herein is the Reformed Arminian

---

[14]David N. Steele and Curtis C. Thomas, *The Five Points of Calvinism Defined, Defended, Documented* (Philadelphia: Presbyterian & Reformed, 1963), 31.

[15]Robert E. Picirilli, *Grace, Faith, Free Will: Contrasting Views of Salvation* (Nashville: Randall House, forthcoming), ch. 11 of unpublished manuscript. This chapter is entitled "Calvinism's Argument for Necessary Perseverance" (italics added).

understanding of how one may be found in Christ. It is simply *by faith* and it is *open to all*. Given the constraints of space, a few scriptural references must suffice in lieu of a more exhaustive listing. With respect to the doctrine of a general atonement and a universal calling, rather than a limited atonement and particular calling, one should consider the following:

- "God was reconciling the world to himself in Christ" (2 Cor. 5:19).
- "For the grace of God that brings salvation has appeared to all men" (Titus 2:11).
- "But I, when I am lifted up from the earth, will draw all men to myself" (John 12:32).
- "The true light [Christ] that gives light to every man was coming into the world" (John 1:9).
- "He is the atoning sacrifice for our sins, and not only for ours but also for the sins of the whole world" (1 John 2:2).
- "The Lord is not slow in keeping his promise, as some understand slowness. He is patient with you, not wanting anyone to perish, but everyone to come to repentance" (2 Peter 3:9).

Likewise, in considering what the Bible teaches about a salvation conditioned on faith, we must note the following passages:

- "... that everyone who believes may have eternal life in him." (John 3:15, NIV text note).
- "Whoever believes in him is not condemned, but whoever does not believe stands condemned already because he has not believed in the name of God's one and only Son" (John 3:18).
- "Whoever believes in the Son has eternal life, but whoever rejects the Son will not see life, for God's wrath remains on him" (John 3:36).
- "They replied, 'Believe in the Lord Jesus, and you will be saved—you and your household'" (Acts 16:31).

Of course, the Calvinist rejoinder is surely that if one says that the call of God goes out to all and that the grace of God comes to all, then one cannot believe in total depravity. But this is not so, for the Calvinist is once again reading in a priori his or her particularistic mindset. Reformed Arminians will agree with

Calvinists on the problem. Fallen humanity is "dead in trespasses and sins." Human beings are unable to perform the least spiritual good on their own. We do not disagree on the problem. Our disagreement is on how God has sovereignly chosen to solve the problem of the human predicament. Calvinists argue that the only way God can be sovereign and gracious is if he *unconditionally* elects certain ones to salvation and then effects their salvation by acting on them with grace that cannot be resisted.

Reformed Arminians, along with other Arminians, respectfully demur from this understanding of God's sovereignty. Once again, we believe that caution is required when considering the eternal counsels of God. Calvinists have generally warned that, when considering God's decrees as relating to the *ordo salutis*, we should keep in mind that we are talking about a *logical, not a chronological,* order. If indeed that is so, then what should follow therefrom? The obvious implication is that we are considering a *logical question* concerning how God would sovereignly choose to effect salvation for humanity. When Calvinists look at fallen individuals, they see them "dead in sins" and "unable to do any spiritual good." Hence, Calvinism teaches that God acts on people in a cause-and-effect relationship with "irresistible grace," thus bringing about their salvation.

Yet if we are talking about logic here, then God could have sovereignly chosen to remedy humanity's situation differently than by the particularistic, cause-and-effect means proposed by Calvinism. In other words, when God saw his fallen human race in as bad a condition as it could possibly be in—"dead in sins" and "unable to do the least spiritual good"—logically, nothing would have precluded him from sovereignly choosing to reach out to all people with enabling grace (often referred to as prevenient grace). In fact, the apostle Paul has said that "the grace of God that brings salvation has appeared to all men" (Titus 2:11).

Nor is there any illogic involved in saying that God's enabling grace might be proffered to fallen humankind in conjunction with God's initiation of salvation on their behalf, that is, by drawing all people toward himself. Indeed, Jesus claimed, "But I, when I am lifted up from the earth, will draw all men to myself" (John 12:32). Of course, the Calvinist recoils and says, "If all are enabled and all are drawn, then universalism must surely result—all would be saved." To which, I would say, "Yes, *if* God's grace were irresistible grace." Once again, however, God can sovereignly choose that his salvation is not going to proceed along the lines of a deterministic, cause-and-effect relationship. Rather, he is going to allow the sinner to resist the offer of grace, which grace he has sovereignly enabled the sinner to accept.

So why would God do such a thing? Arminius states:

> ... beside his own omnipotent and internal action, God is both able and willing to employ the following argument: "God justifies no persons except such as believe: Believe therefore, that thou mayest be justified." With respect, then, to this argument, *faith will* arise from *suasion*. ... In his omnipotent act God employs [or uses] this argument; and by this argument, when rightly understood, He efficaciously produces [operates] faith. If it were otherwise, the operation would be expended on a *stone* or a *lifeless body*, and not upon the *intellect* of a *man*.[16]

F. Leroy Forlines has done an excellent job of developing the idea that God has sovereignly chosen to interact with his human creation in accordance with an "influence and response" model rather than by employing "cause and effect."[17] This is true not only in incidental matters but also in matters related to salvation. God respects the personhood of his human creation. He does not act on persons as on a "stone" or a "lifeless body." I want to reiterate that nothing proposed here diminishes from God's sovereignty or his grace. True, it is not a particularistic schema, nor is the grace viewed thus irresistible. Nevertheless, upon realizing that the ordering of the decrees is a logical ordering rather than a chronological one, the foregoing is a perfectly logical construct of how a sovereign God might choose to effect his gracious salvation for a sinful humanity.

REFORMED ARMINIANISM'S
SIMILARITY TO OTHER ARMINIANISMS

I do not need to go into as great a depth at this point, since much of the argument proceeds along the same general lines

---

[16]*Works of Arminius*, 1:746–47.
[17]F. Leroy Forlines, *The Quest for Truth: Answering Life's Inescapable Questions* (Nashville: Randall House, 2001), 313–21.

between Reformed Arminians and other types of Arminians. A brief laundry list, then, must suffice with reference to areas of overlap. I will take a greater sense of care in the next section to show the distinctiveness of the Reformed Arminian position as over against other Arminian views, which veer from Arminius himself.

Reformed Arminians agree with nearly every conservative Arminian writer on the philosophical question of determinism and free will. In this view God is sovereign, but he has chosen that his foreknowledge will be conditioned on the actual and contingent actions of his free creatures.[18] One should not infer from this that humankind, prior to being excited and enabled by God's grace, has the power of alternative choice with reference to doing spiritual good. Total depravity, inherited from our first father Adam, has rendered the natural human being spiritually dead and helpless before a holy God.[19] Freedom, for Arminius and for all who have a right to the ascription Arminian, is not some sort of absolute freedom or a Pelagian sort of freedom.[20] Rather, it means "freedom from deterministic necessity."

In relation to soteriology, all Arminians agree that salvation is conditional. God's election to salvation is thus conditional. While there is a difference of opinion among Arminians concerning whether election is corporate or individual,[21] the conditional nature of salvation and hence election is not in debate. Reformed Arminians, along with other Arminians, eschew a view of salvation that is rooted in a presupposed particularism. Christ's atoning work is universal in its scope and may be obtained by *any* sinner who will not resist the drawing and enabling power of the Holy Spirit. That right response is a response of faith and repentance, two sides of the same coin, which produces God's regenerating grace in the life of the sinner, rendering him or her a child of God.

---

[18]I have benefited from Robert E. Picirilli's "Foreknowledge, Freedom, and the Future," *Journal of the Evangelical Theological Society* 43 (2000): 259–71.

[19]I would emphasize at this point that unlike much of the more popular expressions of Anglo-Arminianism, Reformed Arminians distance themselves from semi-Pelagian and ultra-synergistic views that claim that sinners can choose what is right if they only will.

[20]*Works of Arminius*, 1:764.

[21]Compare Robert Shank, *Elect in the Son* (Springfield, Mo.: Westcott, 1970), 45–55 with Forlines, *The Quest for Truth*, 364–67, 371–74, 382–83. This distinction can result in nuanced differences with regard to the nature of the condition.

All Arminians hold, however, that people can resist God's saving grace. Divine grace does not function like a tsunami tidal wave, totally overwhelming the sinner's will in its wake. Rather, God's grace works through "suasion," *influencing* sinners, *drawing* them toward God, *enabling* them to respond in faith. Yet when people respond in faith and repentance, it is truly their response, *one that might have been otherwise*. The reason for this is that God works with his human creation in light of the creature's personhood. God's grace is thus resistible grace, from start to finish, both before and after salvation.

REFORMED ARMINIANISM'S
DIFFERENCES WITH OTHER ARMINIANISMS

At this point in the discussion I must refer to certain things already mentioned. While the section immediately preceding shows numerous teachings that all those called Arminians hold in common, important differences exist between Reformed Arminians and other Arminians. Chief among them are divergent views of the meaning of Christ's atonement and how it is applied. As mentioned above, Reformed Arminians hold to a *penal satisfaction* view of the atonement and to the imputation of Christ's perfect obedience to believers. This imputation serves as the only ground of their justification before a holy God. They enter into this legal standing before God by faith. Hence, they stand justified solely on the merits of Christ's righteousness and death, which God graciously accounts to those who trust him.

Most Arminians do not hold this view of atonement and its application in justification. Among those Arminians who are not satisfactionists, it is typical to demean this view by calling it the "Hyper-Calvinistic or Antinomian theory of justification."[22] Though Wesley at times used the phrase "imputation of righteousness" with regard to justification, he disagreed with the Reformed view of the imputation of Christ's righteousness to the believer—that Christ fulfilled the law on the believer's behalf, thereby rendering the believer judicially righteous through imputation. "The judgment of an all-wise God," Wesley argued, "is always according to truth; neither can it ever consist with His

---

[22]See Thomas N. Ralston, *Elements of Divinity* (Nashville: Cokesbury, 1924), 374, 383. Cf. Wiley, *Christian Theology*, 2:396.

unerring wisdom to think that I am innocent, to judge that I am righteous or holy because another is so. He can no more confound me with Christ than with David or Abraham."[23]

Arminius, as I have already shown, would have strongly disagreed with Wesley's perspective.[24] Wesleyan theologian Thomas Ralston quotes from what he calls "leading Arminians" on this subject, *but he never quotes from Arminius himself.*[25] Yet after two pages of quotations and arguments against the imputation of Christ's righteousness to the believer, amazingly, Ralston says that "the Calvinistic notion on this subject [imputation] is now sufficiently clear and distinct from the Arminian view."[26] This is simply false. Arminius held the same Reformed view of the atonement that Calvin and his followers held: Christ's obedience to the law and his obedience to the death of the cross satisfied the just demands of a holy God, and this positive obedience is imputed to believers.

So what view do Arminians hold if they cannot accept the penal satisfaction view? Most accept a governmental view, a concept Hugo Grotius developed in the early 1600s. Wesley himself, and a few Wesleyans after him, did not adhere to a fullblown governmental theory. Yet they incorporated key elements of that view and always distanced themselves from the satisfaction view of Reformed theology. According to the governmental concept, "the atonement was not a satisfaction to any internal principle of the divine nature, but to the necessities of government."[27] Key elements of this view are:

1. God cannot pardon the sins of human beings without some *adequate exhibition of his displeasure.*
2. Christ's sufferings were *an example* of what sin deserved.
3. The sufferings and death of Christ were *intended to teach* that in the estimation of God, sin deserves to be punished.[28]

---

[23]Sermon by Wesley, "Justification by Faith," in *The Works of John Wesley*, ed. Thomas Jackson, 14 vols. (London: Wesley Methodist Book Room, 1872; repr., Grand Rapids: Baker, 1986), 5:57.

[24]*Works of Arminius*, 2:43–44, 253–58.

[25]Ralston, *Elements of Divinity*, 384–85.

[26]Ibid., 385.

[27]Wiley, *Christian Theology*, 2:252.

[28]Ibid., 2:254. Cf. Millard J. Erickson, *Christian Theology* (Grand Rapids: Baker, 1986), 788–92, where Erickson explains and evaluates the governmental view of the atonement.

None of these elements by itself is problematic. However, when the emphasis of Christ's atonement is thought to be merely a public display whereby a moral lesson is being taught, it becomes highly problematic. To say, as noted in Wiley above, that "the atonement was not a satisfaction to any internal principle of the divine nature" tends toward the diminishment, on the one hand, of how bad sin really is and, on the other hand, of the holiness of God.[29] One wonders, in fact, if according to the governmental view, Christ's death was even necessary.

In arguing the governmentalist position, Methodist theologian John Miley says, "While thus asserting the intrinsic evil of sin, Grotius denies an absolute necessity arising therefrom for its punishment. The punishment of sin is just, but not in itself an obligation."[30] A little later Miley himself says, "we do not believe—that in the resources of infinite wisdom the precise manner of the mediation of Christ was the only possible manner of human redemption."[31] These are serious statements, which should not go uncontested.

To view matters relating to Christ's atonement negatively, the governmental theory asserts:

1. There was no necessity that sin be punished.
2. Christ's atonement did not satisfy any internal principle in the divine nature.
3. Christ's death was not the necessary means of human redemption.
4. Christ's righteousness (active obedience) and his death (passive obedience) are *not* imputed to the believer.

Reformed Arminians strenuously object to each of these four statements. Governmentalism,[32] however, views Christ's atonement positively by saying:

---

[29]Ibid. Herein Erickson evaluates this view thusly: "the loving nature of God wishes to forgive sin. It is almost as if, in his desire to forgive sin, God was looking for an excuse not to enforce the full consequences. He found his opportunity in the death of Christ, regarding it as sufficient to preserve his moral government."

[30]John Miley, *Systematic Theology*, 2 vols. (New York: Eaton & Mains, 1894), 2:162.

[31]Ibid., 2:165.

[32]H. Ray Dunning, *Grace, Faith and Holiness: A Wesleyan Systematic Theology* (Kansas City, Mo.: Beacon Hill, 1988), 337.

1. It is *an exhibition* of God's displeasure.
2. It provides *an example* of what sin deserves.
3. Christ's sufferings and death were *pedagogical tools* used by God to teach us that God thinks sin deserves punishment.
4. It maintains the public justice, while allowing God to pardon sinners.

As already stated, these four statements in themselves are not wrong; they simply do not go far enough. The penal satisfaction view is essential to Reformed Arminianism because the necessity of the atonement emanates from God's very nature and thus cannot be seen as mere pageantry or symbolism.[33]

Another important distinction between Reformed Arminianism and Wesleyan Arminianism relates to the doctrine of sanctification. Dunning is correct when he states that "Augustine, Luther, and Calvin all propose a full sanctification in this life in terms of imputation. While the sinner himself is not so completely changed, the perfect righteousness of Christ is accounted to him, and thus, positionally, he is considered perfect in God's sight."[34] Anthony Hoekema has done an excellent job of explaining this concept when he says, "We note first that we are sanctified *in union with Christ*. Paul teaches that we are made holy through being united with Christ in his death and resurrection."[35] Though Dunning is correct in saying that this view of imputation "involves a transaction that occurs external to the person," he is far from correct when he says that "it does not entail a real change" and that "no necessary moral transformation need occur."[36] Hoekema continues:

> Certain opponents of Paul had been twisting his teachings about justification by faith so as to make them mean,

---

[33]Shank, *Elect in the Son*, 35–36. I would note in passing that some recent Wesleyan scholars, such as H. Ray Dunning, have diverged from governmentalism. Dunning, while tipping his hat to Paul's forensic categories (e.g., "in Adam" vs. "in Christ"), proposes a *Christus Victor* (ransom) theory, strenuously avoiding penal satisfaction (*Grace, Faith and Holiness*, 362–65, 386–90). As Dunning has stated, his is a Wesleyan view of the atonement. Yet, it is not essentially Reformed, and it radically diverges from Arminius's view.

[34]Dunning, *Grace, Faith and Holiness*, 462.

[35]Anthony A. Hoekema, "The Reformed Perspective," in *Five Views on Sanctification* (Grand Rapids: Zondervan, 1987), 63.

[36]Dunning, *Grace, Faith and Holiness*, 463.

Let's go on sinning so that grace may increase (see Rom 6:1). Paul replies, "By no means! We died to sin; how can we live in it any longer?" (v. 2). He goes on to show that we died to sin in union with Christ, who died for us on the cross: "We were therefore buried with him through baptism into death.... Our old self [old man] was crucified with him" (vv. 4, 6). Sanctification, therefore must be understood as a dying to sin in Christ and with Christ, who also died to sin. (v. 10)[37]

The next several pages of Hoekema's discussion are insightful and deserve close scrutiny. We will have to be content by noting that Christ *is* our sanctification (1 Cor. 1:30). Redemptive-historically, on the ledger of God, our sanctification is complete in Christ Jesus. Yet on the practical level, it remains for us to appropriate all the blessings that are ours in him. "If we are one with Christ, we are being sanctified; and the only way we can be sanctified is through being one with Christ."[38] God uses *the truth* in this process of sanctification (John 17:17; 2 Tim. 3:16–17). And we are sanctified *by faith* as we more and more grasp our union with Christ (Gal. 2:20), believe that sin is not our master (Rom. 6:6), and appropriate the enabling power of the Holy Spirit, thus producing the fruit of the Spirit in our lives (Gal. 5:16, 22–23).

Hoekema's description is correct. Arminius could not have said it better, but he did say it as well:

The object of sanctification is man, a sinner, and yet a believer: a *sinner*, because, being contaminated through sin and addicted to a life of sin he is unfit to serve the living God. A *believer*, because he is united with Christ through faith in him on whom our holiness is founded; and he is planted together with Christ and joined to Him in a conformity with his death and resurrection.....The External Instrument is the word of God; the Internal one is faith yielded to the word preached: For the word does not sanctify, only as it is preached, unless the faith be added by which the hearts of men are purified.[39]

---

[37]Hoekema, "The Reformed Perspective," 63.
[38]Ibid., 64.
[39]*Works of Arminius*, 2:409.

When looking at a Wesleyan view of sanctification, the view that has characterized much of the Arminianism known today, we find substantial departure from Reformed categories. As shown above, Wesley and those in his train have no use for the Reformed concept of imputation. They refer to it as a "legal and absurd fiction."[40] It is interesting that they adopt this terminology to describe the Reformed view, for this is exactly the claim that Rome made against Luther and the Reformers, who argued that we stand righteous before a holy God based on the merits of Christ's righteousness alone.

The issue was simple: Is my acceptance before God based entirely on what Christ has done (imputed to my account), or am I accepted based partly on what Christ has done and partly on what I do (inherent righteousness within me)?[41] Reformed thought, and I include Reformed Arminianism here, takes as staunch a stand as Luther took when he said, "Here I stand; I can do no other." My acceptance before a holy God is predicated on the standard of absolute perfection—a standard I cannot achieve. But the standard has been achieved, and it can be accounted to me as though I had achieved it when, by faith, I am brought into union with Christ.

According to Dunning, Wesley's views were a synthesis of the Catholic ethic of holiness (love), the Protestant ethic of grace (law), and the Eastern Orthodox understanding of the Christian life (transformation of being).[42] Dunning is likely correct here. For when the Wesleyan understanding of "entire sanctification" or "Christian perfection" is broached, one is regularly confronted with the idea of the heart of the sanctified person acting out of "perfect love." However, one cannot overlook the fact that the popular understanding of this Wesleyan doctrine is that sinlessness is what should be achieved via a definitive second work of grace in the life of the sinner who has been pardoned. Furthermore, if Dunning is right concerning Wesley's synthesis, it is not difficult to see how the Orthodox view of *theosis* (deification) is brought to bear.

---

[40]See Wiley, *Christian Theology*, 2:382; cf. Ralston, *Elements of Divinity*, 375.
[41]R. C. Sproul, *Faith Alone* (Grand Rapids: Baker, 1995), 105–8.
[42]Dunning, *Grace, Faith and Holiness*, 463.

CLASSICAL CALVINISM AND PERSEVERANCE

If *sovereignty* can only be sovereign when God acts in a
cause-and-effect relationship with his creation, even
his human creation,
and if *grace* can only be gracious when it is applied in a
manner that cannot be resisted,
and if *election* can only be of God when it is unconditional
and particularistic,

then Calvinism is obviously correct. However, we should realize that these are assumptions that the Calvinist brings to the
text of Scripture. The system is logically tight. If one subscribes
to this system, then it logically follows that those whom God has
chosen and to whom he has applied his grace irresistibly will
unalterably persevere in salvation.
On the contrary,

if God in his *sovereignty* is powerful enough and his knowledge is great enough to maintain control and accomplish his purposes while allowing real contingency
into his universe,
and if God's *grace* is still unmerited favor though he allows
his human creatures the possibility of resisting its
application,
and if the *election* of God for salvation is conditioned on
faith in Christ, and if salvation is offered to all and
made possible by the drawing power and enabling
grace of his Holy Spirit,

then Calvinism is not correct. Hence, I suggest that, whereas
Calvinism is a logically tight system, Reformed Arminianism is
also logically consistent. Salvation is conditioned on faith in
Christ.
Since God has chosen to deal with his human creation in
terms of their personhood, by influence and response rather than
through cause and effect, he allows us to resist his grace—though
he has enabled us to receive it. However, our personhood, along
with God's method of dealing with his free creatures, does not
end at the moment of salvation. He requires that in order to be
brought into Christ, we must believe in him. If, however, as persons, we exercise our God-given, personal freedom after salvation

and reject the Christ who saved us, then logically we must admit that it is possible for one who has been *in Christ* to exit by the same door that God has ordained as being the way into union with Christ.

Again, it should be remembered that all of the benefits of salvation are ours solely by means of our being *in Christ Jesus*. If it is possible for one who was truly saved ever to reach the point where he or she is no longer in Christ, then the benefits of salvation are forfeited at that point as well. I believe the Bible teaches this to be a real possibility. Though not probable, and though God gives everything necessary for life and godliness, human beings can use the freedom God has given them to insult the Spirit of grace (Heb. 10:29) and to make shipwreck of their faith (1 Tim. 1:19).

At this point I will move forward from a discussion of my view as it relates to Calvinism. In essence, I have granted the Calvinists their case, given their presuppositions. However, I would reiterate one last time that I do not accept their assumptions (1) concerning what constitutes God's sovereignty, that is, a cause-and-effect determinism over his human creation; (2) concerning God's grace, that is, that it is irresistible in its call to salvation and particularistic concerning to whom the call is extended; and (3) concerning God's election, that is, that it is unconditional. Lacking these assumptions, Calvinism cannot stand. I believe that Calvinism is wrong on each of the above points. Hence, its view of perseverance should logically be brought into question. This should be obvious since the underpinning for a Calvinistic understanding of perseverance is based on the other planks within the system as a whole.

MODERATE CALVINISM AND ETERNAL SECURITY

Up to this point, I have been arguing the *conditional* nature of salvation—that salvation is conditioned on faith in Christ. I have conceded to the Calvinist that if one believes in the *unconditional* nature of salvation—that God has unconditionally elected particular individuals to salvation while predestinating others to be reprobates—then the certain perseverance of those thus elected to salvation is assured. For who can thwart the purposes of God?

In contrast to the above concession, I would assert that "Moderate Calvinism," the so-called "once saved, always saved" position, lacks in logical consistency. Indeed, if one believes in the conditional nature of salvation (as Moderate Calvinists do, that condition being faith), and if the particularism of Calvinism is rejected (Moderate Calvinists hold that Christ died for all), and if God's grace comes to humankind through persuasion, that is, acting in conjunction with human personhood (not overwhelming the individual through compulsion), then it logically follows that it would be possible for a person, after conversion, who is still as much a person as he or she was before conversion, to resist the persuasive influence of the Holy Spirit, even to the point of rejecting his or her faith in Christ.[43]

In his *Chosen But Free*, Norman Geisler seeks to show that his view is Calvinistic (he gives a brief, point-by-point explanation on each of the first four points of the TULIP). However, he redefines the meaning so as to empty the system of its classical intent. He is actually a one-point Calvinist—*the last*. According to his measure, Reformed Arminians can also be called Calvinists. I also hold to one point of the TULIP—*the first*. (As I argued earlier, Reformed Arminians hold to the doctrine of total depravity as strenuously as does any Calvinist.) Geisler, by contrast, has defined away both the classical Calvinist and the classical Arminian understanding of depravity, replacing it instead with a sort of semi-Pelagian notion of natural human ability. It seems to me that his logical mind presses him toward an unconscious acknowledgment that his brand of Calvinism is in actuality a one-point Calvinism. For without giving careful argumentation for his redefinitions of the system, he simply jumps into a several-page "Defense of Eternal Security," citing and explaining fifteen proof texts.

Geisler should have made clear how he justifies the sea change that he asserts. He argues that the sinner's will is free to

---

[43]Norman Geisler, *Chosen But Free* (Minneapolis: Bethany House, 1999). On p. 116 Geisler gives a chart that contrasts Moderate Calvinism with that of extreme Calvinism. The chart evidences a conditional understanding of salvation, a general instead of a limited atonement, and resistible grace. However, when he comes to the doctrine of perseverance, he deviates from a logically consistent position, vaulting immediately into "A Defense of Eternal Security."

act in alternative ways, so as to choose God, or conversely, to resist God. He has not attempted to explain, however, why or how a person who is free before salvation is no longer free after salvation. If the character of God's grace is that it is resistible before salvation, acting persuasively in accordance with one's will, then why should God's grace be viewed as irresistible after one is saved, compelling the individual, though his or her will might turn against God and his grace?

One other point with reference to this sea change relates to faith. Giesler says that those who receive the gift of salvation must believe in Christ and that faith is the one condition that the one who receives salvation must meet. However, in arguing against Arminian objections to his view, he eschews what he calls the "symmetrical nature of faith":

> Arminians contend that if we can exercise faith to "get in" Christ then we can use the same faith to "get out" of Christ. Just like getting on and off a bus headed for heaven, we can exercise our free choice at either end. Not to be able to do this, they insist, would mean that once we get saved, we are no longer free. Freedom is symmetrical; if you have freedom to get saved, then you have the freedom to get lost again.[44]

Geisler is partially correct and partially incorrect here. He is correct with respect to the idea he is trying to express, yet incorrect with respect to the expression of the idea. For Reformed Arminians, freedom means *freedom from deterministic necessity*. As I mentioned above, Geisler's view of depravity seems much closer to a semi-Pelagian notion than mine or Arminius's view. He seems to hold that the individual is *able* in one's natural condition to respond rightly to God in faith. My view of depravity is that *the will is bound by sin* until it is drawn, enabled, and excited by grace. However, when God enables, his call is by *influence* or *suasion* (Geisler agrees; his word is persuasion). God does not call to salvation by *coercion—irresistibly* (Geisler agrees; his term is compulsively). Thus, when one responds to God in faith, it is truly *a person's own response*. One's faith is not simply the effect of a determining external or a determining internal cause.

---

[44]Ibid.

However, Geisler's similitude of a bus headed for heaven in no way approximates the Reformed Arminian understanding. Rather, Reformed Arminians propose the following rubric:

1. Prior to being *drawn and enabled,*
   one is *unable to believe . . . able only to resist.*
2. *Having been drawn and enabled,* but prior to regeneration,
   one is *able to believe . . . able also to resist.*
3. After one *believes,* God then *regenerates;*
   one is *able to continue believing . . . able also to resist.*
4. Upon *resisting* to the point of *unbelief,*
   one is *unable again to believe . . . able only to resist.*

The reason persons 1 and 4 are unable to believe and are able only to resist God is that God is not drawing or enabling them. And "apart from [him] you can do nothing" (John 15:5).

Over against what is generally a good treatment by Geisler, Charles Stanley makes some outrageous claims—and he does this with so much repetition that it is obviously not a slip. He asks what he calls a sobering question: "Do I believe I have the power to thwart the purposes of God? . . . To believe that a man or woman can lose his or her salvation is to believe that a human being can frustrate the eternal purpose of God."[45] That would certainly be true if, as the five-point Calvinist says, salvation has no conditions—if God irresistibly applies his grace to unregenerate and willful sinners. But like Geisler, Stanley holds that sinners are saved when they express faith in Christ. In other words, "Faith is simply the way we say yes to God's free gift of eternal life. . . . Forgiveness/salvation is applied at the moment of faith."[46]

Thus, Stanley, like Geisler, believes that God has made his gift of salvation, forgiveness of sins, and eternal life contingent (conditioned) on one's believing in Christ. I would readily agree! But the question once again leaps out: How is it that salvation, which is thought to be *conditional* (the one condition being faith) prior to salvation, all of a sudden is understood as being *unconditional* after salvation? What has happened to the human will in the process? Do people have free will prior to salvation but lose that free will after they are saved? And what about grace? Is it resistible before salvation but irresistible after one is saved?

---

[45]Charles Stanley, *Eternal Security* (Nashville: Thomas Nelson, 1990), 77.
[46]Ibid., 80.

Stanley, like Geisler, shows a lack of logical consistency at this point. However, this is not what is so egregious about his position. Rather, like Zane Hodges and others who argue against the notion of "lordship salvation," Stanley is intent on showing that a person is not saved by grace and then kept by works. Again I would agree. So where is the rub? Stanley goes on to argue his case with a series of outlandish claims. To list a few:

> The Bible clearly teaches that God's love for his people is of such magnitude that *even those who walk away from the faith* have not the slightest chance of slipping from His hand.[47]

> In all probability, a Christian who has expressed faith in Christ and experienced forgiveness of sin will always believe that forgiveness is found through Christ. But *even if he does not*, the fact remains that he is forgiven![48]

> Saving faith is not necessarily a sustained attitude of gratefulness for God's gift. *It is a singular moment in time* wherein we take what God has offered.[49]

Stanley gives an analogy of getting a tattoo in which he states:

> ... that would involve a one-time-act on my part. Yet the tattoo would remain with me indefinitely. I don't have to maintain an attitude of fondness for tattoos to ensure that the tattoo remains on my arm. In fact *I may change my mind the minute I receive it*. But that does not change the fact that I have a tattoo on my arm.... Forgiveness/salvation is applied at the moment of faith. It is not the same thing as faith. *And its permanence is not contingent upon the permanence of one's faith*.[50]

It is somehow hard for me to believe that this is the notion that so overwhelmed Martin Luther and spawned the Protes-

---

[47]Ibid., 74 (italics added).

[48]Ibid., 79 (italics added).

[49]Ibid., 81 (italics added). Cf. Dale Moody, who states: "Those who glibly talk about 'once-saved, always-saved,' as if it is a past transaction so that now one cannot lose 'his salvation' miss most of the meaning of salvation. A salvation that is solely in the past tense is a perversion of the New Testament meaning of salvation" (*Apostasy: A Study in the Epistle to the Hebrews and in Baptist History* [Greenville, S.C.: Smyth & Helwys, 1991], 17).

[50]Stanley, *Eternal Security*, 80 (italics added).

tant Reformation. For Luther's study of Romans convinced him that "the just shall live by faith" (Rom. 1:17, KJV), not that the just will "walk away from the faith" or "change their minds the minute they receive it," as Stanley states. One may wonder whether I am selectively choosing obscure and tangential quotations that do not truly express Stanley's position. Yet he clarifies the issue when he asks: "Does the Scripture actually teach that regardless of the consistency of our faith, our salvation is secure? Yes, it does." He uses 2 Timothy 2:11–13 to make his case:

> If we died with him,
>> we will also live with him;
> If we endure,
>> we will also reign with him;
> If we disown [deny] him,
>> he will also disown [deny] us;
> If we are faithless,
>> he will remain faithful,
>> for he cannot disown [deny] himself.

In commenting on the fourth couplet, Stanley states: "The apostle's meaning is evident. Even if a believer for all practical purposes becomes an unbeliever, his salvation is not in jeopardy. Christ will remain faithful."[51] Stanley's position could not be clearer. He is not arguing that "the just shall live by faith." Rather, he is arguing for *saved unbelievers*. In other words, it would take only a momentary lapse in one's unbelief, "a singular moment in time ... in fact, I may change my mind the minute I receive it [salvation] ... and indeed, walk away from the faith." This sounds strangely akin to what just a few years ago was being called "easy believism." D. A. Carson remarks:

> Zane Hodges is happy to speak of Christians ceasing to name the name of Christ and denying the faith completely, even though (he insists) God keeps such people "saved," that is, in the faith. From a pastoral point of view, what is one to say of these *unbelieving believers*, these *Christ-denying Christians*?[52]

[51]Ibid., 92–93.
[52]Carson, "Reflections on Assurance," 275 (italics added).

Forlines responds to Stanley's treatment of 2 Timothy 2:11–13 by saying that Stanley does not address the statement "If we deny Him, He will also deny us." In fact, Forlines argues,

> Stanley is saying that a person who is a Christian could deny Him, and He will not deny that person. With regard to the last part of verse 13, "If we are faithless, He remains faithful, for he cannot deny Himself," I would give the following explanation: If we become faithless, Christ will remain faithful to His character and will deny us.[53]

This view, which Stanley blatantly asserts, is certainly far from any classical understanding of Calvinism. Indeed, as J. Oliver Buswell remarks, "No wonder the Arminians are scandalized by what is falsely called Calvinism."[54]

Stanley's treatment rightly leaves him open to accusations of antinomianism. Further, he fails to establish how salvation changes from being conditional to unconditional. Geisler, while less overt in his claims, also fails at these same two points. What seems to me to be a better treatment of this view is R. T. Kendall's *Once Saved, Always Saved*. Kendall does an excellent job of arguing a historic Reformed position of justification by faith. He strongly emphasizes the forensic character of the believer's justification. He carefully distinguishes the meritorious cause (the ground) and the instrumental cause (the means) of justification. The meritorious cause is Jesus Christ—alone. The instrumental cause is our faith—alone. He rightly insists on the necessity of Christ's righteousness (both active and passive obedience) being imputed to the believer's account.[55]

Reformed Arminians would agree with all this. Yet Kendall does make a leap in logic. He writes:

> We may ask, then, just what kind of "righteousness" is put to our credit? What precisely is "imputed" to us? Our first answer must be that what God calls "righteous" is righteous enough! If the most holy God declares me *righteous*,

---

[53]Forlines, *The Quest for Truth*, 272. Forlines notes that this perspective concurs with that of M. R. Vincent, who states that God will be "true to his own nature, righteous character, and requirements, according to which he cannot accept as faithful one who has proved untrue to him. To do so would be to deny himself" (ibid.).

[54]J. Oliver Buswell Jr., *A Systematic Theology of the Christian Religion* (Grand Rapids: Zondervan, 1962), 146.

[55]R. T. Kendall, *Once Saved, Always Saved* (Chicago: Moody, 1983), 83–95.

that is good enough for me. That alone makes me eternally secure. For what He in His sovereign pleasure has pronounced cannot be undone. His judgment is irrevocable.[56]

The problem, once again, is that Kendall has not established that salvation is unconditional prior to making those statements. In fact, God does not simply "declare me righteous." It is *me-in-Christ* who is declared righteous. For God has "blessed us in the heavenly realms with every spiritual blessing *in Christ*" (Eph. 1:3, italics added). Eternal life is in the Son. It is ours if we have him (1 John 5:11–13). It is the same with "wisdom . . . righteousness, holiness [i.e., sanctification] and redemption" (1 Cor. 1:30). These are ours by being in Christ Jesus. None of these are abstract entities that I possess.

These benefits and blessings are mine only and always because I am in Christ. And how am I in Christ? *By faith*! As Kendall has said, Jesus Christ alone serves as the meritorious cause of our justification. But there is an instrumental cause, that being faith alone. It is not merely God's "declaring me righteous" that somehow magically or mystically makes me righteous. God has ordained that there be an instrumental cause in salvation—faith in Christ. This is the condition of salvation. And the need for it does not vanish the moment an individual is saved. If salvation is conditional, it is conditional throughout ("a righteousness that is by faith from first to last"—Rom. 1:17).

That conditionality applies to the doctrine of perseverance as well. The issue in question is whether one is in Christ or not. One is to be found in Christ *only by faith*. If one is outside of Christ, he or she is unjustified. If one is in Christ, he or she is justified. To the justified ones are rendered all the benefits of salvation. Yet the instrumental cause of justification is *faith in Christ*.

Calvin and Arminius make interesting statements that seem conversely parallel. According to Calvin: "God is the fountainhead of all righteousness. Hence man, *so long as he remains a sinner*, must consider him an enemy and a judge."[57] According to Arminius: "It is impossible for believers, *as long as they remain believers*, to decline from salvation."[58] Calvin here is talking about the one who is unjustified, whereas Arminius is talking about the

---

[56]Ibid., 93.
[57]Calvin, *Institutes of the Christian Religion*, 1:530.
[58]*Works of Arminius*, 2:42.

one who is justified. Human beings do not possess a righteousness of their own—not inherent, infused, or declared. For "God is the fountainhead of all righteousness." We are enabled to tap into that as we meet the one condition God has placed on salvation—faith in Christ. As long as a believer remains a believer, it is impossible for him or her to decline from salvation. For the just one will live by faith (Hab. 2:4; Rom 1:17; Gal. 3:11; Heb. 10:38).

The Scriptural Case for Eternal Security: A Response

I will try to address with as much care as possible in a work of this length the primary categories of texts typically used to support the "once saved, always saved" position. It should be mentioned that these texts are generally the same ones classical Calvinists employ to support the unalterable perseverance of the elect. However, Moderate Calvinists hold that salvation is conditioned on faith; they argue that God's grace is resistible. They insist that the human will must be exercised in response to God's persuasion. Further, to say, "Why would a saved person ever want to abandon the faith?" is to ask a hypothetical and cognitively meaningless question. Eternal securitists are on their own to make their case. Now to the categories:

1. What Jesus means by "belief." Eternal securitists generally use a large number of proof texts that say that eternal life results from belief in Christ. We have already seen that Charles Stanley holds this to be a one-time, momentary act. On the contrary, however, almost all of these texts use the present tense when speaking of the belief that yields eternal life. Students of elementary Greek learn that the primary characteristic of the present tense is its linear nature, its progressive action. Though one could provide many examples, a few will suffice:

- John 3:15: ". . . that everyone who believes [present participle, is believing] may have eternal life in him" (cf. NIV text note).
- John 3:16: "For God so loved the world that he gave his one and only Son, that whoever believes [present participle, is believing] in him shall not perish but have eternal life."
- John 5:24: "I tell you the truth, whoever hears [present participle, is hearing] my word and believes [is believing] him who sent me has eternal life. . . ."

- John 6:35: ". . . he who believes [present participle, is believing] in me will never be thirsty."
- John 6:40: "For my Father's will is that everyone who looks [present participle, is looking] to the Son and believes [is believing] in him shall have eternal life."
- John 10:27–28: "My sheep listen to my voice; I know them, and they follow me. I give them eternal life. . . ." All of the verbs used here are present indicatives and thus are best rendered as follows: "My sheep are listening to my voice; I am knowing them, and they are following me. I am giving them eternal life. . . ."

It is not a small thing to change the scriptural emphasis from *believing as a process*, which is yielding eternal life, to *belief as a momentary act*, which one may walk away from one moment after believing with no adverse consequences.

2. The possibility that one's spiritual condition may change. Eternal securitists often cite verses such as John 5:24 and John 10:27–28, claiming the absolute unalterability of the promises given, that these "will not be condemned" or that "they shall never perish." However, what they are arguing may prove too much. Picirilli rightly compares the grammar and syntax of John 5:24 to that of 3:36 and shows that they are exactly parallel in their structure:

John 5:24	John 3:36
He that believes	He that believes not
shall not	*shall not*
come into condemnation	see life

Picirilli states:

> Gramatically, if the first means that the condition of the believer *cannot* be changed, then the second means that the condition of the unbeliever likewise *cannot* be changed. In fact, neither passage is even speaking to that issue. . . . Each promise applies with equal force to those who persist in the respective state described.[59]

Forlines effectively makes the same sort of argument regarding the phrase "they shall never perish" (John 10:28). He

---

[59]Picirilli, *Grace, Faith, Free Will*, ch. 12, p. 6.

166 I Four Views on Eternal Security

does not do so based on parallel syntax but rather on the parallelism of the idea expressed in John 10:28 to that of John 3:36. He states:

> No one says that, since it is said of the unbeliever that he shall not see life he is permanently bound without hope in that condition. It is a fact that as an unbeliever, he shall not see life, but if he becomes a believer, he will see life. Now, if the words "shall not see life," which describe the unbeliever, are not contradicted when the unbeliever becomes a believer and sees life, where is the contradiction when it is said that a believer "shall not perish," but if he becomes an unbeliever he will perish? The fact is that a believer, as long as he remains a believer, "shall not perish."[60]

One of the most common proof texts used by supporters of eternal security is that found in John 10:28. In speaking about his sheep, Jesus says, "I give them [am giving them] eternal life; and they shall never perish, neither shall any man pluck them out of my hand" (KJV). Of course, this sounds like unconditional continuance in salvation, if taken alone. The image is often invoked of Jesus whose strong grasp is unyielding on his sheep: No one can pluck them out of my hand or out of my Father's hand (vv. 28–29). Yet the context for this statement was dealt with in the previous section. Those being spoken of, who have this security, are described as those who are hearing his voice (v. 27), those who are following him (v. 27). It is to them that he is giving eternal life (v. 28); they are the ones who will never perish (v. 28). Thus, those who continue believing cannot be plucked from God's hand.

3. Texts giving assurance that all true believers will be saved. Several of the texts within this category are John 17:12; Ephesians 1:13–14; 1 Peter 1:5; 1 John 5:13. Reformed Arminians can read these texts in church and give their "Yea and Amen" without further comment, for each of these passages within their respective contexts clearly delimits who is being referred to: believers. We do not argue for *saved unbelievers*, as do some Moderate Calvinists. Rather, we insist that God will not turn away a single believer. Of those who are believers, not one will be lost—

---

[60]Forlines, *The Quest for Truth*, 274–75.

for they are "kept by the power of God *through faith* unto salvation" (1 Peter 1:5, KJV).

4. Texts not teaching what is being argued. Some texts used to support eternal security simply do not teach what is argued. For example, Geisler points to Romans 8:16 for support. This verse is not speaking to the issue of unconditional security. Rather, it concerns the benefits possessed by those who are in Christ (no condemnation—8:1; minding the things of the Spirit—8:5; witness of the Spirit—8:16; joint inheritance with Christ—8:17). These are not abstract entities that I possess. They result from my *union with Christ*. If that union is broken by unbelief, then the benefits are gone.

Romans 8:35–39 also fits into this category. This passage is not dealing with whether a saved person can ever be lost again. It is teaching that one who is a child of God can never at the same time be separated from the love of God.

5. Texts indicating that God will continue the work he has begun. Such verses as Philippians 1:6; 2 Thessalonians 3:3; 2 Timothy 1:12, 4:18; and Jude 24–25 are thought to show the unalterable perseverance of believers. However, these verses, and others like them, are expressions of thanksgiving and confidence that God will remain faithful in doing his part. But the paraenetic sections of Scripture show that he demands that his free creatures continue in the faith in order to partake in his blessings fully and finally.

Logical Arguments for Eternal Security: A Response

Analogical or logical arguments are common among those who hold to the "once saved, always saved" position. These arguments are often based on analogy with human experience rather than scriptural teaching. With that said, I will interact briefly with a few of the arguments.

1. If one could be removed from the body of Christ, Christ's body would be maimed. Scripture does not teach that he is complete in us, as such an argument would imply; rather, Paul says that we are complete *in him* (Col. 2:10).

2. If one is a child of God, then no matter what happens one cannot cease to be a child of God. This argument proceeds thusly:

Premise:	Your name is Stephen M. Ashby, right?–Yes.
Premise:	Your father was Hobert C. Ashby, right?–Yes.
Conclusion:	Well, no matter where you go, no matter what you do, you cannot cease to be the son of Hobert Ashby.

There is a problem with trying to make an absolute correlation between a spiritual relationship and a natural relationship. For if a spiritual relationship can never be broken, then it would be impossible for anyone ever to be saved. Note the following verses, where Jesus said, "You belong to your father, the devil" (John 8:44). Again, "This is how we know who the children of God are and who the children of the devil are: Anyone who does not do what is right is not a child of God; nor is anyone who does not love his brother" (1 John 3:10). In Ephesians 2:1–3 (KJV), Paul characterizes the unsaved as those who have walked according to the prince of the power of the air, as children of disobedience, and as children of wrath. If it is true that a spiritual relationship cannot be broken when applied to a "child of God," then logical consistency would demand that "children of the devil" must always remain children of the devil. Thus, no one could ever become a child of God. "Once a child, always a child" is simply an invalid argument.

3. One who is born again can never become unborn. If a person becomes an apostate, that person does not become unborn—*he or she dies!* Prior to conversion people are spiritually dead (Eph. 2:1). Through apostasy, one returns to that spiritually dead state. As John 3:36 says: "Whoever believes [present participle, is believing] in the Son has eternal life, but whoever rejects [is not believing] the Son will not see life, for God's wrath remains on him."

4. The believer is said to have eternal life as a present possession; it would not be eternal if you could lose it. Many texts are used to make this argument (e.g., John 3:15–16; 3:36; 5:24; 6:54; 10:28). With many of these passages, I noted above the progressive action of the present tense verbs. However, the point here is a different one. These verses speak of *eternal life*. Thus, we must ask ourselves what eternal life is. The answer may seem obvious, but is it really? Is eternal life a quantity of life? Does it merely mean that I am going to live forever? Further, do unbelievers have eternal life? Not according to the Bible! There is not a single verse of Scripture that attributes eternal life to an unbeliever. Of course, unbelievers are going to exist forever. But that is not what the Bible means when it speaks of eternal life. Several verses from the apostle John are helpful:

- John 1:4: *"In him was life*, and that life was the light of men."[61]
- John 5:26: "For as the Father has *life in himself*; so he has granted the Son to have *life in himself*."
- John 5:39–40: "You diligently study the Scriptures because you think that by them you possess eternal life. These are the Scriptures that testify about me, yet you refuse to *come to me to have life*."
- John 10:10: "I have come that they *may have life*, and have it to the full."
- John 12:50: "I know that his command *leads to eternal life*. . . ." The entire context of verses 44–50 is important here. Belief in Christ is obviously the key to eternal life.
- 1 John 5:11–13: Here John says that *"[eternal] life is in [God's] Son"* and that *"he who has the Son has life."* He concludes by saying that the key to having the Son, and thus eternal life, is believing in the Son of God.

Faith in Christ is what places one in Christ. Eternal life is not merely perpetual existence; it is the very life of God. I participate in that life because I am forensically *in Christ*. No one who is outside of Christ has eternal life. The life of God was eternal before I got it, and it will continue to be eternal, even if I were to forfeit it by rejecting Christ Jesus.

CONDITIONAL CONTINUANCE IN SALVATION

Conditional Continuance in Salvation: The Logical Case

I have earlier conceded classical Calvinists their case, granted their presuppositions. Since they believe that salvation is unconditional—that God has unconditionally elected particular ones to salvation while choosing to reprobate all the rest— the necessary perseverance of the elect logically follows. However, for those who reject the Calvinist's belief in unconditional

---

[61]The italics in any Scripture verses are all added.

election, there must be a willingness to consider the implications of conditional salvation. The condition of salvation is faith in Christ. Further, faith conditions the whole of salvation, not just its inception.

If divine grace is resistible prior to conversion, it is also resistible after conversion. God does not take away our free will at the moment of conversion (bear in mind that Reformed Arminians hold free will to be "freedom from deterministic necessity"). Forlines clearly shows both logically and theologically why those who believe that salvation is conditional should also believe that the condition pertains throughout—even to the point that salvation could be lost. He states:

> Being made in the image of God means that we are personal beings. We think, feel, and act. A person makes decisions or choices. Regardless of how much influence is brought to bear upon the will or how much assistance is given, a person's actions are in a very real sense his own. That is what it means to be a person. While there is divine aid for the Christian, it is possible for him to resist this aid and make wrong choices. Among these wrong choices is the possibility of turning back to unbelief. God made us persons. In His relationship with us, He never violates our personhood. While I do not think that the likelihood is high that a person who is saved will become an unbeliever again, I do believe that because we are persons, the possibility remains open ... the real issue is whether a Christian is a genuine, personal being. Does he think, feel, and make choices (both good and bad)?[62]

If God did not consider Christians to be persons who make choices (both good and bad), which are truly and significantly their own choices, then the volume of paraenetic and hortatory writings that deal with Christian behavior would not be needed. Hence, we should now look at the scriptural case for the possibility of apostasy.

Conditional Continuance in Salvation: The Scriptural Case

On strictly logical grounds, the Reformed Arminian position I am arguing coheres at least as well as does Calvinism.

---

[62]Forlines, *The Quest for Truth*, 276–77.

However, when viewed beside the "once-saved, always-saved" position or the Wesleyan Arminian perspective, the Reformed Arminian view sharply distinguishes itself. Only Reformed Arminianism is logically consistent and classically Arminian. Nevertheless, the question of whether saved individuals can ever again be lost should not be decided primarily on logical grounds but rather by examining the scriptural basis for the doctrine. In doing this I will propose several categories of texts that indicate that apostasy is a real possibility and then treat six key passages in more depth.

1. Numerous warning passages throughout the book of Hebrews. Hebrews is filled with warnings to believers to be careful not to fall away from salvation by ceasing to believe in Christ. Picirilli notes that "each main section has a hortatory 'center' assuming the possibility of apostasy. These are: chs. 1, 2, with 2:1–4 at the heart; chs. 3, 4, with 3:7–4:2 at the heart; chs. 5–7, with 5:11–6:12 at the heart, especially 6:4–6; chs. 8–12, with 10:19–39 and 12:1–29 at the heart."[63] I will look with more detail at some of these passages, along with a couple of other passages, after concluding the present categories.

When considering apostasy or perseverance, Hebrews should be the primary focus of one's attention, since it is in Hebrews that this subject takes center stage. As Dale Moody has said, if one understands the warning passages in Hebrews, he or she will have no problem making sense of the warning passages throughout the New Testament. "It is when one tries to twist Hebrews to fit traditional systems based on false philosophy and dogma that difficulties arise. Few passages in the New Testament have been twisted with more violence than the five warnings on apostasy in Hebrews."[64]

---

[63]Picirilli, *Grace, Faith, Free Will*, ch. 12, pp. 3–4. Cf. Scot McKnight, "The Warning Passages of Hebrews: A Formal Analysis and Theological Conclusion," *Trinity Journal* 13 NS (1992): 21–59. Cf. Grant R. Osborn, "Soteriology in the Epistle to the Hebrews," in *Grace Unlimited*, ed. Clark H. Pinnock (Minneapolis: Bethany Fellowship, 1975), 144–61.

[64]Dale Moody, *The Word of Truth: A Summary of Christian Doctrine Based on Biblical Revelation* (Grand Rapids: Eerdmans, 1981), 352. After examining the overall teaching of the five warning passages of Hebrews (not unlike Scot McKnight's synthetic approach), Moody concludes three things: "(1) It is possible to press on to maturity and full assurance (6:1, 11; 10:22); (2) it is possible for believers who do not press on to commit apostasy; and (3) there is no remedy for the sin of apostasy" (355).

2. Texts that indicate one's final salvation is conditioned on continuance in faith. The primary text within this grouping is Colossians 1:21–23. The audience Paul is addressing here is those who were "once ... alienated from God" but are "now ... reconciled" to him. The goal he sets forth is that they may be presented in eternity "holy ... without blemish and free from accusation." The means for accomplishing the goal is found in verse 23: "if you continue in your faith, established and firm, not moved from the hope held out in the gospel."

To understand the Reformed Arminian position, we must recognize that one is not saved by quitting sinning. Nor does committing sin or failing to confess sin cause one to lose salvation.[65] It is all on the basis of faith in Christ. This is what brings about *union with Christ,* thus rendering to the believer the benefits of salvation. In union with Christ, the believer stands righteous, not by his or her own merit but solely by the perfect obedience of Christ. Other passages in this category include 1 Peter 1:5 and Hebrews 3:14.

3. Passages that name individuals who have renounced faith in Christ and are endangering others. In 1 Timothy 1:18–20, Paul is charging Timothy to continue to fight the good fight by holding fast to faith and a good conscience. He names Hymenaeus and Alexander as examples of some who have departed from the faith, thus having made shipwreck of their faith. Paul adds Philetus to this list in 2 Timothy 2:16–18. Such shipwreck makes it apparent that these individuals have apostatized and are about to lead others to depart from the faith.

4. Texts in which Paul expresses concern that his labor among believers might be in vain. Several of these passages can be found in Galatians 4:9–11; Philippians 2:15–16; 1 Thessalonians 3:5. The reasons for Paul's concern were varied. His converts were encountering affliction and tribulation (1 Thess. 3:3–4). They were being bombarded by false teaching (Gal. 3:1–3). They were being tempted as they lived for God in a crooked and perverse nation (Phil. 2:15). Paul's concern was over their faith (1 Thess. 3:5), over the possibility of their turning to another way of salvation, that is, other than the grace of Christ (Gal. 1:6; 4:9), and over their holding forth the word of life (Phil. 2:16). He did

---

[65]The obvious and only exception to this statement is the sin of apostasy, which is the position taken throughout this entire chapter.

not want his labor that had produced true believers ultimately to be in vain.

5. Texts that speak of the possibility of a person's name being blotted out of the book of life. John warns of this possibility in Revelation 3:5 and 22:18–19. In order for one's part to be taken out of the book of life, that name must have been written there to begin with.

A Closer Look at Some Key Texts

As we now turn our attention to consider several key passages indicating that continuance in salvation is conditioned on continuance in faith, let me reiterate a point I made earlier. In referring to many of the proof texts used to support the "once-saved, always-saved" view, I stated that Reformed Arminians, believing that salvation is conditional from beginning to end, are able to read those texts (e.g., John 3:15–16; 5:24; 10:27–28) and add their *Amen* without further comment. However, the same cannot be said for eternal securitists regarding the texts we are about to consider. To look at these passages in light of the clear sense of the text, those holding to an unconditional continuance in salvation need to give extensive explanations in order to buttress their position. Now to the texts.

1. Hebrews 3:6b, 12–14.

And we are his house, if we hold on to our courage and the hope of which we boast. . . . See to it, brothers, that none of you has a sinful, unbelieving heart that turns away from the living God. But encourage one another daily, as long as it is called Today, so that none of you may be hardened by sin's deceitfulness. We have come to share in Christ if we hold firmly till the end the confidence we had at first.

The conditionality is clear within this passage. We are God's house *if* we hold fast our "confidence." Again in verse 14, our sharing in Christ is ultimately conditioned on *if* we hold firmly till the end the confidence we had at the first. Philip E. Hughes is to the point when he states:

Admonitions such as our author gives here serve to emphasize the seriousness of the Christian's calling and are thoroughly in line with God's covenant relationship with his people in former times (cf., for example, Dt. 30). God is not beholden to any person or nation: obedience to the terms of the covenant brings blessings; unfaithfulness and apostasy lead to judgment.[66]

One may wonder how long the Christian must hold the confidence spoken of above. The writer of Hebrews says: "till the end" (v. 14). Whom is the writer addressing? He identifies his readers as "brothers" (v. 12), and he even includes himself within the admonition by using the pronoun "we" (vv. 6, 14). And what is the warning against? It is against developing a "sinful, unbelieving heart" (v. 12), because the consequences are tragic: "turning away from the living God" (v. 12).

2. Hebrews 6:4–6.

It is impossible for those who have once been enlightened, who have tasted the heavenly gift, who have shared in the Holy Spirit, who have tasted the goodness of the word of God and the powers of the coming age, if they fall away, to be brought back to repentance, because to their loss they are crucifying the Son of God all over again and subjecting him to public disgrace.

Several positions are put forward regarding this passage by those who are unwilling to accept the clear sense of the text:

a. The writer is speaking hypothetically. According to this view, the situation described here would certainly be serious if it could happen, but it cannot happen. In effect, this view holds that God is using this passage as a means of scaring people into obedience. Hughes rightly says that this would be "the invention of a bogey for the purpose of frightening them into being better Christians. But the end does not justify the means, and to resort to subterfuge and deception, and that too within so solemn a context, would be subchristian."[67] Such a modus operandi is beneath God! Jesus said, "You will know *the truth*, and the truth will set you free" (John 8:32). As D. A. Carson remarks, the argu-

---

[66]Philip E. Hughes, *A Commentary on the Epistle to the Hebrews* (Grand Rapids: Eerdmans, 1977), 138. The covenant relationship of which Hughes speaks here does have "terms," what I have referred to in this chapter as the condition of salvation. The condition (the "terms") of salvation is faith in Christ.

[67]Ibid., 212.

ment that the warning passages "are merely hypothetical or that the turning aside . . . is from useful service but not from salvation, are desperate expedients that responsible exegesis will happily avoid."[68]

b. *The writer is speaking to first-century Jewish Christians.* This view argues that those being addressed were thinking about going back to the ritual of temple worship. Of course, all commentators recognize this. However, the next step of those who argue this view is to say that this cannot possibly apply to people today (not even Jewish Christians), since there is at present no temple to which they might return.

This perspective simply begs the question. Is it or is it not possible to commit apostasy by going back to one's former way of life? Obviously, every Christian has a former way of life. The Thessalonians turned to God from idols (1 Thess. 1:9). There are many lifestyles, not merely the ceremonial law and temple worship, wherein if a Christian were to return to that in preference to Christ, it would subject Christ to public disgrace.

c. *Those described here got close to salvation but never actually experienced it.* This view is often held by those Calvinists who refer to "children of the covenant." In other words, it is said that children of saved parents within the covenant community experience the overflow of blessings from being in close proximity to believers.[69] This would necessitate our considering whether the people described in Hebrews 6:4–6 were actually saved or lost. Five things are said of those being described:

  i. They were once-for-all enlightened.
  ii. They tasted the heavenly gift.
  iii. They became sharers of the Holy Spirit.
  iv. They tasted the good word of God and the powerful deeds of the coming age.
  v. They fell away.

It is hard to imagine finding any clearer statement that describes believers anywhere in all of Scripture. The *tasting* spoken of here is a full experience of the heavenly gift, the good

---

[68]Carson, "Reflections on Assurance," 261.

[69]This position is clearly developed by Pastor Petros Roukas in a sermon entitled "Can We Lose Our Salvation?" preached May 9, 1999, at Westminster Presbyterian Church, Muncie, Indiana.

Word of God, and the powers of the coming age. The writer of Hebrews earlier used the same term *taste* to describe Jesus' experience of death, saying "that by the grace of God he might *taste* death for everyone" (2:9). Surely everyone who holds the faith dear believes that when Jesus tasted death, he in fact *fully experienced* death. Clearly, those described in 6:4–6 had fully experienced salvation, as is evidenced by their being sharers in the Holy Spirit. To be a sharer in the Holy Spirit is to be a full-fledged participant in salvation (Rom. 8:9). Theirs was a once-for-all enlightenment that had exhibited the powers of the new creation in their lives.[70]

Now the question is asked: What happened to these addressees of Hebrews *when* (not *if*, as in the KJV or NIV) they fell away?[71] It became impossible for them again to be renewed to repentance. The fact that they cannot be renewed to repentance shows that they had repented previously. Hence, the one who has thus fallen away cannot be restored to faith (repentance/faith being two sides of the same coin); he or she cannot be saved again.

Many Arminians disagree with this understanding.[72] They maintain, "It is impossible to renew them to repentance while they are crucifying [Him] . . . and while they are shaming Him publicly." Picirilli cogently points out that "this almost amounts to saying that it is impossible to bring him to repentance so long as he persists in an attitude that makes it impossible to bring him to repentance."[73] That is mere tautology. This passage is speaking of those who were saved. They have fallen away. Now they cannot be saved again. The apostasy spoken of here is irremediable.

3. Hebrews 10:26–29.

If we deliberately keep on sinning after we have received the knowledge of the truth, no sacrifice for sins is left, but only a fearful expectation of judgment and of

---

[70]Hughes, *Epistle to the Hebrews*, 212.

[71]What the writer of Hebrews gives us here is a series of five equal aorist participles, which should be understood according to the rendering I gave them above. There is no conditional *if* in the original Greek, as related to the falling away. Rather, these have fallen away.

[72]Robert Shank, *Life in the Son* (Springfield, Mo.: Westcott, 1960), 318.

[73]Robert E. Picirilli, "Hebrews 6:4–6 and the Possibility of Apostasy," *Dimension* 2 (Fall 1985): 10.

raging fire that will consume the enemies of God. Anyone who rejected the law of Moses died without mercy on the testimony of two or three witnesses. How much more severely do you think a man deserves to be punished who has trampled the Son of God under foot, who has treated as an unholy thing the blood of the covenant that sanctified him, and who has insulted the Spirit of grace?

The person spoken of in this passage is said to have been "sanctified." This is clearly referring to a saved person, because his or her sanctification has been accomplished by the blood of Christ. However, because of a change of mind about the efficacious blood of Christ (apostasy), this individual sets a course on the path of willful sinning. Since he or she has rejected the only way of salvation, "no sacrifice for sins is left." Such apostasy is irremediable.[74] As William Lane says, "The sin of apostasy entails irreversible consequences."[75]

4. Hebrews 10:23, 35–36, 38–39.

Let us hold unswervingly to the hope we profess, for he who promised is faithful.... So do not throw away your confidence; it will be richly rewarded. You need to persevere so that when you have done the will of God, you will receive what he has promised.... "But my righteous one [the just person] will live by faith. And if he shrinks back, I will not be pleased with him." But we are not of those who shrink back and are destroyed, but of those who believe and are saved.

Some would suggest that "those who shrink back" refers to those who will lose rewards at the judgment seat of Christ.[76] It is difficult to believe that anyone who is committed to the plain sense of the text could find this interpretation satisfying. Indeed,

---

[74]See Forlines, *The Quest for Truth*, 280–83. He makes a strong case that what is being spoken of here is the new covenant equivalent of "presumptuous sin," not a "sin of ignorance." It should be remembered that presumptuous sins were committed with a "high hand" of arrogant and defiant unbelief. No sacrifice was available for this sort of sin (Num. 15:30–31).

[75]William Lane, *Hebrews: A Call to Commitment* (Peabody, Mass.: Hendrickson, 1985), 142.

[76]See Geisler, *Chosen But Free*, 126–27.

it should be noted that a contrast is being drawn within the passage between "those who shrink back and are destroyed" and "those who believe and are saved." When we look at how the passage characterizes those being contrasted, the picture becomes clearer:

The just	Those who shrink back
Live by faith (v. 38)	Throw away their confidence (v. 35)
Encouraged to hold fast to their confession of hope (v. 23)	God has no pleasure in them (v. 38)
They are of those who believe (v. 39)	(Conversely implied) They do not continue to believe (v. 39)
Belief results in salvation (v. 39)	Their end is destruction (v. 39)

Hughes rightly states that "to 'shrink back' is to renounce the life of faith, and in the man who does this God *has no pleasure*, for as our author will shortly explain (11:6), 'without faith it is impossible to please God.' . . . Destruction is the appointed end of those who desert the faith."[77]

5. 2 Peter 2:20–22.

> If they have escaped the corruption of the world by knowing our Lord and Savior Jesus Christ and are again entangled in it and overcome, they are worse off at the end than they were at the beginning. It would have been better for them not to have known the way of righteousness, than to have known it and then to turn their backs on the sacred command that was passed on to them. Of them the proverbs are true: "A dog returns to its vomit," and, "A sow that is washed goes back to her wallowing in the mud."

Peter is teaching that the people mentioned here were saved persons, for they have "escaped the corruption of the world"

---

[77]Hughes, *Epistle to the Hebrews*, 436–37. It should be noted that Hughes does not hold to the view I am arguing. Nevertheless, he has done some excellent exegesis and seemingly cannot refrain from making statements that would support the Reformed Arminian approach. Yet, after acknowledging where his exegesis leads, he time and again veers away from such a position, preferring instead dogmatic conclusions.

and made their escape "by knowing our Lord and Savior Jesus Christ." He makes clear that they are saved by using the same phraseology for these individuals as that found in 1:4, where he includes himself within the group he is addressing. Having made clear that they were saved, he warns that there are horrible consequences in store for those who abandon the truth that is found in Christ, preferring false teaching instead.

The entirety of 2 Peter 2 serves as the context for the warning given at the end of the chapter: If they are overcome, "they are worse off at the end than they were at the beginning" (v. 20). Now at the beginning, before having "known the way of righteousness" and before having "escaped the corruption of the world by knowing our Lord and Savior Jesus Christ," they were unsaved, lost, and under the wrath of God. What could possibly be worse than being lost? In conjunction with the other texts already seen, the answer becomes clear. What is worse than being lost and hell-bound is to be lost *with no hope of being saved*. Those who have been saved and then have turned their backs on faith in Christ are worse off because of the irremediability of their condition (cf. Heb. 6:4–6; 10:26, 39).

6. John 15:1–6.

> I am the true vine, and my Father is the gardener. He cuts off every branch in me that bears no fruit, while every branch that does bear fruit he prunes so it will be even more fruitful. You are already clean because of the word I have spoken to you. Remain in me, and I will remain in you. No branch can bear fruit by itself; it must remain in the vine. Neither can you bear fruit unless you remain in me. I am the vine; you are the branches. If a man remains in me and I in him, he will bear much fruit; apart from me you can do nothing. If anyone does not remain in me, he is like a branch that is thrown away and withers; such branches are picked up, thrown into the fire and burned.

This particular passage is speaking poignantly about the believer's union with Christ. This union serves as the basis for all fruitfulness in the Christian's experience, for apart from him we can do nothing. However, as I. Howard Marshall states:

> John thus uses the verb "abide" [remain] to express the need for disciples to continue in their personal commitment

to Jesus; the abiding of Jesus in them is not an automatic process which is independent of their attitude to Him, but is the reverse side of their abiding in Him. Just as men are summoned to believe in Jesus, so they are summoned to abide in Jesus, i.e., to continue believing.[78]

In other words, the branch's attachment to the vine—indeed, the individual's union with Christ—is what makes possible a life characterized by Christian virtue and fruitfulness. C. K. Barrett proclaims that "this union, originating in his initiative and sealed by his death on their behalf, is completed by the believer's responsive love and obedience, and is the essence of Christianity."[79] Nevertheless, the figure presented by Jesus speaks of two kinds of branches: those that bear fruit, yet are pruned so that they will be more productive; and those that bear no fruit, causing them to be cut off by the gardener. Again, Barrett states:

> The interpretation of the unfruitful branches may be twofold. The original branches in God's vine were the Jews; these, being unfruitful (unbelieving), God removed. Cf. Matt. 21:41, where the thought is very similar, and Rom. 11:17.... This seems to have been the earliest Christian interpretation of the vine–symbolism, and it may well have been at the back of John's mind; but [*en emoi*] shows that his primary thought was of apostate Christians.... An unfaithful Christian suffers the fate of an unfruitful branch.[80]

Hence, Christians who do not choose to remain in Christ will find themselves cut off from union with Christ by the Father. The end of such individuals is to be "thrown away ... and burned."

REFORMED ARMINIANS AND OTHER ARMINIANS ON THE LOSS OF SALVATION

Two questions distinguish Reformed Arminianism from other expressions of Arminianism, most notably Wesleyan Arminianism. "Is the loss of salvation remediable?" and "How

---

[78]I. Howard Marshall, *Kept by the Power of God* (Minneapolis: Bethany, 1969), 183.

[79]C. K. Barrett, *The Gospel According to St. John*, 2d ed. (Philadelphia: Westminster, 1978), 470.

[80]Ibid., 473–75.

does an individual lose his or her salvation?" The discerning reader will already know the Reformed Arminian answer to these questions. However, it is important to go into greater detail on these two important questions, if only to distinguish Reformed Arminianism from the more commonly known forms of Arminianism.

The Irremediable Nature of Apostasy

As was argued in the foregoing section, the New Testament affirms one species of loss of salvation: apostasy through defection from faith. Furthermore, such apostasy is irreparable. When one begins discussing the possibility of apostasy, the question naturally arises: "Does any remedy exist for someone who was saved and now has made shipwreck of faith? *Can this one be saved again?*"

The view that is typically and most widely referred to as Arminian would answer the latter question in the affirmative. Adam Clarke, the Methodist theologian and younger associate of John Wesley, wrote: "In a state of probation everything may change. While we are in life we may stand or fall.... There can be no truer proverb than 'While there is life there is hope.' Probation necessarily implies the possibility of change."[81] In commenting on the apostasy referred to in Hebrews 6, Robert Shank remarks that such apostasy "takes its character not merely from a past act of defection, but also from a present deliberate hostility toward Christ.... The present condition of deliberate, open hostility may conceivably be remedied and the persons renewed to repentance and salvation."[82]

John Wesley was in tension regarding the remediability of apostasy. In his *Notes* concerning Hebrews 6:4–6 and in his "Serious Thoughts on the Perseverance of the Saints," Wesley indicated that he believed a "total" or "final" apostasy resulted from a renunciation of the atonement of Christ. He claimed that such was without remedy.[83] Conversely, however, in his sermon, "A Call to Backsliders," he poses the issue thus:

---

[81]Adam Clarke, *Christian Theology* (Salem, Ohio: Convention Book Store, repr. 1967), 366–67.

[82]Shank, *Life in the Son*, 318.

[83]"Serious Thoughts on the Perseverance of the Saints," in *Works*, 10:284–98.

If it be asked, "Do any real apostates find mercy from God? Do any that have 'made shipwreck of faith and a good conscience,' recover what they have lost? Do you know, have you seen, any instance of persons who found redemption in the blood of Jesus, and afterwards fell away, and yet were restored,—'renewed again unto repentance?'" Yea, verily and not one or an hundred only, but, I am persuaded several thousands.... Indeed, it is so far from being an uncommon thing for a believer to fall and be restored, that it is rather uncommon to find any believers who are not conscious of having been backsliders from God, in a higher or lower degree, and perhaps more than once, before they were established in faith.[84]

By using the phrase "renewed again unto repentance" and by placing it in quotes, Wesley is obviously alluding to Hebrews 6:6 as he speaks here of ones who fall away and are afterward restored. So, in different contexts, he makes conflicting claims concerning the remediability of the apostasy found in Hebrews 6. However, that notwithstanding, he clearly held that the lost condition of the backslider could be remedied, and that many times over.

Like Wesley himself, Wesleyans typically conflate the categories of "backsliding" and "apostasy" without explaining the differences. In Wesley's view, most cases of the loss of salvation involve what he called "backsliding," in which the believer is living in a state of unconfessed sin. In "A Call to Backsliders," Wesley makes clear that he believes backsliders are in a lost condition.[85] Thus, even if Wesley believed there are cases in which one so totally renounces the atonement of Christ as to be in a state of irremediable apostasy, most cases of loss of salvation (i.e., backsliding) are remediable through penitence.

Reformed Arminians, on the contrary, insist that there is only one way for a believer to lose salvation: a decisive act of

---

[84]Sermon, "A Call to Backsliders," in *Works*, 6:525.

[85]Many Arminians, Wesleyan and otherwise, insist that if a believer dies in a state of unconfessed sin, he or she will be damned. Reformed Arminians would argue that, at death, one is either saved or lost; there is no in-between state wherein death somehow becomes the arbitrator. There are only two kinds of people: justified people (in Christ) and unjustified people (outside of Christ). If one is in Christ at the time of one's death, whether or not he or she is in a state of unconfessed sin, such a person will be glorified. Physical death does not affect one's "in Christ" status.

apostasy—departing from the living God through unbelief (Heb. 3:12). If a saved individual ever rejects Christ, he or she will at that point have cast aside the God-appointed instrumental cause of salvation. For it is on the condition of faith in Christ that the substitutionary death and absolute righteousness of Christ is imputed to the sinner. Faith is the means whereby the sinner is brought into union with Christ and is the instrumental cause through which the benefits of salvation are mediated. My exegesis of the Scripture texts mentioned above (see "A Closer Look at Some Key Texts") leads me to believe that when one abandons the one condition God places upon salvation, he or she thereby enters into a spiritually lost state from which there is no possibility of returning.

The Cause of Apostasy

Reformed Arminians, like Arminius, would wish to maintain the greatest possible distance from Pelagianism. The Roman Catholic view of "inherent righteousness" within the believer was also held by Grotius and the governmentalists who follow after him. This is not the Reformed view of the righteousness that saves. Reformed Arminians are squarely within the Reformed tradition, which claims that people are justified by Christ's righteousness alone, imputed to them by God because of their faith in Christ. Inherent righteousness, the Christian's obedience to the commands of Scripture, is related to the believer's growth in grace. It is a matter of progressive sanctification, not of salvation.

The governmental view of the atonement has been the prevailing understanding of those in the Wesleyan Arminian tradition. While Wesley himself cannot be strictly termed a governmentalist, his vacillation on the critical issue of the imputation of Christ's righteousness to the believer belies his ongoing struggle with this approach. A few brief quotes will suffice to illustrate this struggle. In his sermon "Thoughts on the Imputed Righteousness of Christ" (1762), Wesley says:

> I dare not insist upon, neither require any one to use [the term, imputed righteousness of Christ] because I cannot find it in the Bible. If any one can, he has better eyes than me.... And doth not this way of speaking naturally tend

to make Christ the minister of sin? For if the very personal obedience of Christ (as those expressions directly lead me to think) be mine the moment I believe, can anything be added thereto? Does my obeying God add any value to the perfect obedience of Christ?[86]

Wesley's final two questions here help to make my point: The merits on which my justification rests are those of Christ alone. "Can anything be added thereto?" Not one thing! A few years later Wesley again disavowed his belief in the imputed righteousness of Christ. This time in his "Preface to a Treatise on Justification," he wrote:

It is not scriptural; it is not necessary. . . . But it has done immense hurt. I have abundant proof, that the frequent use of this unnecessary phrase [imputed righteousness of Christ], instead of "furthering men's progress in vital holiness," has made them satisfied without any holiness at all.[87]

The reason Wesley wished to distance himself from the Reformed notion that Christ's righteousness was imputed to the believer was grounded in his concern that this doctrine would logically lead to antinomianism.[88] Further, he held in common with the Church of Rome and governmentalists that the Reformed view of imputation constituted a "legal fiction." In his sermon on "Justification by Faith" Wesley proclaims:

Least of all does justification imply, that God is deceived in those whom he justifies; that he thinks them to be what, in fact they are not; that he accounts them to be otherwise than they are. . . . The judgment of the all-wise God is always according to truth. Neither can it ever consist with his unerring wisdom, to think that I am innocent, to judge that I am righteous or holy, because another is so. He can no more, in this manner, confound me with Christ than with David or Abraham.[89]

Nevertheless, in his sermon entitled "The Lord Our Righteousness" Wesley proclaimed:

---

[86]Sermon, "Thoughts on the Imputed Righteousness of Christ," in *Works*, 10:315.

[87]"Preface to a Treatise on Justification," in *Works*, 10:318.

[88]See *Works*, 10:315, 326, 328.

[89]Sermon, "Justification by Faith," in *Works*, 5:57.

I therefore no more deny the righteousness of Christ, than I deny the Godhead of Christ. . . . Neither do I deny imputed righteousness: This is another unkind and unjust accusation. I always did, and do still continually affirm, that the righteousness of Christ is imputed to every believer. But who deny it? Why, all Infidels. . . .[90]

It seems obvious that Wesley was unsettled on this critical issue of the Reformed faith. At various times, he used the language of the "imputation of Christ's righteousness," yet via his characteristic phrase "for the sake of" he emptied the idea of its Reformation content. He wrote:

But in what sense is this righteousness imputed to believers? In this: all believers are forgiven and accepted, not for the sake of anything in them . . . but wholly and solely *for the sake of* what Christ hath done and suffered for them. . . . The meaning is, God justifies the believer *for the sake of* Christ's righteousness.[91]

Wesley's view is not the Reformed view. He did not embrace a forensic understanding of justification, wherein Christ's righteousness is accounted to the believer. Rather, he held that "the plain scriptural notion of justification is *pardon*, the forgiveness of sins. It is the act of God the Father, whereby, for the sake of the propitiation made by the blood of his Son, he showeth forth his righteousness (or mercy) by the *remission of sins that are past.*"[92] Indeed, in Wesley's approach, when the sinner is justified, his or her sinful condition is not dealt with, and the curse of original sin is not removed. Rather, the justified one receives forgiveness (pardon) for every sin committed up to the moment when he or she trusted in Christ.

Wesley's assertion that Christ's atonement when applied to the believer is efficacious only for the forgiveness of past sins had far-ranging implications for one's continuance in the Christian life. Indeed, what actually happens when the Christian sins? Wesley broaches that subject in his sermon "The Fruits of the Spirit":

Wilt thou say, "But I have again committed sin, since I had redemption through his blood?" . . . It is meet that thou

---

[90]Sermon, "The Lord Our Righteousness," in *Works*, 5:242.
[91]*Works*, 5:238–40.
[92]Sermon, "Justification by Faith," in *Works*, 5:57 (italics added).

shouldst abhor thyself.... But, dost thou now believe?...
At whatsoever time thou truly believest in the name of the
Son of God, all thy sins antecedent to that hour vanish
away.... And think not to say, "I was justified once; my
sins were forgiven me:" I know not that; neither will I dispute whether they were or no. Perhaps at this distance in
time, it is impossible to know.... But this I know, with the
utmost degree of certainty, "he that committeth sin is of
the devil." Therefore, thou art of thy father the devil.[93]

So, for Wesley, if a believer sins, he cannot know if he was previously saved—maybe yes, maybe no. He can only know that
having sinned, he is of his father, the devil.

I do not know how to interpret such a view other than to
say that if a believer commits a single sin, that sin renders him
lost—he being once again a child of the devil, until the moment
he repents. If this is the view that Wesley espoused, it is a stark
view indeed. It is apparent that many in the Wesleyan tradition
profess this approach. W. T. Purkiser, for example, in commenting on 1 John 2:1–2, states that John

gives encouragement to the soul impulsively plunged
into some sin under the pressure of strong temptation,
who immediately confesses and renounces his sin and
avails himself of the services of the Advocate for his forgiveness. Such sin as this, thus renounced, causes *only a
momentary break with the Father*.[94]

This notion of a "break with the Father," momentary or not,
sounds ominous to me. Yet it hints at one of the major differences
between Reformed Arminians and Wesleyan Arminians. For
Reformed Arminians, only one kind of "break with the Father"
can occur. It occurs through apostasy, and it has no remedy.

Summary

Let me close by summarizing the main differences between
Reformed Arminians and Wesleyan Arminians and asking two
questions.

---

[93]Sermon, "The Fruits of the Spirit," in *Works*, 5:95.
[94]W. T. Purkiser, *Security: The False and the True* (Kansas City, Mo: Beacon Hill,
1956), 24 (italics added).

What causes one to lose salvation? Wesleyans say that willful and unconfessed sin constitutes a backslidden condition, which renders the individual lost. Reformed Arminians, by contrast, hold that rejection of faith in Christ, and that alone, removes one from union with Christ. But, short of that solitary act of apostasy, the believer is to be found in union with Christ and thus stands justified in the merits of Christ alone.[95]

Is loss of salvation remediable? Wesleyans would say yes. For each time one repents, God reissues his pardon anew, and it avails for every past sin committed up to that point. Reformed Arminians say no! According to this view, God's salvation, provided in Christ Jesus, is not tenuously teetering in the balance. One's salvation rests securely in the fact that one is *in Christ* by faith. Thus, "there is now no condemnation for those who are in Christ Jesus" (Rom. 8:1).

Sin in the life of the believer is a serious matter. God takes it seriously, the church should take it seriously, and the individual must take it seriously as well. Nevertheless, we must recognize what sin does and what it does not do. The Bible is clear that all are sinners (Rom. 3:10–18). Yet one does not receive God's salvation simply by turning over a new leaf. It is not by quitting sinning that one becomes *justified* before God. It is, instead, by faith in Christ. Neither does committing sin after one is saved cause one to become *unjustified* before God. That can happen only as the individual rejects and renounces faith in Christ, God's one and only condition for salvation, for faith in Christ is what brings the individual into union with Christ.

Everyone who is justified by faith has the merits of Christ's righteous life and his substitutionary death imputed to him or her, that is, placed on one's account. Thus, *believers* are justified by God for salvation solely on the merits of Christ and not their own. Nevertheless, if one again becomes an *unbeliever*, which is not probable but yet is possible since he or she is a personal being, then God removes that individual from the true vine, Christ Jesus (John 15:2, 6). Hence, the singular act of apostasy is irreversible (Heb. 6:4–6).

---

[95]Judith Gundry Volf, a Calvinist, makes a succinct statement about Paul's understanding of postconversion sin that reflects the Reformed Arminian position: "Paul does not make Christians' final salvation dependent on their repentance from post-conversion sins, though he by all means views their repentance as desirable" (*Paul and Perseverance: Staying In and Falling Away* [Louisville, Ky.: Westminster/John Knox, 1990], 157).

A CLASSICAL CALVINIST RESPONSE TO STEPHEN M. ASHBY

Michael S. Horton

Stephen Ashby's contribution represents a much-needed correction of the caricatures of Arminius's views. His own citation of standard Wesleyan Arminian sources reveals that the dominant Arminian position represents a pull toward Pelagius with respect to total depravity, the substitutionary atonement, and justification by an imputed righteousness. Recent studies, however, seem to substantiate Ashby's attempt to recover Arminius from Arminianism.[1]

Ashby begins by observing the similarities between Arminius's views and Calvinism. His account justifies his conclusion that "this view of total depravity is Reformed to the core," even if Reformed readers may question its consistency with Arminius's doctrine of prevenient rather than effectual grace. Ashby's defense of justification and the substitutionary atonement, well-supported by citations from Arminius, shows how un-Arminian most of subsequent Arminianism really has become. (Most card-carrying Arminians today would probably regard Arminius's views as too Reformed!)

So where do the roads diverge? Ashby puts his finger on the right questions: "How can one be found *in Christ*? What effects this imputation? Is it by a particularistic understanding

---

[1]See especially Richard A. Muller, *God, Creation and Providence in the Thought of Jacob Arminius* (Grand Rapids: Baker, 1991).

of God's unalterable decree, which is grounded in nothing else but God's good pleasure? If so, then Calvinists are correct in asserting their views of unconditional election, irresistible grace, and the necessary perseverance of the saints." Of course, Ashby does not think that this is so. Rather, he argues, "This view, however, presupposes particularism in setting forth the *ordo salutis* (order of salvation)." Like many critics, Ashby accuses Reformed theology of imposing presuppositions (usually derived from logic rather than Scripture) on the texts. Since this is a tendency that I have criticized in another essay, it would hardly be appropriate to pass over his charge lightly.

First, it should not be controversial to suggest that everyone comes to Scripture with presuppositions. If one came with an entirely blank slate, there would be no such thing as interpretation. Furthermore, the analogy of Scripture ("Scripture interprets Scripture") requires us to come to particular texts in the widest possible recognition of other texts—and indeed, as much as possible, the whole teaching of Scripture. The real issue, then, is not whether one comes to the text with presuppositions but whether one comes with the right ones, the most scriptural ones.

Why do Calvinists presuppose "a particularistic understanding of God's unalterable decree, which is grounded in nothing else but God's good pleasure?" If it is bare logical inference from hypothetical conjecture, that would certainly make reason a lord rather than a servant of God's Word. Reformed theology maintains this presupposition, however, because it is persuaded (not coerced) by Scripture on this matter. Here are some examples of the biblical presuppositions we bring to disputed passages on the subject of human inability and the new birth:

- Isaiah 65:1: "I revealed myself to those who did not ask for me; I was found by those who did not seek me."
- Ezekiel 11:19: "I will give them an undivided heart and will put a new spirit in them; I will remove from them their heart of stone and give them a heart of flesh."
- Ezekiel 37:3–6: "He asked me, 'Son of man, can these bones live?' I said, 'O Sovereign LORD, you alone know.' Then he said to me, 'Prophesy to these bones and say to them, "Dry bones, hear the word of the LORD! This is what the Sovereign LORD says to these bones: I will make

breath enter you, and you will come to life. I will attach tendons to you and make flesh come upon you and cover you with skin; I will put breath in you, and you will come to life. Then you will know that I am the LORD.""

- Daniel 4:35: "All the peoples of the earth are regarded as nothing. He does as he pleases with the powers of heaven and the peoples of the earth. No one can hold back his hand or say to him: 'What have you done?'"
- Luke 17:5: "And the apostles said to the Lord, 'Increase our faith!'"
- John 1:12–13: "Yet to all who received him, to those who believed in his name, he gave the right to become children of God—children born not of natural descent, nor of human decision or a husband's will, but born of God."
- John 6:37, 44: "All that the Father gives me will come to me, and whoever comes to me I will never drive away.... No one can come to me unless the Father who sent me draws him, and I will raise him up at the last day."
- John 15:5, 16, 19: ". . . apart from me you can do nothing.... You did not choose me, but I chose you.... I have chosen you out of the world."
- Acts 13:48: "When the Gentiles heard this, they were glad and honored the word of the Lord; and all who were appointed for eternal life believed."
- Acts 16:14: "The Lord opened [Lydia's] heart to respond to Paul's message."
- Romans 2:4: "God's kindness leads you toward repentance."
- Romans 8:30: "And those he predestined, he also called; those he called, he also justified; those he justified, he also glorified."
- Romans 9:15–16: "For he says to Moses, 'I will have mercy on whom I have mercy, and I will have compassion on whom I have compassion.' It does not, therefore, depend on man's desire or effort, but on God's mercy."
- Romans 11:5–7: "So too, at the present time there is a remnant chosen by grace. And if by grace, then it is no longer by works; if it were, grace would no longer be grace. What then? What Israel sought so earnestly it did not obtain, but the elect did. The others were hardened."

- 1 Corinthians 2:14: "The man without the Spirit does not accept the things that come from the Spirit of God, for they are foolishness to him, and he cannot understand them, because they are spiritually discerned."
- Ephesians 1:11: "In him we were also chosen, having been predestined according to the plan of him who works out everything in conformity with the purpose of his will...."
- Ephesians 1:19: We believe according to "his incomparably great power."
- Ephesians 2:1–5: "As for you, you were dead in your transgressions and sins.... Like the rest, we were by nature objects of wrath. But because of his great love for us, God, who is rich in mercy, made us alive with Christ *even when we were dead in transgressions*—it is by grace you have been saved" (emphasis added).
- Philippians 2:13: "For it is God who works in you to will and to act according to his good purpose."
- 2 Timothy 2:25: "... in the hope that God will grant them repentance leading them to a knowledge of the truth."
- James 1:18: "He chose to give us birth through the word of truth."

Furthermore, it is not just proof texts but the systematic teaching of Scripture on related points that seems to us to be woven into a coherent tapestry, not by logic-chopping Calvinists but by the primary author of Scripture. While Ashby is largely fair to the Reformed position, he does make a few mistakes in stating it. For instance, he says that Berkhof (a leading twentieth-century Reformed theologian), concerning the covenant of grace, denied "that the offer of the covenant comes to all." If Ashby means by this that Berkhof denied that this offer is made to all (which I think is his intention here), he is incorrect. In fact, Berkhof, typical of Reformed theologians, lists as the first characteristic of God's external calling, "It is general or universal."[2]

Later, Ashby repeats this mistake: "Of course, the Calvinist rejoinder is surely that if one says that the call of God goes out to all and that the grace of God comes to all, then one cannot

---

[2]Louis Berkhof, *Systematic Theology* (Grand Rapids: Eerdmans, 1941), 460–61.

believe in total depravity." Ashby may think that this logically follows, but it is not the Reformed position. The universal free offer of the gospel is a prized doctrine of every major system in the Reformed tradition. Even the Canons of Dort, from which we derive the so-called TULIP, declare:

> This death of God's Son is the only and entirely complete sacrifice and satisfaction for sins; it is of infinite value and worth, more than sufficient to atone for the sins of the whole world.... Moreover, it is the promise of the gospel that whoever believes in Christ crucified shall not perish but have eternal life. This promise, together with the command to repent and believe, ought to be announced and declared without differentiation or discrimination to all nations and people, to whom God in his good pleasure sends the gospel.[3]

In contrast to hyper-Calvinist groups, Calvinistic churches make evangelistic appeals that in many cases can hardly be distinguished in their scope and earnestness from appeals in other churches. If Ashby's characterization were correct, how could it be that so many of the evangelists and the principal leaders of the modern missionary movement were Calvinists? "Come to me, all you who are weary." "Whoever wills, let him come"— these are repeated without crossed fingers or a bad conscience.

We understand those appeals in their fullest sense: God does not discriminate in his invitation to his marriage feast. Election is a divine secret, not to be searched out by us. "Those he predestined, he also called," Paul says, yet we do not know who is predestined or called inwardly. That is none of our business. We are simply to invite everyone to the feast and pray that God will bring them all to a saving knowledge of Christ. That God calls only those who are predestined does not mean that we call only those who are predestined. Christ's "external call" goes out indiscriminately, while "no one can come to me unless the Father ... draws him" (John 6:44).

Furthermore, Calvinists do not deny that sinners resist God's invitation (the external call). How can we, when Scripture clearly teaches this? In fact, that confirms our understanding of

---

[3]Canons of the Synod of Dort, *Ecumenical Creeds and Reformed Confessions* (Grand Rapids: Christian Reformed Board of Publications, 1979), 2.4–5.

total depravity. We are "always resisting," as Jesus said of the Pharisees. This is our contribution to salvation: sin and resistance! However, effectual grace is different from common grace, and the effectual call is different from the universal call. It seems apparent in Scripture that Christ invites all to be saved and yet only the elect come. So this distinction seems founded exegetically and confirmed by our own experience. But why some come and others do not cannot be attributed to our own disposition or moral ability. It must be credited to God's marvelous grace.

A further misunderstanding appears in a quote from Robert E. Picirilli: "If, then, the New Testament makes clear that salvation really is conditional, then we dare not 'read' the unrevealed terms of an implied covenant of redemption in such a way as to destroy that conditionality." The Reformed do maintain that salvation (i.e., justification) is conditional in the sense that one must believe in order to be justified. Further, to believe one must ordinarily hear the gospel preached—that is a condition also. However, a condition is not an effectual cause. In other words, if one closes the door, that act actually causes the effect of the door being closed, but when one trusts in Christ, this is a passive receiving. To be sure, it is a passive receiving that immediately becomes an active faith bringing forth good fruit. Yet in the matter of justification, it does not do anything but rather receives something that is done. It makes a big difference how one understands that word "condition."

Furthermore, repentance and faith are conditions of the covenant of grace, not of the covenant of redemption. Since I have already defended these distinctions in my chapter, I will only reiterate them here. The covenant of redemption is an eternal and unconditional covenant made between the Father, the Son, and the Holy Spirit. It is clearly in view in a number of passages to which I referred in that chapter. The Father elects his people "in Christ." To him the Father entrusts their salvation, and the Holy Spirit is charged with the application of redemption and their preservation in Christ.

The covenant of grace is made, however, between God and his people. The latter are not stones but moral agents and are treated as partners—even though the repentance and faith that are necessary for their salvation are themselves his gifts. They must respond. Belonging to the covenant community is not sufficient apart from personal faith (Heb. 4:2). Therefore, the "conditionality" that Picirilli and Ashby rightly insist on is upheld in covenant theology. By confusing the covenant of redemption and the covenant of grace, their criticism falls wide of the mark.

Further along in his argument, Ashby returns to his representation of Calvinism as following logical assumptions rather than Scripture: "'But I, when I am lifted up from the earth, will draw all men to myself' (John 12:32). Of course, the Calvinist recoils and says, 'If all are enabled and all are drawn, then universalism must surely result—all would be saved.'" I do not doubt that there may be misinformed Calvinists who would offer this argument, but it is not the way we typically argue in our representative systems.

Instead of offering a logical (actually, a speculative) rebuttal, we say, "Let's look at John 6: Does God in fact enable and in fact draw everyone savingly to himself?" There are other passages, such as the list above, to which we would turn to in order to interpret John 12:32. Unless Scripture is self-contradictory, John cannot be saying something that other apostles, Jesus, or even he himself elsewhere rejects. If it is clear from Scripture that God enables, draws, and effectually calls only "those he predestined," those "appointed for eternal life," and so forth, then can we not see John 12:32 referring to the full range of those whom he will draw?

There is surely a sense in which the whole world will be saved—not in an each-and-every-person sense, but in terms of representation. In the context of John's Gospel, which is particularly aimed at the universal mission of the church beyond Palestine, can we not see this marvelous announcement as indicating that on his cross Jesus was held up in the wilderness this time not only for Israel but for the nations? This is the authentic universalism that Calvinists joyfully embrace. It moves outward from Jerusalem to Judea, Samaria, and the uttermost parts of the earth. It is those who look to this outstretched Lamb of God who are Abraham's offspring, whether Jew or Gentile. He is the Light of the world!

And if the world can be said to have been saved through such a small remnant as Noah and his family, then John has all the more reason to report the heavenly anthem to the Lamb:

"You were slain, and with your blood you purchased men for God *from every tribe and language and people and nation*" (Rev. 5:9).[4] Even if Arminians are not persuaded by our exegesis, hopefully we can get beyond the caricature that one school appeals to Scripture while the other depends on philosophical-logical hypotheses.

The author's analysis of Geisler's position, illustrated in the latter's *Chosen But Free*, is insightful and fair. He correctly observes that Geisler's position is "one-point Calvinism," which makes for an odd claim to be "Moderate Calvinism." I would only add, as I have done in my response to Geisler, that his position is not even "one-point Calvinism," as his notion of eternal security is not the Reformed doctrine of the perseverance of the saints. Furthermore, Ashby's careful analysis of the relevant passages shares much in common with Reformed exegesis. However, as I have argued in my proposal, the covenantal model provides a context in which to understand these passages and to take them with the same seriousness without adopting an Arminian position.

As much as Ashby identifies with classical Reformed theology (on depravity, justification, atonement, and the necessity of prevenient grace), he concludes that "Reformed Arminians agree with nearly every conservative Arminian writer on the philosophical question of determinism/free will." But since the Arminian understanding of determinism/free will is based on the popular Arminian understanding of depravity and grace from which Ashby wants to distance himself, the result can only lead to inconsistency. After all, that is not a philosophical question but a theological one. Whether the will is bound to sin as a result of the Fall and can therefore only be freed from the outside by God is at the heart of what we mean by "saved by grace."

To rest God's saving determination on something in us (even faith) rather than something in God (mercy), by denying unconditional election, is to substitute a philosophical doctrine of human liberty for a biblical one. It is to transform faith from a divine gift to a divine possibility, the "one thing" that we do—or actually one of several things that we do—in order to make salvation effective. This lies at the heart of all synergistic approaches that eventually undermine the clear proclamation of God's saving grace in Christ.

It is certainly true that Arminius was an ordained minister and a professor in the Dutch Reformed Church. However, the Remonstrants were ejected from their ministry and subsequently founded their own denomination. The term "Reformed" has been stretched so far these days that even an Arminian can identify himself by it. But two brief points must be noted in this connection. First, Reformed theology is not defined by an individual—not even the Reformers—but is circumscribed by its confessions. The Canons of Dort and the Westminster Standards, following on the heels of the Arminian debate, directly rejected "Five Points" of Arminianism.

Second, the areas of Arminius's (and Ashby's) solid agreement with Calvinism are not distinctively Reformed. That is to say, we are not the only ones who embrace as central to our system the doctrines of total depravity, the substitutionary atonement, and justification by an imputed righteousness. Confessional Lutherans and Baptists, not to mention the great majority of evangelicals, have affirmed these truths as well. It is what Calvinism (as a synonym for "Reformed") holds in distinction from other Reformation bodies that makes it something more than evangelical. While Ashby is certainly an evangelical Arminian, to my mind he has not sufficiently demonstrated that he is a "Reformed Arminian"—or that such a hybrid exists.

Reformed theology has typically maintained that Arminians do not necessarily deny the gospel because of a "felicitous inconsistency." Ashby's admirable defense of depravity, penal satisfaction, and justification underscores the evangelical side of at least Arminius's thought, while his remaining commitment to conditional election and an autonomous view of human freedom represent Arminianism's perennial threat.

A MODERATE CALVINIST RESPONSE TO STEPHEN M. ASHBY

Norman L. Geisler

AREAS OF AGREEMENT

First of all, we agree that classical Arminianism is a "Reformed" view. Here again, strong Calvinists have no copyright on the term. In addition, Reformed Arminians are correct in the claim that strong Calvinists often construct "straw men" in their polemics against others. Even a casual reading of Arminius reveals the extent to which he was Calvinistic and Reformed. Certainly, the popular stereotype of Arminianism simply does not fit him.

Likewise, we agree that many have often misread Wesleyanism into Arminius's views. Indeed, Arminius held a strong view of human depravity, insisting on the necessity of God's grace. In this same vein, Reformed Arminianism is correct in denying the label "Pelagian," which is a common but false characterization given by strong Calvinists.

Further, we agree with the Reformed Arminian against the strong Calvinists that the latter often wrongly assume limited atonement ("particularism") a priori. Strong Calvinists often read this into the biblical text, not out of it. They systematically assume it and then make the biblical text to fit with it. The limitation of the word "world" to the elect (noted above) is only one example. Making "all" mean "some" in 1 Timothy 2:4 is another instance. Strong Calvinists bring a logically tight system to the text of Scripture. But it is not one that can be derived from Scripture alone.

We also have accord with the statement that, although there are no conditions for giving salvation, nevertheless, faith is the condition for receiving it. This is because God operates on sinners in salvation by "influence and response" and not like "a tsunami tidal wave." That is, God does not use irresistible grace on the unwilling. He does not violate our free will at the moment of conversion.

Furthermore, Reformed Arminians are right in noting that fallen humans are "dead in sin" and unable to perform any spiritual good on their own. That is to say, they can neither initiate nor attain their own salvation. They can merely receive it as a gift of God. One is able to believe only after God works on one's hearts, not before.

What is more, we concur that Charles Stanley is wrong in affirming that one who ceases to believe in Christ is truly a saved person. This view, originating with Zane Hodges, lacks biblical support, as we demonstrated in our chapter.

In addition, there is agreement that the question of the loss of salvation should not be decided primarily on logical but biblical grounds. This is not to say that good arguments that are logically consistent with Scripture cannot be used to support it, as we have attempted to do.

In contrast to many Wesleyan Arminians, we agree that committing sin or failing to confess it does not lead to loss of salvation. This is true even if the sins are deliberate. Thus, sins do not cause one to be unjustified after salvation.

Finally, we concur that faith is an instrumental cause of salvation. That is, God uses faith as a secondary cause to receive the gift of salvation. So God is the primary Cause and free choice is the secondary cause for our *receiving* salvation. And God alone is the primary Cause of the *source* of salvation.

AREAS OF DISAGREEMENT

These agreements notwithstanding, Moderate Calvinists disagree with Reformed Arminians in many significant ways. First, we deny that there can be no "cause-and-effect" relation between God and free creatures in salvation. This fails to understand the difference between the primary Cause (God) and the secondary cause (free creatures), which even the Westminster Confession of Faith recognizes (3.1). Since on the classical view of God,[1] all effects (including free agency) preexist in God, then even free acts can be the effects of God without the primary Cause destroying the freedom he gave these free agents. God provides the *fact* of freedom, but humans perform the *acts* of freedom. The *power* of free choice comes from God, but the *exercise* of that power is from humans.

Furthermore, contrary to Reformed Arminians, full and complete sovereignty (control) over all events is not possible without a cause-and-effect relationship between God and creatures. For without it God is dependent for what he wills on what he merely foresees free creatures will do. But a dependent being is not a completely independent Being that is in full and complete sovereign control of everything, including free acts, as God is.[2]

What is more, we disagree with the contention that election is "conditioned on faith in Christ." Like the strong Calvinists, this is reading meaning into the text from one's system, not reading the true meaning out of the text in its context. Salvation is a completely unconditional gift (Rom. 11:29), as Calvinists of both varieties claim. If it were conditional, then God would not be the sovereign and ultimate cause of all things, as the Bible affirms he is.[3] Nor could there be unconditional grace, as the Bible clearly teaches there is (Rom. 11:6; Eph. 2:8–9; Titus 3:5–7).

In addition, moderate Calvinism does not lack "logical consistency" because it holds both free will and the impossibility of losing one's salvation. No contradiction exists between these two premises: (1) It is certain that all the regenerate will persevere, and (2) all the regenerate will persevere freely. Even Arminians admit that God knows for sure (i.e., it is determined) who will freely accept Christ. Hence, one and the same event can be both determined from God's standpoint and yet be free from ours.

Further, there is no necessary symmetrical relation between belief and disbelief so that, once one believes and is saved, one

---

[1]The classical view of God was held by all major church teachers (including Augustine, Anselm, and Aquinas) up to and through the Reformation.

[2]See Norman L. Geisler, *Chosen But Free* (Minneapolis: Bethany, 1999), ch. 1.

[3]Ibid.

must thereby be able later to disbelieve and be lost. Some decisions in life are one way. For example, one can will to commit suicide, but one cannot will to reverse it. Indeed, even Reformed Arminians believe that the free choice to apostatize is irreversible, so they are inconsistent in claiming that some free choices cannot be reversed. Finally, in heaven we will be in an irreversible state of free choice by God's grace. Why cannot God do the same by his grace to us while we are still on earth?

Also, Reformed Arminianism has failed to demonstrate that there is no valid correlation between natural and spiritual sonship so that neither can be lost. On the contrary, it is a good analogy that is used repeatedly in Scripture (cf. John 1:12; Rom. 8:15; Gal. 4:6–7). There are strong similarities between natural and spiritual sonship.

Likewise, salvation is not, as the Reformed Arminian claims, conditioned on the continuance of our faith. Rather, as we have shown in our chapter, the reception of salvation is conditioned on our faith. But it is not necessary to have a continuous act of faith to receive the gift of salvation. Nevertheless, continued faith, while not a *condition* for receiving salvation, is a *manifestation* of someone who is truly saved.

Finally, as we have shown in our chapter, none of the biblical passages (e.g., Heb. 6 and 10) that Reformed Arminians use refer to a loss of salvation. They are clearly speaking about a loss of maturity or reward, not a loss of salvation. As indicated in our chapter, 2 Peter 2 is not speaking of truly saved individuals but only professing believers who were never truly saved from the beginning.

A WESLEYAN ARMINIAN
RESPONSE TO
STEPHEN M. ASHBY

J. Steven Harper

Like Stephen Ashby's Presbyterian friend, I was intrigued to hear Dr. Ashby describe himself as a "Reformed Arminian." He had my attention from the start. I was not surprised when he defined Reformed Arminianism as none other than the view of Jacobus Arminius himself. By doing so, Ashby rooted his chapter in the primary representative of the position, as I believe each of the chapters should have done. In the course of the chapter, Ashby further helped me by continuing to shed light on the differences between classical and Moderate Calvinism. But even more, he helped me differentiate between Reformed Arminianism and Wesleyan Arminianism.

But before I move on to refer to some of the differences, I must say that early on in the chapter, I found myself thinking, "John Wesley sounds like a Reformed Arminian on that point." This should not be surprising, for whenever Wesley drew directly from Arminius, we would expect their views to look similar. Nevertheless, Ashby helped me to see specific ways in which it is entirely appropriate to link the words "Wesleyan" and "Arminian." Even more, in doing that, he helped me to see how Wesley was indebted to significant perspectives within Reformed theology, something Wesley himself acknowledged from time to time.

Before comparing Reformed and Wesleyan Arminianism, I believe it is important to show the contributions Ashby's chapter makes in relation to the chapters on classical and Moderate Calvinism. Perhaps most important, he puts into words what I have personally believed for years—namely, that Calvinism is fueled by a priori philosophical presuppositions that cause it to become the theological perspective it is. Ashby believes that the a priori presuppositions are particularism and an unconditional notion of salvation. He goes on to point out how those assumptions actually control Reformed readings of many biblical texts.

I know in advance that both Ashby's assertion and my agreement with it will not endear us to our Calvinistic friends. Yet I think this is an important thing to point out as a significant strength of his chapter. I also know that Calvinists have placed the same charge (i.e., that a priori presuppositions control interpretation) at the feet of Wesleyans. Both Reformed and Wesleyan theologians quickly and passionately assert that if we have such assumptions, they are drawn from what the Bible first says. But because our respected "other" in the theological debate does not think so, the discussion easily becomes circular and unending. We may simply be stuck. The point for you as a reader of these chapters is to ask yourself, "If, in fact, a priori presuppositions influence the way we read the Bible, which set of presuppositions seem most clearly to connect to the prior and ultimate biblical revelation?" None of us contributors can determine how you will finally answer that question, but it is a question you must not bypass. Ashby writes in such a way that we have to deal with it.

In this respect, Ashby correctly points out the caution (if not the downright humility) required whenever we set about describing "the eternal counsels of God." This is true regardless of our theological tradition. He shows that there is danger in taking soteriology (God's desire and plan to save human beings through Christ) and reformatting into a matter where "logic" ultimately governs the discussion. Logic becomes a substitute for mystery, explanation a substitute for wonder. We must be careful when we take the *ordo salutis* and try to pin it down in every detail. When the main tenets of a theological position are "logical," the problem is that someone else can present another set of doctrines with equal logic. If particularism and an unconditional notion of salvation "logically" produce the main points of Calvinistic theology, Ashby is correct in contending that, on the basis of logic, "God could have sovereignly chosen to remedy humanity's situation differently than by the particularistic, cause-and-effect means proposed by Calvinism."

We see this very thing happening in our day when theologians who have thrown overboard every notion of particularism are left with nothing other than the "logic" of universalism to interpret the salvific work of God in the world. Again, it is important for you as the reader to recognize the caution in building too much of your theological system on "logic." Ashby believes that Calvinism, whether in its classical or moderate expressions, has too much embraced this tendency. The result is too great an "either/or" mentality, when the God of mystery and wonder may be more into a "both/and" mentality.

For example, Calvinism may call us to choose between divine sovereignty and human responsibility, whereas Arminianism may encourage us to hold the two together. By using "logic" as the starting point, Calvinism may *appear* to be clearer and Arminianism *appear* to be inconsistent. But that is only true if mystery, wonder, and creative tension are excluded as formative elements in theological interpretation. It may turn out that God can indeed be sovereign without having to elect particular persons to salvation in divine counsels before creation. Again, Ashby's chapter keeps this kind of thinking before us and raises important questions about *how* we go about "doing theology."

Having viewed his chapter in relation to the Reformed tradition, I will use the rest of my space to make selected comments about his writing in relation to the Wesleyan tradition. I must again remind you of the many ways that Ashby helped me see the connections of Wesley to Arminius, and I am personally grateful for those insights. He also made a number of correct observations concerning differences between Wesleyan Arminianism and Reformed Arminianism. However, there are some places where I was disappointed.

Perhaps the greatest point of dissatisfaction has to do with his statements related to the atonement. He too greatly overplays distinctions with respect to penal satisfaction and the imputed righteousness of Christ. He leaves the impression that Reformed Arminians believe in both while Wesleyan Arminians believe in neither. As you will see when you read my chapter, this is simply not the case. Wesley included elements of the penal satisfaction theory of the atonement into his theology, and he surely believed that part of the story of righteousness is that it is imputed to us. I regret Ashby's impression that the two theological traditions are distinct. They are closer than his chapter implies.

There are other errors and exaggerations. One has to do with the place of the governmental theory of the atonement in Wesleyan Arminianism. Ashby quite rightly states that Wesley did not hold to a full-blown governmental theory. However, he argues that Wesley incorporated key elements of the theory to the extent that he distanced himself from the satisfaction elements in Reformed theology. I hate to say it, but this is an example of Ashby's "either/or" thinking on the subject. Wesley's ability to hold elements of the governmental theory in tension with penal satisfaction comes nearer to the truth of the Wesleyan Arminian position. This resulted in a theology of the atonement that Wesley believed was more biblically accurate and more substantive than any of the other theories considered alone.

Unfortunately, here is one place in Wesleyan theology where Wesley's successors have equated their views with his. John Miley, H. Orton Wiley, and John Wesley are not the same theologians. There are times and points of discussion when I wish my Reformed friends understood that in a more sophisticated way than they do. The result would actually be a "coming closer" in our points of view and a lessening of apparent separations between our positions. As you read my chapter, you will see a few places where I try to make that point.

Before I exhaust my space, I must also note that Ashby overplays the assertion that the Wesleyan position leads to the belief that a single sin renders a believer lost. You will see in my chapter that this is clearly not the case, and it is unfortunate that Ashby leaves that impression in his chapter. This apparent difference is simply not, as Ashby maintains, one of the major differences between Reformed Arminians and Wesleyan Arminians. Or perhaps to say it more accurately, it would not have been as major a difference between Arminius and Wesley as it may have come to be between certain of their successors.

Coming to the end of Ashby's chapter, I felt I had generally read the views of one who has lived *within* the Reformed tradition sufficiently to see and critique its own problems and inconsistencies. This is something those of us who are not Reformed in our views must be more cautious in doing. In that respect, I believe his chapter plays a key role in the overall development of this book. I also came to the end of the chapter with the belief that Dr. Ashby knows the Wesleyan tradition better than some Reformed theologians with whom I have dealt over the years, and perhaps with a greater commitment to represent our view (and the differences in our views) more charitably and fairly than others I have known. If that is the case, then I hope that he will see the same intent on my part in this response to his chapter.

Chapter Four

A WESLEYAN
ARMINIAN VIEW

J. Steven Harper

A WESLEYAN ARMINIAN VIEW

J. Steven Harper

THE CONCEPT OF THEOLOGY

Theology cannot be chopped into pieces. It is the unified story of God's nature and activity in relation to all he has made. Specific doctrines are connected to each other, drawing from and contributing to other elements of the story. This is particularly true with respect to the Wesleyan view of theology, which sees the whole as an "order of salvation" running from creation to consummation.[1] The Wesleyan system is not a set of topics arranged in a way that produces a theological book but rather an interpretation of God's work in the world that produces a theological life. As an "order of salvation," soteriology is the keynote—that is, God's desire, fulfilled in Christ, to save people in time and for eternity. This story begins before we draw our first breath, and it continues after we have taken our last one.

When we examine a particular topic, it must always be in relation to that larger perspective. The subject of eternal security and the perseverance of the saints is no exception. We cannot "camp out" at the end of the theological story and take a snapshot of this one doctrine when God has made a videotape of the

---

[1]The understanding of theology as an "order of salvation" (*ordo salutis*) is not Wesley's creation but rather a concept that can be traced back to the early church. See Thomas C. Oden, *The Word of Life* (San Francisco: Harper, 1989), for numerous references to it in his index. Indeed, Oden writes, "Systematic ecumenical theology looks for a cohesive grasp of the whole of classic Christian teaching, so that each part is seen in relation to the whole" (x).

total message. Final perseverance must be interpreted in the larger flow of God's comprehensive plan to deliver us from evil and to effect a new creation, essentially defined in Wesleyan theology as holiness of heart and life—that is, life in Christ. In some ways this makes theological inquiry more complicated, because we cannot capture the total truth of any particular doctrine by studying it in isolation. But it saves the exploration of a particular truth from becoming myopic and detached. In this chapter I will attempt to write from this synthetic point of view, both as a means to study our subject properly and also as an exercise in "doing theology" from a Wesleyan perspective.

For me this means that, while a four-view approach to the subject is interesting and helpful, we must not conclude that any single view completely encompasses the topic. The fact is that elements of truth are found in each of the views described in this book. Such is the richness of the subject, and such is the contribution that multiple traditions have made to it over the centuries. We must not approach our topic with a "who's right–who's wrong" attitude. John Wesley realized this in his own day when he wrote to Mr. Alexander Coates on July 7, 1761: "Remember, as sure as you are that 'believers cannot fall from grace,' others (wise and holy men too) are equally sure that they can; and you are as much obliged to bear with them as they are to bear with you."[2] While doing my best to set forth the Wesleyan Arminian position as clearly as I can, I aim to write with this same spirit in relation to the other authors of this book.

In addition to the substance ("order of salvation") and spirit (irenic) of Wesleyan theology, a Wesleyan methodology guides the way a particular topic is studied. This method is sometimes called the quadrilateral—composed of Scripture, Tradition, Reason, and Experience. Again, this fourfold methodology was not Wesley's invention, but it was one that he regularly used, both

---

[2]John Wesley, "Letter to Mr. Alexander Coates," *The Works of John Wesley*, ed. Thomas Jackson, 14 vols. (London: Wesley Methodist Book Room, 1872; repr., Grand Rapids: Baker, 1986), 12:240. (In this chapter I will use two different editions of Wesley's *Works*: the earlier fourteen-volume edition edited by Thomas Jackson and referred to as the Jackson edition [originally published between 1829–31, and subsequently by various publishers], and the multivolume edition commonly called the Bicentennial edition, currently being produced by Abingdon Press. In making references to either edition, the first number is the volume; the second is the page. Hereafter, I will cite Wesley's works as simply *Works*.)

explicitly and implicitly.[3] After I have dealt with the constellation of doctrines that help us interpret the topic of eternal security, I will conclude this chapter using the quadrilateral as an
organizing principle to summarize our examination of the Wesleyan Arminian position on the perseverance of the saints.

This concept of theology must include a few remarks about
style, both for Wesley and for myself. He once remarked that he
intended to write "plain truth for plain people."[4] This statement
was more than a cliché; it was an indication of his commitment
to a particular approach to communication (both oral and written). That method sought a mediating ground between ornate
complexity on the one hand and uneducated superficiality on
the other. The style arose in the seventeenth century as a means
to promote clarity of thought and the maintenance of substance.[5]
Plain-style communication could bear the weight of scholarly
scrutiny while remaining intelligible to the average person. I
hope to write with that same style in this chapter, so that
whether you are an academically trained theologian or not, you
will find beneficial information for your journey with God. My
ultimate desire in writing is that you will understand what I
write in a way that makes a difference in your life.

Finally, I wish to make some comments about sources. All
theological interpretations are related to primary texts that precede them. For the purposes of this chapter, the Bible and Wesley's works constitute the two key primary texts. These will
shape the core of what I write. This means that it is not my
intention to carry the discussion of eternal security of believers
and the perseverance of the saints into a consideration of all the
subsequent Wesleyan theologians who have written on the subject. I will do this only where such references bear directly on
or have influence in relation to the more primary view of Wesley himself.

---

[3]Donald Thorsen, *The Wesleyan Quadrilateral* (Grand Rapids: Zondervan, 1990).
The Anglican tradition trained its priests to use a trilateral (Scripture, tradition, and
reason), although it was never seen as a determinative formula for theological reflection. From his writings it can be seen that Wesley added "Experience" as a fourth
dimension of interpretation, realizing full well that some of his contemporaries
would view such an addition as too subjective. Nevertheless, he persisted, believing that doctrine must necessarily bear witness in actual life.

[4]"Preface to the Sermons on Several Occasions," *Works* (Bicentennial), 1:104.

[5]*Works* (Bicentennial), 1:20–29.

As a reader, you must understand that my choice to do this is both deliberate and descriptive. It is deliberate in that I am consciously leaving out large portions of the Wesleyan Arminian tradition. My expertise is in Wesley, not those who have come after him. I will leave it to others to compare and contrast what I have written with what post-Wesley scholars have written. The choice also illustrates the kind of Wesley scholar I view myself to be and where I place myself in relation to other reputable Wesleyan scholars. I believe that when a substantial theological topic (like the perseverance of the saints) is under study, we must first examine it in relation to the primary exponents and the sources that shaped it. One of the problems in doing theological study is that the primary spokespersons can easily get lost or misrepresented by their "interpreters." Thus, the first step in presenting a person's views is to let that person speak for himself or herself. In this case, that is John Wesley.

I am a scholar who stands in what Albert Outler referred to as "Phase III Wesley Studies."[6] I was trained in this method by Frank Baker at Duke University and have chosen to represent it for the past twenty years. This method says we must read the words of the primary person before we use the words of subsequent interpreters to color (or cloud) our thinking. As often as we can, we must avoid "reading back into Wesley." I want your reading of this chapter to root you in what Wesley himself believed and taught and to show you how he believed his interpretation was a reflection of biblical truth. This approach virtually guarantees that various "interpreters" will determine that what I have written is not "the real Wesley." In some cases, they may prove to be correct. I do not propose that all my views of

---

[6]Outler posited three phases of Wesley-related scholarship. Phase 1 was "Wesley the Hero," with all of the obvious problems in glamorizing or uncritically assessing him. Phase 2 was "Wesley As Viewed by His Interpreters," with the potential for an interpreter to make Wesley end up looking more like the interpreter than himself. Phase 3 was the phase in which Outler felt Wesleyan scholarship stood in our time—a phase that called for scholars who know and present Wesley on his own terms and in relation to the sources that shaped him. It must be noted that Outler did not believe the previous two phases were either to be discounted or abandoned. Valuable work has been done and can still be done in the two phases. What he urged on the Wesleyan world was the addition of phase 3 as a means to allow Wesley to "critique" his interpreters, more than the other way around. That is the approach I am taking in this chapter.

him are correct, even though that is my intention whenever I write about him.

This does, however, raise the question about where and how you are to separate me as the author from Wesley as the source. I do not write using a lot of first-person language. So, some may wonder whether I am describing what I think or what Wesley thought. As a general rule for reading this chapter, you should assume that the generic sentences reflect my thinking. The sentences that are "pure Wesley" either directly or indirectly refer to his writings. Obviously, I hope that my views will also accurately represent Wesley. Yet I do not want you to read every sentence as if it is unquestionably from the mind of Wesley himself. You must allow the views of others to help you draw your conclusions, and in the Wesleyan world today, those other views are often quite diverse.

THE CONTEXT OF THEOLOGY

Just as theology cannot be chopped into pieces, neither does it exist in a vacuum. Theology is always produced in relation to elements that exist outside the theological enterprise. Whenever we study theology, we must ask, "What is fueling this concern and influencing the particular way it is being expressed?" In other words, we must set theology in its formative context. In this section I will briefly examine three elements in relation to theology in general and to our topic in particular: culture, ecclesiology, and the internal dynamics of early Methodism in which Wesley lived and worked.

(1) Culturally, the eighteenth century was bearing the distinctively humanistic fruit of the Enlightenment. With amazing advances in almost every area of life (e.g., travel, science, industry, law, and politics), the eighteenth century dawned with an equally strong belief in the ability of human beings to shape their lives and forge their destinies.[7] Philosophers such as David Hume, Richard Price, Thomas Reid, Joseph Priestly, and Lord Kames were contributing to the subject as they debated the nature and extent of moral responsibility. Overall, a belief in natural ability eclipsed one of graced enablement. Reason superseded revelation. Ironically, the determinists also played into the

---

[7]Gerald Cragg, *The Church and the Age of Reason* (New York: Penguin, 1970).

214 | Four Views on Eternal Security

picture by positing an arrangement of reality that ended up with humanity "off the hook" with respect to their responsibility in shaping that reality.[8]

The result was a confusing mixture of human potential and passivity. This set English society on a particular course. However, it also shaped Wesley's approach to the subject of the perseverance of the saints. He resolutely disavowed any notions of "natural" free will (which he felt resulted in antinomianism) or of divine fore-counseled decree (which he felt resulted in passivity). The former, Wesley believed, elevated human beings too high; the latter pushed them too low. At either level, something unbiblical and unfortunate happened to the understanding of *imago dei*, of persons being made in the image of God. As we will see, he thought his view of the perseverance of the saints honored the doctrine without going to either extreme. He believed he preserved a proper doctrine of both God's sovereignty and human nature. Because he was out of step with the naturalists and the determinists, his views were controversial in the culture. But he was convinced that it was a theology in keeping with scriptural Christianity.

(2) Ecclesiastically, Wesley found himself in the midst of a varied but strong Calvinistic theology in England. Scholars have sometimes differentiated the views as high Calvinism, hyper-Calvinism, and moderate Calvinism.[9] Proponents identified largely with the Nonconformists (e.g., Puritans, Baptists, and Presbyterians), but there were also representatives within the Church of England. Wesley had family roots in Puritanism, and

---

[8]In my doctoral study at Duke University, I read many of the seventeenth- and eighteenth-century sermons preached in the Church of England. One recurring thread was a reliance—explicitly and implicitly—upon the Aristotelian "chain of being." In effect, people were told to find their place in that scheme and stay there. At the same time, England was moving toward an entirely different way of perceiving reality—one that included a new philosophy of the individual, of private ownership, and so forth. Wesley lived, ministered, and developed his theology in "a time between times."

[9]It is not the purpose of this chapter or within the ability of this writer to define each major segment of the Calvinistic view, much less to portray the nuances that differentiated them. Allan Coppedge gives a good summary of these three views in his book, *John Wesley in Theological Debate* (Wilmore, Ky.: Wesley Heritage, 1987), 37–40. The point of the statement is to show that the Calvinistic position was noticeably present through a variety of views and proponents.

he was familiar with other advocates of Calvinism, either through their writings or through personal acquaintance.[10] Thus, he was not ignorant of the fact that his views would fly in the face of equally competent, devout, and passionate interpreters of Christian belief. As we will see in a moment, this happened within his own ranks (Anglicanism and Methodism) and among his close friends.

When we turn to the Church of England, we find a body that reflected the cultural and religious pluralism of the times. Anglicans spanned the spectrum from conservatism to liberalism. What was even more telling, however, was the church's unwillingness and inability to come to terms with controversial theological issues, preferring to push for a "middle way." The prevailing thought of Anglican theologians at the opening of the eighteenth century could more accurately be called latitudinarian than dogmatic.[11] The result is what Outler called "an Erastian establishment in a demoralized environment."[12] In short, the Church of England had become domesticated in ways that stunted its ability to proclaim a clear or univocal theological message to the age.

In contrast, other denominations and free churches sometimes went to the opposite extreme of having theological interpretations that smacked of a "we're the only true church" mentality. Again, Wesley stood between the extremes, choosing to advocate universal truths but attempting to do so in ways that avoided driving wedges between legitimate segments of the body of Christ. To some of his fellow Anglicans, he appeared too conservative, and to some of his fellow Christians he seemed too liberal. Yet he chose his course deliberately and resolutely.

(3) Finally, Wesley could not escape the context of early Methodism itself. Before the Methodist movement was ten years old, Wesley was already having to deal with variant leaders—

---

[10]Robert Monk, *John Wesley: His Puritan Heritage* (Nashville: Abingdon, 1966), provides one of the best examinations of Wesley's knowledge of Calvinism as mediated through the Puritan heritage, broadly conceived.

[11]"Speculative latitudinarianism" was a phrase used in Wesley's day to describe an undefined and largely unbounded spectrum of belief. It was "speculative" in that it saw conviction as untenable, and it was "latitudinarian" in its assumption that widely divergent views could be simultaneously held both in the society and the church.

[12]Albert Outler, *John Wesley* (New York: Oxford Univ. Press, 1964), 20.

some Calvinistic and others Arminian.[13] In 1752 he wrote a summary of his views entitled "Predestination Calmly Considered."[14] This treatise established the main lines along which his beliefs flowed. Other writings shed further light on the subject both before and after that watershed document, such as "A Dialog Between a Predestinarian and His Friend" (1745), "Serious Thoughts on the Perseverance of the Saints" (1751), and "Thoughts upon Necessity" (1774). The index to Wesley's *Works* shows additional comments scattered throughout his sermons, letters, and miscellaneous writings.

Things within Methodism came to a head in 1770 with what is now termed the "Minute controversy." Preachers within Methodist ranks pressured Wesley for some response to the differences between Calvinism and his own views regarding predestination. The conference minutes of 1770 included a poorly drafted statement and the record of a disappointing discussion that effectively ended what little hope there might have been for a reconciliation between the Calvinists and the Arminians inside Methodism. John Fletcher joined Wesley in arguing against predestinarianism and antinomianism through his series of essays he called "Checks." In Fletcher's writings we can see a similar attempt to that of Wesley, that is, attempting to fuse and balance God's sovereign grace and human moral responsibility.

The Calvinists counterattacked with a spate of pamphlets and journals. So in 1778, Wesley began publishing his own journal, *The Arminian Magazine*, through which he sought to advance the view of God's willingness to save all people from sin, not just the elect. His use of the word "Arminian" in the magazine's title erroneously made it appear that Arminius was a more substantial theological source than he actually was. It also made Wesley appear (then and now) that he was more an interpreter of Arminius's theological views than a presenter of his own. The fact is, John Wesley was "a Church of England man," and we

---

[13]Coppedge, *John Wesley in Theological Debate* provides what is likely the most detailed analysis of theological differences between Wesleyans and Calvinists in relation to two major doctrines: predestination and perfection. The sections of the book are framed around the time periods in which particular aspects of the debate were going on: (1) the free-grace controversy (1739–1744), the minor controversies (1745–1770), and the Conference Minute controversy (1770–1778).

[14]See "Predestination Calmly Considered," *Works* (Jackson), 10:204–59.

must understand his views (shaped to be sure by multiple traditions) more in that light than in the light of any single person or position.

The long and short of it was that *The Arminian Magazine* became both a means to propagate his views and a vehicle to keep the fires of controversy burning. When Wesley died in 1791, the Calvinistic and Arminian segments of Methodism remained divided. The schism enabled subsequent interpreters to go in different directions, all the while claiming that their later views were rooted in "Methodism." It was not long before Wesley was relegated to the status of "founding hero," which frequently meant that more attention was given to the words of his successors than to his own words. And it is possible to see subsequent theologians claiming to be Wesleyan but with scant references to Wesley in what they write. This is one of the reasons why I want to root this chapter in Wesley's words. It is important to get back to the views of the one from whom succeeding generations of interpretations have flowed. Yet even then we must realize that Wesley lived at a particular time, faced particular issues, and advocated scriptural Christianity within a specific context.

THE CONTOURS OF THEOLOGY

Continuing the motif that theology cannot be chopped into pieces, I turn now to the realization that theological positions are enriched through their interaction with one another. Independent theology is limited theology. Ecumenical theology is enriched theology. The fact is, Christians have much more in common than they have in disagreement. Even with respect to the doctrine of the perseverance of the saints, we must take note of significant areas of agreement. Before I launch into an extended presentation of the Wesleyan Arminian position, I believe it is necessary to state some key areas on which all Christians agree.

First, we all agree on the sovereignty of God. Even if Wesley's approach differs from that of others, he in no way believed less in God's sovereignty. Nor did he have any interest in proposing theological views that would diminish that sovereignty. He has been accused of doing so by critics, but an examination of his works reveals the fallacy of such a charge. For all Christians, "God's *fundamental* designs of creation and redemption cannot be finally frustrated."[15]

Second, we agree on the freedom of humanity. No Christians settle for a "robot" or "puppet" concept of humanity, even if they disagree as to the nature, scope, and operation of that freedom. In the same way, no Christians believe that human freedom is "natural" in its makeup and expression. Even though he was accused of believing in and teaching the freedom of the will, Wesley himself said that "natural free will" was a term he did not understand.[16] Along with other Christians, he maintained that whatever freedom we may possess is the result of God's grace.

Third, we agree on the efficacy of the atonement. Christ's death is sufficient; nothing more is needed or required in order for us to be saved. With Paul we enthusiastically "preach Christ crucified" (1 Cor. 1:23). We may hold varying theories of the atonement, and we may even disagree as to its operative nature on the human being. But for all Christians, the atonement is the objective cause of our salvation, exerting subjective influence on us. Christ died for us while we were yet sinners (Rom. 5:8).

Fourth, we all admit some kind of perseverance of the saints. This may appear surprising in a book of this nature, but it is important to point it out. No Christians hold to a tentative salvation—here today and gone tomorrow. We do not have a "hope so, think so, maybe so" faith. We are secure in Christ, even though we may differ as to the nature and extent of that security and whether or not there is anything that can cause us to lose it. The simple fact is this: True saints persevere! This belief is rooted in God and not in ourselves, and it produces a healthy commitment to doing God's will on earth as it is in heaven. Furthermore, it gives us the assurance that we are not in some whimsical relationship with God.

Finally, we agree that equally genuine and devout Christians may nevertheless disagree on the matter of eternal security and the perseverance of the saints. To restate Wesley's words cited above, we agree that "wise and holy men" stand on dif-

---

[15]Charles W. Carter, ed., *A Contemporary Wesleyan Theology*, 2 vols. (Grand Rapids: Francis Asbury [Zondervan], 1983), 1:123.

[16]"Predestination Calmly Considered," *Works* (Jackson), 10:229.

ferent sides of this issue. We also note that none of the norma-
tive creeds of ecumenical Christendom (Apostles', Nicene, or
Athanasian) has a statement about the perseverance of the
saints, even though subsequent statements of faith have included such.[17] Personally, I take this to mean that the doctrine of
the perseverance of the saints is an important doctrine, but that
no particular interpretation of it is a required article of faith. I
allow that Christians can interpret it in more than one way.

As this book points out, however, there have been (and continue to be) longstanding differences with respect to the doctrine
of the perseverance of the saints. And as we have seen in this
brief introduction, those differences have sometimes erupted
into bitter controversy and spawned unfortunate schism in the
body of Christ. This book is not intended to contribute to either
of those things. The following focus on the Wesleyan Arminian
interpretation of the doctrine is not intended to add to contemporary arguments between believers. I understand this book to
be an example of doing theology in Christian community, even
as each of us is charged with the responsibility of providing a
particular view on the subject.

THE CONNECTEDNESS OF THEOLOGY

The fact that theology cannot be chopped into pieces also
means that one doctrine is connected to others. As I said earlier,
God makes theological videotapes, not snapshots. So we must
look at some of the doctrines that naturally and necessarily
accompany any discussion of eternal security. In doing so, I
intend to show how theology is a "connected" enterprise, made
up of a dynamic interaction between and among particular
beliefs. In this section Wesley's theology of perseverance will
emerge. I will show how selected doctrines interface with each
other and how Wesley's articulation of them differed from other
advocates. The doctrine of eternal security is like any other
belief: It is a combination of specific doctrines (each of which is
dynamic in its own right) to provide the larger view of the particular doctrine under study.

---

[17]Wesley notes three examples of subsequent statements that include references to God's elective decree: "The Protestant Confession of Faith" (1559), the Synod
of Dort (1618), and the Westminster Confession of Faith (1646).

The Doctrine of Grace

Surely grace is the broadest and deepest doctrine that gives rise to Wesley's view of eternal security and the perseverance of the saints. The doctrine of grace is rooted in the nature of God, especially regarding such things as the nature and extent of God's sovereignty, love, favor, and bestowal of freedom. Without going into all these aspects, we can point to them through our discussion of grace, for it is God's grace that brings all these things to bear on us.

Perhaps more than anything else, we must strongly emphasize from the beginning what Thomas Oden has properly noted, that "it is completely contrary to Wesley's intent to think of grace as natural to humanity, or inherent in our nature. Grace remains a radical gift wholly unmerited by us in our natural fallenness. Grace comes before any of our natural competencies or responses."[18] On too many occasions, persons outside the Wesleyan tradition have caricatured both Wesley and the tradition as advocating some sort of "natural" free will. Nothing could be further from the truth. Obviously, stating this does not uncomplicate Wesley's views or mean that they will now be consonant with other interpretations. But it does mean that Wesley is (and must be) freed from the erroneous charge of being a closet naturalist. Whatever points of agreement or disagreement may exist in the theology of grace between Wesley and other Christians, the matter of graced enablement must not be one of them.

This leads us to an immediate consideration of the activity of grace. For Wesley, a proper understanding of grace begins in God's ultimate intent, expressed through this unchangeable fact: "He that believeth shall be saved; he that believeth not shall be damned."[19] God sovereignly establishes the way of salvation. Nothing supersedes it, and no one can resist it. However, this saving intention is not initiated or maintained by election, but rather by God's judgment as to whether or not a person has met the condition for salvation—that is, faith in the Lord Jesus Christ. By taking this approach, Wesley believed he was advocating the proper relationship between God's

---

[18]Thomas C. Oden, *John Wesley's Scriptural Christianity* (Grand Rapids: Zondervan, 1994), 53.

[19]"Predestination Calmly Considered," *Works* (Jackson), 10:235.

sovereignty and human responsibility. By grace, God establishes the irrevocable intention that all may be saved and that all who believe shall indeed be saved.[20] This perspective understands God's sovereignty more in terms of governance, not of predeterminism.

To make this eternal intention real in human existence, God sheds his love abroad in our hearts through prevenient grace. Prevenient grace literally means the "grace that comes before." Before what? Before our first conscious awareness of God's existence or God's love.[21] This is yet another way to reinforce the fact that self-salvation is impossible. The first move is God's, not ours. This eliminates "all imagination of merit from man."[22] It means that "it is not possible for men to do anything well till God raises them from the dead.... It is impossible for us to come out of our sins, yea, or to make the least motion toward it, till He who hath all power in heaven and earth call our dead souls into life."[23]

So far, this sounds like a way of merely repeating God's ultimate intention declared from eternity, which we described previously. However, prevenient grace also includes two other significant aspects. First, it is grace that "prevents." But what does it prevent? The absolute, "tee-total depravity" of the human being.[24] Or to say it a bit more technically, prevenient grace prevents the Fall from being so *intensive* that even the ability to respond is lost. The Fall is extensive; that is, no aspect of existence escapes it. Yet because of grace, it is not so complete in humanity that people lose all ability to recognize and respond to God.

Just as Wesley used governance to interpret divine sovereignty, so also he used prevenient grace to explain depravity. He summarized his position in a letter using these words:

---

[20]Further along in the chapter I will provide more detail concerning the nature of "belief" and what it means to "have faith."

[21]Sermon "On Working Out Our Own Salvation," *Works* (Jackson), 6:511–13.

[22]Ibid., 6:508.

[23]Ibid., 6:511.

[24]Albert Outler, *Theology in the Wesleyan Spirit* (Nashville: Tidings, 1975), 34. Outler makes an accurate and essential differentiation between "total depravity" (every part affected; that is, extensively) and "tee-total depravity" (every part completely affected; that is, intensively). For more on this distinction, see Carter, ed., *A Contemporary Wesleyan Theology*, 1:268–70.

I always did clearly assert the total fall of man and his utter inability to do any good of himself; the absolute necessity of the grace of the Spirit to raise even a good thought or desire in our hearts; the Lord's regarding no work and accepting of none but so far as they proceed from His preventing, convincing, and converting grace through the Beloved; the blood and righteousness of Christ being the sole meritorious cause of our salvation.[25]

Under the heading of grace we could continue to look at other doctrines connected to and contributing to Wesley's theology of perseverance. As we noted early in the chapter, his theology is a theology of grace, and his system is an order of salvation. Therefore, we could proceed to view other specific doctrines under the heading of grace. However, I am choosing at this point to explore other particular doctrines in their own right, so that we may clearly see their contribution to the doctrine under study. I offer this first subsection merely to emphasize that God's grace is the root of Wesley's theology, not Pelagianism or any other notion of natural free will.

The Nature of Humanity

From what we have already said about God's grace, we are already in a position rightly to discern key aspects of Wesley's view of humanity. For the sake of analysis, however, it is important to state explicitly certain things in relation to the doctrine of eternal security. First, Wesley believed in "a measure of free will supernaturally restored."[26] This supernatural restoration was essential if men and women were to continue to be called "human" and maintain their fundamental distinction from the animals.

The Fall destroyed the moral dimension of the *imago dei* (righteousness and holiness), thus rendering people utterly helpless before God. But God intervened and "prevented" a Fall so

---

[25]*The Letters of Rev. John Wesley*, ed. John Telford 8 vols. (London: Epworth, 1931), 5:231. (In citing Wesley's letters, I will also use two editions. The first is that of John Telford and to date the most complete. The second is that section of the Bicentennial Edition of Wesley's *Works* wherein several volumes of letters (25–27) edited by Frank Baker are extant. As with other primary citations, the first number is the volume; the second is the page.

[26]"Predestination Calmly Considered," *Works* (Jackson), 10:229–30.

complete and tragic that people totally lost the natural and political dimensions of the image.[27] By grace, human beings are still capable of recognizing and responding to God. This creational fact has implications for the doctrines of atonement and spiritual growth. In terms of the perseverance of the saints, it means that human beings are genuinely "response-able" and thus accountable for the choices they make relative to God.

It also means (and this is an important contrast with traditional Calvinism) that grace is resistible. In restoring our "measure of freedom," God took the risk and made the allowance for us to remain capable of saying "yes" or "no" to the divine message and influence. We must continue to avail ourselves of grace and be actually involved in working out our own salvation (Phil. 2:12), or God will cease working.[28] We will come back to this point and explore it in greater detail futher along in the chapter. For now it is enough to emphasize that by gracious provision, human nature is preserved, including the necessary capacity to recognize and respond to God—or to refuse to do so.

The Atonement of Christ

By now you will recognize Wesley's intention to synthesize elements in theology that are sometimes separated. In terms of God, Wesley brought together sovereignty and allowance through a theology of governance. In terms of humanity, he combined depravity and responsibility through a theology of graced enablement. When we turn to the atonement, we again discover that it is not possible to place Wesley into a single theory of it. As we will see, his views are more synthetic and dynamic than one particular position can describe.

With all other Christians, Wesley affirmed the centrality of Christ's death on the cross for our redemption. For him, the essence of the gospel was this: Jesus Christ came into the world

---

[27]Carter, ed., *A Contemporary Wesleyan Theology*, 1:204–7.

[28]Sermon "On Working Out Our Own Salvation," *Works* (Bicentennial), 3:208. By all accounts, this is a landmark message in Wesley's theology, both showing that he is not Pelagian and at the same time showing wherein he stands apart from Calvinism. This sermon must be read and studied carefully if we are to understand Wesley's anthropology, especially as it relates to the order of salvation.

to save sinners. Thus, he could write: "Nothing in the Christian system is of greater consequence than the doctrine of the Atonement. It is properly the distinguishing point between Deism and Christianity."[29] That statement is not only sufficiently strong to show Wesley's conviction, but also its reference to Deism is important to show his absolute separation from prevailing "natural will" theories of his time.

Wesley based his commitment to the atonement on three indisputable facts: (1) All humanity by nature is separated from God and evil in God's sight. (2) God sent Jesus to die for every person, and Christ enlightens everyone who comes into the world. (3) The benefits of Christ's death are extended even to those who are excluded from a direct knowledge of Jesus.[30] In stating his belief, Wesley was quick to point out the ultimate mystery of the atonement. He wrote, "I can no more comprehend it than [Christ's] lordship. . . . Our reason is quickly bewildered. If we attempt to expatiate in this field, we 'find no end, in wandering mazes lost.'"[31]

This quotation reveals Wesley's recognition that some doctrines must be maintained as *facts* without our going "across the line" to insist on *explanations*. The atonement was one such doctrine for him, so we must not try to force him into a particular camp or limit him to a single theory. We discover that his interpretation of the atonement has connections to the several major positions that theologians have advanced through the centuries. We will briefly look at them and apply them to the Wesleyan view of atonement in relation to eternal security.[32]

---

[29]*Letters* (Telford), 6:297–98.

[30]Ibid., 2:117–18. The three points are a summary of an extended statement made by Wesley to show where Christianity and Quakerism are alike. The statement should be read in its entirety, especially his remarks summarized in point 3. He did not believe in universalism, but he did believe that God (in order to be just) had to make some kind of provision for those who (for whatever reason) never had the opportunity to hear about Christ. The fact that he connects the atonement even to this gracious benefit is significant.

[31]Ibid., 6:298.

[32]For a more extensive study of Wesley's views on the atonement, see the following sources: William R. Cannon, *The Theology of John Wesley* (Nashville: Abingdon, 1946); Colin Williams, *John Wesley's Theology Today* (Nashville: Abingdon, 1960); Mildred Bangs Wynkoop, *A Theology of Love* (Kansas City, Mo.: Beacon Hill, 1972); Charles W. Carter, ed., *A Contemporary Wesleyan Theology*, vol. 1; Allan Coppedge, *John Wesley in Theological Debate*; and Thomas C. Oden, *John Wesley's Scriptural Christianity*.

First, we look at *the moral influence theory*. If we remember Wesley's commitment to human depravity (including the loss of the moral dimension of the image of God), we might think that notions of "moral influence" would have little place in his theology of the atonement. This is not the case, however. For Wesley, Christ is the pattern sent by God for us to follow all along the journey of salvation. He is the example of what life looks like when properly lived. As such, Christ models sacrificial service, even the "suffering servant" motif, through his death on the cross.

Because grace enables us to recognize and respond to God, Christ's example provides moral influence by stirring us not only to make a response to him but also to make it in relation to God's design (that is, Christlikeness). The atonement reveals how God intends to save us and how we are to live in relation to our salvation. In these respects, the cross "influences" us (since we are capable of being influenced) to respond to God's offer of salvation in Christ and to follow him for the rest of our lives.

With respect to eternal security and the perseverance of the saints, moral influence means that when we truly gaze on Christ and his saving work on the cross, the grace of God moves in our hearts, stirring us both to a profound recognition of who God is and who we are. When Christ is lifted up (John 3:14–15), God establishes the means by which we are "influenced" to consider our true estate, God's provision for a Savior, our need to receive the benefits of this salvation, and ultimately the commission to be sent from the cross to preach and live Christ and him crucified.

We turn next to the *penal substitution theory*. Along with Christians in the Reformed tradition, Wesley held that Christ died for sin in our place. Christ died in part as a means of satisfying God's demand for justice (that sin be atoned for) and also to accomplish what we could never do by ourselves. A belief in God's anger toward sin is totally accurate, and we can do nothing (in and of ourselves) to assuage that anger. In that sense, atonement is propitiation. It is also the ultimate proof we can give nothing in exchange for our souls. Jesus has taken our place to effect our pardon.

But this raises the question: "Pardon from what?" The simple answer is, of course, pardon from sin. But this leads further to the question: "What sin?" Unfortunately, some have mistakenly concluded that Wesley modified the classic penal substitution theory by holding to a belief that Christ atoned only for the believer's past sins, not for the *condition of sin* (original sin) or for sins committed by believers after their conversion. This error springs from a misreading of two statements in Wesley's writings. The first misreading occurs in "A Dialogue Between an Antinomian and His Friend," in which Wesley (the friend) replies to the Antinomian: "Did he then heal the wound before it was made and put an end to our sins before they had a beginning? This is so glaring, palpable an absurdity, that I cannot conceive how you can swallow it."[33]

But such a false reading is quickly seen if the statement is placed in its context. For just before it, Wesley affirms that Christ died to "take away, put an end to, blot out, and utterly destroy *all our sins for ever*."[34] There is no distinction between past, present, and future sinfulness. Furthermore, to make the conclusion Wesley does (i.e., his conviction that the atonement deals with "all sins"), he would have to connect it to the originating source, the condition of our sinfulness. Otherwise, the atonement would not deal with the sins that flow from that source, regardless of timing. Perhaps most unfortunate is the fact that this misreading leaves open the question of what kind of "atonement" is required and/or sufficient for sins that believers commit after their conversion. Or to say it more clearly, nothing in Wesley's writings supposes anything other than the all-sufficiency of Christ (through his atoning death on the cross) for our redemption from whatever condition, expression, or timing of sin.

What Wesley is obviously referring to in his misread quotation is the necessity of not excluding human subjective response to Christ's objective work. His substitutionary death for our sins totally accomplishes our deliverance, but the efficacy of that deliverance must include our ongoing appropriation of it. Hence, "when the wound is made" (as per Wesley's quotation above), the only fitting connection with the atonement by a believer is immediate repentance. Here we can see the relation between imputed and imparted righteousness in Wesley's

---

[33]"A Dialogue Between an Antinomian and His Friend," *Works* (Jackson), 10:267.

[34]Ibid. Italics added.

view. If a believer should falsely assert that he or she has no need of repentance for recent sin (because the righteousness of Christ has been imputed), this would not destroy the objective reality of the atonement. However, it would undermine its subjective benefit (the impartation of righteousness)—that is, the work of Christ to deal decisively with sin "once and for all."

The second misreading occurs in relation to Wesley's explanatory note for Romans 3:25. Commenting on Paul's phrase (as it was translated in the New Testament used by Wesley for his *Explanatory Notes upon the New Testament*), "by the remission of past sins," Wesley adds this comment: "All the sins antecedent to their believing." Some non-Wesleyans use his comment to say that Wesley believed Christ's propitiation applied only to a believer's past sins. But this lifts the phrase out of context (as has been done with Wesley's earlier-cited phrase) and treats the "explanatory note" as if it were somehow limiting the efficacy of the atonement. There are three immediate problems with that conclusion. The first is that if interpreters of Wesley lay this belief at his feet, they must also accuse Paul of the same thing, for it is Paul's phrase—"the remission of past sins"—that Wesley is commenting on.

Second, the interpretation of the Bible's phrase "past sins" and Wesley's term "antecedent to their believing" as pertaining to timing both turn the scriptural phrase away from its intended aim. Both phrases correctly mean that prior to Christ, unbelievers trusted in the law (the context of Rom. 3)—the "antecedent" to salvation by faith in Christ, the system for the "remission of past sins" before the cross of Christ. To continue to trust the law is to miss the substitutionary death of Christ and continue to rely on something that never could save to the full extent needed.

Third, Wesley's statement about Romans 3:25 is a "note," not a full exposition of his larger theology of atonement or his narrower belief in penal substitution. Interestingly, the notes that both precede and follow Wesley's comment for 3:25 establish his belief in justification, "whose essential character is to punish sin" without regard to its being before or after belief in Christ. As the other notes that surround the misread comment show, Wesley's interpretive phrase in 3:25 is dealing with the timing of Christ's coming into the world to die for sin, not the limiting of the atonement to sins one has committed in the past.[35] Here again, the proper reading and correct conclusion is that Christ's substitutionary death covers all our sins, not just some of them.

Thus, we see penal substitution in Wesley's view of the atonement, and it is atonement for all sin, not just past sins. Yet it is true that on another front he deals with penal substitution differently from his Reformed friends. In fact, for the purposes of this chapter it is important to note that Wesley does not place the substitutionary element primarily within a legal framework. Christ's satisfaction of God's demand for justice is not the satisfaction of a demand based on an eternal and unchangeable decree. Rather, it is the justice that resides in God's own nature—that is, the need to bring into proper relationship the "justice" between God's love for persons and God's hatred of sin. That kind of "at-one-ment" could be achieved only by Christ. Penal substitution is more properly placed in Christ's priestly ministry than in the legal-requirement context. It is not the satisfaction of a legal demand for justice so much as it is an act of mediated reconciliation.[36] With regard to penal substitution, the proviso is that we believe in the One "who hath given Himself a 'propitiation for our sins, for the sins of the whole world.'"

With respect to eternal security and the perseverance of the saints, penal substitution establishes the objective basis for our salvation. Christ has died for us—once and for all. Christ has done something we could never do for ourselves. Christ has done something that needs no further additions. Christ is the atoning sacrifice. We are "secure" because of him. We "persevere" because of him. When coupled with the resurrection, it is the proof that "sin" is not the final word, "salvation" is; "wrath" is not the final word, "love" is. Christ has died in our place to move us from the problem to the solution.

To view the atonement in this way is forever to abandon two deadly notions: (1) that we are now somehow excused from responsibility for sins we commit after our initial confession of faith in Christ, and (2) that any notion of works righteousness can

---

[35]A reading of Romans 3:25 in newer translations makes this abundantly clear from the Bible itself. See the NIV, Good News Bible, and NLT, which show that the reference is not to a believer's past sins but rather to believers "in the past" who sinned.

[36]Williams, *John Wesley's Theology Today*, 84.

deal with such sins. To believe in Christ's substitutionary atonement is, instead, to profess faith in our Lord and Savior Jesus Christ, who loved us and gave himself for our sins (Gal. 1:4).

We now look at the *ransom theory*. This view of the atonement relates to the penal substitution theory in that it recognizes the need for another to do something for us that we could never do for ourselves. But it builds on the actual meaning of the word "redemption," which means "to buy back." In its early and technical expressions, the "ransom" was associated with the struggle of Christ against Satan and the demonic evil powers and the Lord's rescue of us from them.[37] Church fathers such as Irenaeus, Origen, and Augustine held that Christ redeemed humanity with his blood and exchanged his soul for our souls. He gave his life to Satan as a ransom for those who were in bondage to the devil.

Wesley did not discount the reality of Christ's struggle with evil, including his struggle on the cross.[38] But this dimension of the atonement does not find an equal place in his theology with the other atonement theories we have examined. This is most likely due to the fact that Wesley chose to put the emphasis more on reconciliation to God than rescue from the devil. The atonement provides the saving base for a conscious cultivation of our relationship with God. As this occurs, there is a lessening need to remain focused on the demonic forces.[39] The ransom theory has value in further reminding us that Christ is the victor over sin and evil. But Wesley did not want the focus to be on "looking back" to a victory that had already been won. Rather, he wanted the atonement to create a "looking forward" to the effects of it: righteousness, peace, and joy in the Holy Spirit (Rom. 14:17).

With regard to eternal security and the perseverance of the saints, the ransom theory served for Wesley as a means to establish the fact that nothing can separate us from the love of God in Christ Jesus (Rom. 8:35). Christ himself has "spoiled the

---

[37]Carter, ed., *A Contemporary Wesleyan Theology*, 1:500.

[38]John Wesley, *Explanatory Notes upon the New Testament*, first published in 1755 and subsequently reprinted by a variety of publishers. The edition used for references in this chapter is that of Alec R. Allenson, Naperville, Ill., 1966. The note that pertains to Christ's ransom of our souls from evil is in relation to Colossians 2:15. Hereafter, I will simply refer to this source as *Notes*.

[39]Williams, *John Wesley's Theology Today*, 88.

principalities and powers" (Col. 2:15), exposing them and triumphing over them before all the hosts of heaven and hell.[40]

Before leaving this section on the atonement, we must look at the *governmental theory*. It arose as a protest against a radical penal substitution theory on the one hand and a defense against the critics of vicarious intervention on the other. At the extreme, critics of substitution (like the Socinians) abandoned the idea of atonement altogether. Critics of satisfaction attempted to show that such a motif was illogical since sinners deserve eternal death but Christ did not suffer eternal death.

In defense of the atonement, Hugo Grotius advocated what has come to be called the governmental theory. Grotius modified the substitutionary theory by viewing justice not as the need to mollify the offended will of a ruler but as the need to establish order and governance in a God-created universe. Grotius rejected the notion that God needed to be compensated, arguing instead that Christ's death was necessary to reestablish and maintain God's moral governance. The governmental theory is a version of an interpretation that tries to hold moral influence, penal substitution, and ransom in a dynamic relationship.[41]

We must include this theory in our discussion, because some outside the Wesleyan tradition have mistakenly claimed that this was John Wesley's primary view of the atonement. This mistake is easily made for a couple of reasons. First, some of Wesley's subsequent interpreters have held to versions of the governmental theory. Among the major adherents are Richard Watson, William Burton Pope, and John Miley. Persons outside the Wesleyan tradition "read back into Wesley" the views of these theologians, in part reasoning that no qualified interpreters of Wesley would hold a view of the atonement that Wesley himself did not hold.

This assumption is further fueled by the legitimate connections between Wesley and these men. But taking it to mean that Wesley held a governmental view of the atonement is taking the

---

[40]This sentence is a virtual rewriting of Wesley's own translation of Col. 2:15 in combination with the interpretive statements he makes in the corresponding explanatory note.

[41]For a more detailed study of the governmental theory, see Carter, ed., *A Contemporary Wesleyan Theology*, 1:502–5; H. Orton Wiley, *Christian Theology*, 3 vols. (Kansas City, Mo.: Beacon Hill, 1952), 2:252–59.

comparisons too far. As both H. Orton Wiley and R. Larry Shelton point out, the governmental theory fails to encompass Wesley's doctrine of the atonement. Wiley lists four objections to the governmental theory as a description of Wesley's view:

- It does not attach sufficient importance to the idea of propitiation and therefore minifies the idea of a real satisfaction of the divine attributes.
- It emphasizes the mercy of God in much the same sense that Calvinism emphasizes the justice of God.
- It is built on a false philosophical principle that utility is the ground of moral obligation.
- It practically ignores the immanent holiness of God and substitutes for the chief aim of the atonement that which is only subordinate.[42]

Shelton provides a more recent critique by pointing out that "all models for these theories of the atonement are drawn from societal and political concepts that are extra-biblical. There is a need to develop an understanding of atonement and salvation that is inductively derived from a biblical model and deals with the essential elements of Christ's work."[43] Shelton's view represents not only a better Wesleyan perspective but also one that Wesley himself would advocate.

Second, the governmental theory puts the reality of God's governance in the wrong place. As we showed at the beginning of the atonement section, governance is the synthesis of the beliefs Wesley held regarding divine sovereignty and the allowance for human freedom. Governance is not based on the atonement but rather on the nature of God to hold these two elements in dynamic tension. Thus, while Wesley would recognize that in certain ways the atonement affects God's ability to govern all things, he would not root in the atonement the causative aspects a full-blown governmental theory presumes.

With respect to eternal security and the perseverance of the saints, we do not need to say a lot about the governmental theory of the atonement, given that it is neither the exclusive nor primary view of Wesley himself. However, we can note that divine governance is an overarching concept in relation to how God effects

---

[42]Wiley, *Christian Theology*, 2:258.
[43]Carter, ed., *A Contemporary Wesleyan Theology*, 1:505.

232 I Four Views on Eternal Security

both our security and our perseverance. We would be amiss if we did not at least acknowledge that the atonement finds its place in the constellation of factors that make God's governance of all things possible. Evil has created chaos. Life is out of control, apart from the redeeming work of God in Christ. But God is a God of order, holding things together through multifaceted providence. To whatever extent the atonement contributes to God's governing providence, Wesley would affirm it. However, he does not root a theology of governance in the atonement.

As a way of leaving this important section, let us briefly review the salient features of Wesley's view of the atonement. Its nature is sacrificial, vicarious, universal, and triumphal. Its benefits include redemption, reconciliation, justification, adoption, regeneration, the rule of God, and the initiation of our sanctification.[44] The cross of Christ stands not only on the hill of Calvary but also at the apex of time, providing the salvation that God intends and we need.

Appropriation of Salvation

It is impossible to consider the subject of eternal security and the perseverance of the saints apart from an examination of how salvation is appropriated. While not minimizing the many elements that figure into the discussion, the simple difference between Wesley and his Calvinist friends lies at this very point: A Calvinistic view of appropriation rests on the basis of decree (predestination), and Wesley's view of appropriation rests on the basis of choice (graced-enablement). Wesley wrote of this fundamental difference and said to the Calvinists, "You are afraid if you do not hold election, you must hold free will, and so rob God of his glory in man's salvation."[45] This is the crux of the issue, and it works itself out in a number of significant ways.

First, it creates a different understanding of grace. Earlier in the chapter we spoke of grace as the root of Wesley's theology and the rationale for his understanding of theology as an order of salvation. This eliminates all notions of natural free will. In that regard he stands with the other Reformers in emphasizing the primacy of grace. Yet he stands in a different place from

[44]Ibid., 1:486–96.
[45]"Predestination Calmly Considered," *Works* (Jackson), 10:229.

the Calvinists when he moves on to describe grace as resistible. Now that we are examining how salvation is appropriated, we can return to a further look at this difference.

When Wesley postulated a genuine free agency through prevenient grace, he restored the idea of choice to the human being. He could not see any evidence that this choice, which could operate quite frequently and broadly (both in terms of acceptance and rejection) prior to conversion, would cease to exist afterward. Harold Lindstrom provided a good summary of Wesley's view:

> The view of salvation as something also dependent on human decisions is emphasized by the idea of repentance before faith as a condition of justification and repentance after faith as a condition of perfect sanctification. In accordance with his Arminian view of election Wesley thus rejects the idea of *gratia irresistibilis*. Grace, that is, does not operate irresistibly; its effectiveness is dependent on human cooperation. In consonance with this basic idea he dismissed the doctrine of an unconditional perseverance. Thus those who believe in Christ are not regarded as incapable of apostasy.[46]

We must return later to see how Wesley conceived of the possibility of apostasy. For now, the quote points to his belief that human choice exists both before and after conversion.

Contrary to the Calvinists, Wesley did not believe resistible grace undermined God's sovereignty. Those who are not Wesleyan marvel at this, because it seems completely illogical to admit that anything or anyone could resist God's grace and yet be subordinate to God. Wesley, however, put his confidence in God's sovereignty at another place, namely, that God's ultimate will for all creation and God's complete rule over all creation can take into account any and all human choices and yet not be undermined. A negative choice works to the "eternal ruin" of the person who makes it, not to the erosion of the nature of God who allows it.[47]

In fact, Wesley actually believed he had a higher concept of divine sovereignty than did the Calvinists. Speaking of saving

---

[46]Harold Lindstrom, *Wesley and Sanctification* (London: Epworth, 1946), 214.
[47]"What Is an Arminian?" *Works* (Jackson), 10:360.

someone who could reject the offer was more glorifying to God than making it all rest on a previously irresistible decree. Irresistible grace produced a deficient anthropology, making "man a mere machine, and consequently, no more rewardable or punishable."[48] Wesley was convinced that we could not properly represent one doctrine (divine sovereignty) by misrepresenting another (anthropology).

Resistible grace speaks a word not only about the nature of human beings, both before and after conversion, but also (and in the final analysis, more importantly) about the nature of God. Irresistible grace, Wesley believed, is founded on an understanding of God in which, in order to be sovereign, God must act on the basis of his arbitrary will. In that view of sovereignty, God is sovereign Creator, choosing to elect some to salvation and the rest to reprobation. A God of that nature has no need or desire to give human beings any part in their salvation. Wesley believed in God as sovereign Creator, but he added the concepts of God as loving Father and just Governor. With these additions, the place and possibility of human choice comes into the picture. As loving Father, God desires for us to respond to the offer of salvation through genuine love and obedience—both of which presuppose some measure of graced-enablement of the will.[49] As just Governor, God is fully capable of receiving all our choices and integrating them into providence without any fear that God's nature or intent will be altered or reduced.

Allowing this, we move to a second difference: the doctrine of justification by faith. With other Christians, Wesley understood that "justification" means the pardon and forgiveness of sins by God through grace. When a person professes faith in Christ, he or she is "justified by faith"—an act of God that makes Christ's salvation efficacious "up to the minute." It is important to note that for Wesley justification is not something God does that is contrary to the real state of things.[50] To make it so would be a violation of God's own nature, resulting in divine self-deception. Justification is not falsification or fantasy but is again the mysterious and marvelous blending of imputed and imparted righteousness. God can authentically justify us because

[48]"Predestination Calmly Considered," *Works* (Jackson), 10:232.

[49]Coppedge, *John Wesley in Theological Debate*, 138.

[50]"Justification by Faith," *Works* (Bicentennial), 1:188.

of Christ, and because of Christ we are *being transformed* from one degree of glory to another. And because justification is viewed by Wesley as initial sanctification, it is also the ongoing means by which God pardons and forgives us. We never outgrow the need to be justified *by faith in Christ*.

In Wesley's theology, however, the act of faith is rooted in one's choice to believe, not in the expression of belief by persons because they were previously elected to do so. For Wesley, "faith" is a fully trusting response to grace, which is itself made possible by grace.[51] Because there are different dimensions of grace, so too there are also differing kinds of faith. Prior to conversion human beings demonstrate rudimentary faith in such things as scientific facts, the material realm, rationalistic conclusions, common human decency, a belief in the necessity of morality, various faith expressions among different religions, and even variations within Christianity itself.[52] All these manifestations may properly be termed "faith" because they meet the generic definition: a fully trusting response to grace. But none of these are properly termed *saving faith*.

Nevertheless, rudimentary faith is important for our discussion because it predisposes us toward fuller expressions of faith in a way comparable to the way exercise predisposes us to greater physical well-being. Any constructive expression of faith is beneficial and has the potential to condition us to become people who live by faith and grow in the expression of faith.

However, a fully trusting response to converting grace requires a different expression of faith. The faith that justifies is faith in Jesus Christ. Saving faith is more than intellectual assent to propositional revelation. It is a disposition of the heart to trust in God through the merits of Christ.[53] It is a profession of faith that results in new birth. Part of the newness is the manifestation of righteousness, and here Wesley's view takes a turn from that of the Calvinists—a turn we need to examine for the purposes of our topic.

Along with the Calvinists, Wesley affirmed imputed righteousness, which he said means that "all believers are forgiven

---

[51]Oden, *John Wesley's Scriptural Christianity*, 192.
[52]Sermon "On Faith," *Works* (Bicentennial), 3:492–97.
[53]Sermon "The Marks of the New Birth," *Works* (Bicentennial), 1:417–19.

236 | **Four Views on Eternal Security**

and accepted, not for the sake of anything in them, or of anything that ever was, that is, or ever can be done by them, but wholly and solely for the sake of what Christ hath done and suffered for them."[54] In terms of philosophical theology, he was one with believers in the Reformed tradition—even though some have thought differently. Such imputation occurs the very moment people believe, precisely because there is no other merit whatsoever to which they can turn other than the righteousness of Christ.

However, as time moved on and Wesley saw increasing misuse and abuse of "imputation" language, he decided not to use it anymore. Unfortunately, some have misread a statement in Wesley's "Remarks on Mr. Hill's 'Farrago Double Distilled.'"[55] Near the end of the treatise, Wesley is astonished that Mr. Hill has determined never to use the phrase "imputed righteousness" again. Wesley shows that he has indeed taught the doctrine for nearly twenty-eight years and maintained the concept for thirty-four years. However, he goes on to note that the phrase "the imputed righteousness of Christ" (note the slightly different terminology) he never did use because it is not a scriptural term and also because he has seen too many instances when it has been abused by certain advocates. He does not explain why the doctrine is acceptable to him while the phrase is not, except for undocumented references to many instances where he has seen the phrase to be hurtful. But the section of the treatise where imputed righteousness is dealt with is sufficient to show his belief in the doctrine.

However, if we look at the doctrine in its larger context, it seems likely that Wesley's problems emerge when Calvinists combine the idea of imputation with a belief in election. If God has predetermined who will be saved, and if all such persons have been clothed in the righteousness of Christ (the eternally sinless Son of God), then it only stands to reason that their security would be eternal. By contrast, Wesley held to imputed righteousness but did not connect it with the eternal decree of God. He felt that to do so was to move in the direction of antinomianism. If we are eternally secure because of God's election, which includes the permanent imputation of Christ's righteousness,

---

[54]Sermon "The Lord Our Righteousness," *Works* (Bicentennial), 1:455.
[55]"Remarks on Mr. Hill's 'Farrago Double Distilled,'" *Works* (Jackson), 10:426–30.

then Wesley believed it was possible to "justify the grossest abominations."[56]

Being fair to the Calvinist view, no genuine Calvinist would allow for this possibility. In fact, committing gross abominations is proof positive that a person is not among the elect, no matter what he or she says to the contrary. But Wesley was not a philosophical theologian so much as a practical one, and what he observed in the eighteenth century was a host of people who used Calvinist theology to rationalize inappropriate behavior. To do this, Wesley maintained, was not to honor a doctrine of security but rather to make Christ a "minister of sin and so build on his righteousness as to live in such ungodliness and unrighteousness as is scarce named even among the Heathens."[57] It is for reasons like this that we may reasonably see the source for his not wanting to be misunderstood (or worse, hurtful) by using the phrase "the imputed righteousness of Christ."

What was the proper answer to this dilemma? Wesley believed it was to view imputed righteousness as the starting point for a life of godliness and true discipleship. When viewed juridically, it was a metaphor comparable to the bang of a judge's gavel and his words, "You are free." The words are spoken, but the declaration in and of itself does not determine the behavior that follows when the person leaves the courtroom. When viewed horticulturally, imputed righteousness is the implantation of righteousness, which requires daily nurturing if it is to continue to live.[58] Consequently, Wesley put the emphasis on imparted righteousness.

Wesley began with imputed righteousness to make clear that he was not advocating any forms of self-righteousness or works righteousness. We are made righteous with the righteousness of Christ. But this righteousness is not simply clothing in which we dress; it is an influence in which we grow. The Spirit works in us to make us righteous not in standing only, but also in actual condition and behavior—both inwardly and outwardly. He termed this real change "inherent righteousness." He viewed it "not as the ground of our acceptance with God, but as the fruit of it; not in place of imputed righteousness, but as

---

[56]"Thoughts on the Imputed Righteousness of Christ," *Works* (Jackson), 10:315.
[57]Ibid.
[58]Oden, *John Wesley's Scriptural Christianity*, 208.

consequent upon it. That is, I believe God implants righteousness in everyone whom he has imputed it."[59]

In both expressions, it is the same righteousness—the righteousness of Christ. Thus, Christ is the meritorious means of our salvation, and Christ is the influencing agent in our growth as faithful disciples. Christlikeness is the goal pursued, and Christ is the one who enables us actually to become what we profess to be. Because Wesley did not link either imputed or imparted righteousness with any notion of God's election, he connected its ongoing effects to human cooperation with the sanctifying grace of God.

Sin After Conversion

Having worked through the previous key doctrines, we are in a position to raise the question, "What about sin after conversion?" I have already made some references to the question in the section dealing with Wesley's theology of the atonement. But we still need to focus on the question because it is the perseverance *of the saints* and the eternal security *of the believer* that are the subjects of our investigation. Contained in this question are two dimensions that we must explore in relation to the subject of eternal security: the nature of sin after conversion and how such sin may lead to the loss of one's salvation.

With respect to the first issue, Wesley maintained that believers—faithful Christians who have been baptized, received new birth, and begun to walk in the life of holiness—remain subject to falling. Sin remains, but it does not reign. Wesley made a threefold distinction regarding sin in believers: the guilt, the power, and the being. Believers are delivered from the guilt and power of sin, but they are not delivered from the being of it.[60]

In other words, two things do not change after conversion. (1) The Adversary does not cease attempting to recapture the now-redeemed individual. (2) Graced-enablement, which preserved the power of choice in the unregenerate, does not take it away in the redeemed. Thus, the possibility of losing what has

---

[59]"Preface to a Treatise on Justification," *Works* (Jackson), 10:320. One of the best secondary studies of the subject of imputed and imparted righteousness is found in Coppedge, *John Wesley in Theological Debate*, 145–55.

[60]"On Sin in Believers," *Works* (Bicentennial), 1:328.

been gained remains a real possibility for the believer. This creates a healthy sense of vigil, self-examination, and believer's repentance. It is healthy because it is not a morbid fixation but rather an ongoing attentiveness that rests in the confidence that "the one who is in you is greater than the one who is in the world" (1 John 4:4).

This leads us to the second issue: how such sin can lead to the loss of salvation. In order to assess this matter properly, we must realize that in Wesley's order of salvation it is possible to depart from whatever grace God has given, because grace does not suppress free choice. But if we are growing in Christlikeness through imparted righteousness, we will also be growing in a sensitivity to movement away from God, in whatever form that movement may take. Furthermore, we are enabled by grace at any moment to repent and receive forgiveness—not the forgiveness of initial salvation but the forgiveness that sets us back on our feet and enables us to continue our journey.

In his treatise "A Call to Backsliders," Wesley alludes to Hebrews 6:4–6; 1 Timothy 1:19–20; and 2 Peter 2:20–22. Yet he says that even the kind of people described in these passages can be restored to salvation—but not apart from their maintaining a sober assessment of their true condition and making appropriate repentance.[61] So the first thing to see is that the act of committing sin is not in itself ground for the loss of salvation. Our standing with Christ and in Christ is not so fragile that a temporary lapse into sin cancels everything God has done for us up to that point. The Spirit who lives in us is the same Spirit who speaks to us regarding our departures from the way and will of God and provides the offer to repent and be restored.

The loss of salvation is much more related to experiences that are profound and prolonged. Wesley saw two primary pathways that could result in a permanent fall from grace: unconfessed sin and the actual expression of apostasy. As we will see, even these two avenues are not without restorative recourse, but they are surely to be guarded against as we grow in the grace and knowledge of our Lord and Savior Jesus Christ. To discount the possibility of either is to make us even more vulnerable to their occurrence.

---

[61]"A Call to Backsliders," *Works* (Bicentennial), 3:211–26.

For Wesley, unconfessed sin is not sin that is unknown but rather sin that is consciously held without repentance and continued without regret. Christ has broken the power of sin over us, but we have not lost the power to return to actions and attitudes that once separated us from God. This will not occur accidentally or apart from our knowledge that we are doing so, but it can happen through a misuse of our capacity to choose.

I believe Wesley was attempting to create another way to view the subject, and he developed his views (once again) in the context of controversy. He did not want to maintain the Lutheran view of *simil justus et peccator*, which seemed to him to put too little emphasis on God's power to deliver us from sin. Nor did he want to go toward the Calvinists, who made eternal security the way around the dilemma of sin after conversion. Finally, he could not follow groups like the Moravians, who were teaching "sinless perfection," in which all the remains of sin are removed in believers.

Instead, he proposed another alternative—one that differentiated between involuntary and voluntary sin. Involuntary transgressions (i.e., sins we commit without the awareness that we have done so) are not held against us by God, unless we discover them and do nothing about them. Voluntary sins—deliberate violations of known laws of God—do, however, become mortal if we do not repent of them.[62] The subject of eternal security rests (in both categories of sin) on the matter of ongoing repentance. Before we look specifically at Wesley's view of the repentance of believers, let us be clear concerning the process by which one fails to deal properly with unconfessed sin.

As long as we live in faith (i.e., in the moment-by-moment unfolding of our lives in both attitude and action), we are not committing sin. However, temptations arise. When they do, the Holy Spirit will admonish us, through a variety of means that lead to a response in our conscience, to remember that we are children of God, not children of the devil. At the point of the temptation, grace comes to provide strength to resist it. But even if we fail to appropriate such grace and commit sin, the Spirit still seeks us out to offer grace to repent and experience restoration. If we are attentive to the Spirit, we will hear the warning signals and call on grace to keep us in the faith that enables us to live as followers of Christ.

---

[62]"On Sin in Believers," *Works* (Bicentennial), 1:315.

If, however, we yield in degrees to the temptation, it will begin to be more pleasing to us. The Spirit will be grieved. Our faith will be weakened. Our love for God will cool. The Spirit will warn us more sharply, but we may persist in the downward spiral, turning further away to the point that we essentially resume a life of rebellion akin to that which we knew before we were born again. In that state, we may properly be said to have "fallen from grace."[63]

It is essential, however, to see that even when we fall *from* grace, we do not fall *beyond* grace. The seed of faith remains planted. The Spirit remains active. The seed may yet be revitalized by repentance and faith. The great privilege of those born of God is not that sin ceases to exist in them, that sin is no longer imputed to them, or that sin (after conversion) proves they were never actually converted. The "great privilege" is that, because of what God has done for us in Christ, we are no longer *bound* to sin—that is, no longer attached to it or inevitably having to commit it. This is why unconfessed sin in Wesley's theology is both so significant and so sad. It flies in the face of what God intends and what God's grace is able to prevent.

The prevention is provided through what Wesley called the repentance of believers.[64] Such repentance was not the same as the initial repentance that resulted in our justification, but there are similarities. Both deal with the acknowledgement of sin and our helplessness to change apart from grace. The difference lies in the awareness of God's willingness to forgive. Prior to conversion we repent without any previous experience of God's pardon. After conversion, our repentance is in the context of confidence that God is a forgiving God. We have tasted the grace of God, and we know it to be better than anything sin has to offer. After conversion, more than ever we see the terribleness of sin and know our need to stay away from it. No matter how much we experience the transforming grace of God, we never outgrow the need to repent, and it becomes part of our journey in the

---

[63]Wesley chronicles this erosion in detail in his sermon, "The Great Privilege of Those That Are Born of God," *Works* (Bicentennial), 1:431–43.

[64]To understand this doctrine properly, we must study both the Wesleyan view of sin in believers and repentance within the Christian life. Randy Maddox provides a good summary of these two doctrines in *Responsible Grace: John Wesley's Practical Theology* (Nashville: Kingswood, 1994), 163–66.

242 | Four Views on Eternal Security

order of salvation. We can always depart from an active appropriation of the grace we have thus far received.

At this point in the journey we are in what Wesley would call a state of "backsliding."[65] The problem for some in this condition is they think that, having sinned after their conversion, they are either unworthy or incapable of forgiveness. Wesley believed that the greater danger for backslidden believers was despair, not further decline. Believers are convicted by the Holy Spirit, as we saw above. How we interpret the conviction determines whether or not we move to repentance or to remorse. Oden captures the Wesleyan view in these words: "More sinners are destroyed by despair than presumption. Many who once fought in spiritual combat now no longer strive, feeling victory impossible to attain."[66] But the possibility of victory is always present, and God offers it to us through his continuing invitation to repent.

But what if we do not repent? What if we choose to let sin remain unconfessed? As amazing as this possibility may seem (laid alongside God's gracious offer of restoration), Wesley saw the possibility in biblical passages that spoke explicitly or implicitly of believers making "shipwreck" of their faith (1 Tim. 1:19).[67] On this he commented, "for ships once wrecked cannot afterwards be saved."[68] Yet even here he could not bring himself to discount completely the possibility of a radical intervention of God's grace (who originally created *ex nihilo* and has the capacity to do it again) breaking into even this dismantled state. In fact, when asked if he had ever seen such happen, he responded, "Yea, verily; and not one, or an hundred only, but I am persuaded, several thousands. . . . Innumerable are the instances of this kind, of those who had fallen, but now stand upright."[69] Such is Wesley's optimism of grace, to the extent that he cannot finally rule out its possible victory.

It must be pointed out that Wesley's theology of grace comes very close to being the same as eternal security; that is,

---

[65]For more on this, see Wesley's sermon, "A Call to Backsliders," *Works* (Bicentennial), 3:211–26.

[66]Oden, *John Wesley's Scriptural Christianity*, 341.

[67]Other passages include John 15:6; Rom. 11:16–22; Heb. 6:4–6; and 2 Peter 2:20.

[68]*Notes*, 1 Tim. 1:19, 774.

[69]"A Call to Backsliders," *Works* (Bicentennial), 3:224.

he can hardly imagine the possibility that grace would ever be eclipsed by human choice—particularly the choice of those who have, in fact, been Christians. Even granting this, however, it is necessary to point out the primary distinction in such optimism. It is confidence, not because of election but because of the nature and activity of grace. It is confidence, not because of God's decree but because of God's relentless pursuit of us. Despite such optimism, however, grace (as we have already said) is not irresistible. It is not automatic. It can be denied—and that everlastingly.

This brings us around again to a consideration of the "shipwreck" motif. It is a metaphor of total loss. If we continue in unconfessed sin, we move from what might be called a temporary lapse (of whatever duration) to a condition of apostasy—a state in which we calculatedly and very demonstrably choose to reject Christ and the merits of his salvation and turn to live once again by our own devices. Wesley called it renouncing the only sacrifice for sin, such that no other sacrifice remains. It is renouncing the sacrifice "by which the Son of God made a full and perfect satisfaction for the sins of the whole world."[70]

In his treatise, "Serious Thoughts upon the Perseverance of the Saints," Wesley proposes eight conditions in which we may so fall from grace as to perish everlastingly. These conditions are rooted in Scripture, and we will examine them in detail when we come to the final section of this chapter. For now, it is sufficient to show that despite his optimism of grace, he also maintained the possibility of an absolute and irrevocable fall. He concluded his treatise with this summary and warning:

> The sum of all is this: If the Scriptures are true, those who are holy or righteous in the judgment of God himself; those who are endued with the faith that purifies the heart, that produces a good conscience; those who are grafted into the good olive tree, the spiritual, invisible Church; those who are branches of the true vine, of whom Christ says, "I am the vine, ye are the branches;" those who effectually know Christ, as by that knowledge to have escaped the pollutions of this world; those who see the light of the glory of God in the face of Jesus Christ, and who have been made partakers of the Holy Ghost, of

---

[70]Ibid., 3:221.

the witness and fruits of the Spirit; those who live by faith in the Son of God; those who are sanctified by the blood of the covenant, may nevertheless so fall from God as to perish everlastingly. Therefore, let him that standeth take heed lest he fall.[71]

Such apostasy may occur in two ways. First, believers may continue to posit the intellectual belief in the salvation offered in Christ but choose to step outside it in preference to their own self-will (cf. John 3:19). This might be called rebellious apostasy. Wesley saw it expressed in Hebrews 6:4–6 and commented on it in this manner:

Here is not a supposition, but a plain relation of fact. The apostle here describes the case of those who have cast away both the power and the form of godliness; who have lost both their faith, hope and love (verse 10, &c), and that willfully (Heb. X.26). Of these willful total apostates he declares *it is impossible to renew them again to repentance* (though they were renewed once), either to the foundation or anything built thereon.[72]

But the second way is through a rejection of God's provision for salvation in Christ. This is called "sin that leads to death" (1 John 5:16). This second means of apostasy is more radical than the first. It is also less possible to be restored in this kind of apostasy, precisely because it is an act of a person to thoroughly reject God's salvation in Christ. The fact that Wesley allows this possibility among believers (yes, even among those who are sanctified), demonstrates his central conviction that perseverance is not held on the basis of God's election, but on the continuance of faith in those who have been saved. To "crucify the Son of God afresh" is not to ask him to die again for us. Rather, it is to deny that he ever did, that is, to declare his death of no account.

Before we leave this section on sin after salvation, we can do Wesley justice only if we conclude the matter where he himself concluded it. At some point in the discussion, he could not go further in describing those whom he called "children of

---

[71]"Serious Thoughts upon the Perseverance of the Saints," *Works* (Jackson), 10:298.

[72]*Notes*, Heb. 6:6, 824.

perdition." He was compelled to return to the optimism of grace
and declare that he was chiefly concerned

> for those who feel "the remembrance of our sins is
> grievous unto us, the burden of them is intolerable." We
> set before these an open door of hope: let them go in, and
> give thanks to the Lord. Let them know that "the Lord is
> gracious and merciful, longsuffering and of great good-
> ness." "Look how high the heavens are from the earth! So
> far will he set their sins from them." "He will not always
> be chiding; neither keepeth he his anger for ever." Only
> settle it in your heart, "I will give all for all," and the
> offering shall be accepted. Give him all your heart! Let all
> that is within you continually cry out, "Thou art my God,
> and I will thank thee: thou art my God, and I will praise
> thee." "This is my God for ever and ever. He shall be my
> guide even unto death."[73]

Wesley preached these words a little more than three years
before he died. They show us that despite his allowance for a
final apostasy, his heart was forever inclined toward the mercy
of God, and his appeal was for any person to respond to God's
unceasing call to be saved, even in the face of the loss itself.

Before we conclude this chapter by looking at Wesley's basis
for his position, we need to let him speak for himself in providing
a summary of all that we have said thus far. He was not unaware
of the differences between his views and those of the Calvinists.
In his treatise, "What Is an Arminian?" he provided an extended
but clear summary of five crucial differences. The first two (that
Arminians deny original sin and justification by faith) he felt
were so glaringly erroneous that they did not even merit attention. The final three differences, however, required a response,
and they formed the essence of the differentiation. He wrote:

> But there is an undeniable difference between the Calvin-
> ists and Arminians, with regard to the three other ques-
> tions. Here they divide; the former believe absolute, the
> latter only conditional predestination. The Calvinists
> hold, (1.) God has absolutely decreed, from all eternity,
> to save such and such persons, and no others; and that
> Christ died for these, and none else. The Arminians hold,

---

[73]"A Call to Backsliders," *Works* (Bicentennial), 3:226.

God has decreed, from all eternity, touching all that have the written word, "He that believeth shall be saved: He that believeth not, shall be condemned:" And in order to this, "Christ died for all, all that were dead in trespasses and sins;" that is, for every child of Adam since "in Adam all died." The Calvinists hold, Secondly, that the saving grace of God is absolutely irresistible; that no man is any more able to resist it, than to resist the stroke of lightning. The Arminians hold, that although there may be some moments wherein the grace of God acts irresistibly, yet, in general, any man may resist, and that to his eternal ruin, the grace whereby it was the will of God he should have been eternally saved. The Calvinists hold, Thirdly, that a true believer in Christ cannot possibly fall from grace. The Arminians hold that a true believer may make "shipwreck of faith and a good conscience;" that he may fall, not only foully, but finally, so as to perish for ever. Indeed, the latter two points, irresistible grace and infallible perseverance are the natural consequence of the former, of the unconditional decree. For if God has eternally and absolutely decreed to save such and such persons, it follows, both that they cannot resist his saving grace, (else they might miss salvation,) and that they cannot finally fall from grace which they cannot resist. So that, in effect, the three questions come into one, "Is predestination absolute or conditional?" The Arminians believe, it is conditional; the Calvinists, that it is absolute.[74]

THE CONSTRUCTION OF THEOLOGY

Theology cannot be chopped into pieces because to do so would be to separate it from its base. All theology rests on some foundation. It is constructed on certain presuppositions and developed in relation to particular methodologies. Having set forth the fundamental affirmations of the Wesleyan position on eternal security and the perseverance of the saints, I want to conclude this chapter with a look at Wesley's foundation for his views. I have chosen to make this the last section of the chapter because I wanted you first to see *what* Wesley believed and then move to show *how* he established his beliefs.

---

[74]"What Is an Arminian?" *Works* (Jackson), 10:359–60.

This calls for a return to the Wesleyan quadrilateral. As with the total scheme of his theology, Wesley drew from Scripture, tradition, reason, and experience in the construction of his beliefs. This final section will examine eternal security under each of those headings. For purposes of space and focus, I will concentrate on Wesley's treatise "Predestination Calmly Considered." Even though it was published in 1752 and was thus prior to certain key aspects to the Calvinist controversy, it still stands as Wesley's most thorough and thoughtful development of his position. Outler is correct in stating that the treatise established "the main lines along which the controversy would thereafter proceed."[75] Viewing this treatise through the lens of the quadrilateral will reveal more about Wesley's position and how he developed it.

Scripture

We live in an age of "free-lance" theology[76]—theology that takes something other than the Bible as its starting point and proceeds to disconnect itself from tradition in favor of contemporary experience. If we are not careful, we may lay a similar charge at Wesley's feet. In fact, some who hold other views have done so concerning him—claiming that his position is not consonant with the biblical revelation. However, this is not the case. It is clear that Wesley always sought to ground his theology in the Bible. Even if his interpretation differs from that of others, we must not make the mistake of saying that his views do not arise from Scripture and his attempt to be a serious and accurate interpreter of it. To see how he constructed his theology of eternal security and the perseverance of the saints, we begin with Scripture.

Up to now, I have made references to key passages in the Bible that Wesley used to promote his views, including his willingness to show how his interpretations differed from those of other Christians. I have done this because his references to Scripture are so frequent that any substantial attempt to exegete the

---

[75]Outler, *John Wesley*, 425.

[76]This was Robert Cushman's favorite term for describing many contemporary theologians and theologies. He meant essentially that such persons and views are disconnected from the very foundations on which good theology rests—the Bible and twenty centuries of tradition. To show my agreement with Cushman and to give him the credit for this term, I continue to use it in my writing today.

passages would take this chapter far beyond its intended bounds. However, we are at a point in the chapter where some words about his exegesis are in order. I will use his interpretation of Romans 9:21 in "Predestination Calmly Considered" as an illustration of his approach to a controversial passage.

The verse reads in Wesley's Bible, "Hath not the potter power over the clay?" Wesley's exegesis of this question includes insights into the basics of his exegetical method. (1) He compares it with another passage in Matthew 20:15 (the conclusion of the parable of the workers in the vineyard). Exegetically, he (like others of his day) often began by comparing one passage of Scripture with another. In this particular case, he connected the two verses because his Calvinist counterparts were doing so, attempting to show that they referred to divine sovereignty as it applied to reprobation. Wesley concluded that the Matthean passage has nothing to do with reprobation and therefore does not serve to shed the intended light on the Romans passage.

(2) He turns exegetically to the examination of context of Romans 9. In this case, he begins with Romans 1 and carries Paul's thought forward to the verse in question. By doing so he is able to set the passage in its largest possible context (the whole book) and to show particularly that the context for 9:21 is actually one of hope as expressed in 8:39—that nothing should be able to separate those who are in Christ Jesus from the love of God.

(3) Wesley then uses a kind of historical-critical method in his exegesis by showing how the Jews and the Gentiles would have understood Paul's words and reacted to them: The Jews would be deeply offended, and the Gentiles would be greatly encouraged. The statement in 9:21 would (for both groups) be rooted in the deep love of God, something the Jews could not see manifested to others as to themselves, and something the Gentiles would receive as incredibly good news. With respect to reprobation, neither group would have understood 9:21 that way in relation to themselves.

(4) His exegesis then turns to a detailed examination of objections. Again, this was a common method in Wesley's day, which rested on the conviction that the proper understanding of a passage is connected to a successful refutation of its inaccurate interpretations. We can see the same hermeneutic at work

in much of Wesley's preaching, when he will often end a sermon by showing how his points successfully silence his objectors.

(5) Finally, as he exegetes Romans 9:21, he comes full circle by comparing Scripture with Scripture—in this case, showing how the Bible never views one attribute of God in isolation from the others—and concluding how dangerous and misleading it is to do so. Without making a direct reference to it, this element of his exegesis also draws on extrabiblical materials, in this case a work of his own: "Thoughts upon God's Sovereignty." In doing so, we see the hermeneutical element of correlation at work in Wesley's exegesis.

It would be good if we could take all the relevant passages and show the exegetical method underlying Wesley's conclusions concerning them. But his handling of Romans 9:21 is essentially accurate in revealing the way he dealt with both data within the Bible, and outside it, in coming to his conclusions. To put it another way, we can see that he was using the same kind of exegetical methodology as those with whom he both agreed and disagreed. That is, Wesley's theological conclusions cannot be dismissed using the inaccurate view that his exegetical method was faulty.

Looking beyond his exegesis of one passage to "Predestination Calmly Considered" as a whole, we can see that Wesley basically approached the Bible in two ways. First, he cited passages he believed effectively ruled out a belief in eternal security, with its particularly unsuitable affirmation of unconditional reprobation. Regarding the passages he thought refuted an ability to reconcile reprobation with God's desire to save anyone and everyone, Wesley put forth a plethora of examples.[77] In a rapid-fire manner (with very little commentary on his part), he listed one passage after another. He concluded by saying that the citations "are but a very small part of the Scriptures which might be brought on each of these heads. But they are enough."[78] However,

---

[77]The citations refer to Gen. 3:17; 4:7; Deut. 7:9, 12; 11:26–28; 30:15–19; 2 Chron. 15:1–2; Ezra 9:13–14; Job 36:5; Ps. 145:9; Prov. 1:23–29; Isa. 6:2–5; Ezek. 18:20–23; Matt. 7:26; 11:20–24; 12:41; 13:11–12; 18:11; 22:8–9; all of chapter 25; Mark 6:15–16; Luke 19:41; John 1:29; 3:17–19; 5:34, 44; 12:47; Acts 8:20ff.; 17:24ff.; Rom. 1:20ff.; 5:18; 10:12; 14:15; 1 Cor. 8:11; 2 Cor. 5:14ff.; 2 Thess. 2:10ff.; 1 Tim. 2:3–6; 4:10; Heb. 2:9; James 1:5; 2 Peter 2:1; 3:9; 1 John 2:1–2; 4:14.

[78]"Predestination Calmly Considered," *Works* (Jackson), 10:215.

he did not limit his list to the ones referred to in the footnote. Rather, he continued the treatise for another fifty pages, virtually making the Bible the thread that held the document together. Here again is strong proof that Wesley cannot be branded as "unscriptural" in his views, even if some disavow his views.

He also used the Bible in a second way, by showing how the Calvinists had wrongly interpreted key passages.[79] He believed that the exegetical problem lay in the fact that they had separated God's attributes, focusing exclusively on sovereignty without sufficient attention to how other attributes define the whole nature of God and thus modify an election motif. He wrote that we must "never speak of the sovereignty of God but in conjunction with his other attributes. For the Scripture nowhere speaks of this single attribute as separate from the rest. Much less does it anywhere speak of the sovereignty of God as singly disposing the eternal states of men."[80]

Beyond these two ways of approaching the Scripture, Wesley made further use of the Bible in an extensive section of the treatise, demonstrating that eight categories of persons may nevertheless fall from grace: true believers, those endued with the faith that produces a good conscience, those who are grafted into the good olive tree (the church), those who are branches of Christ, those who know Christ to the extent that they have escaped the pollutions of the world, those who see the light of the glory of God in the face of Jesus Christ, those who live by faith, and those who are sanctified by the blood of the covenant.[81] By using categories of persons who were undeniably Christian, he felt that the biblical foundation was laid in a way that made a doctrine of eternal security virtually impossible to hold.

The preceding comments do not exhaust Wesley's references to the Bible in developing his views of eternal security and refuting conflicting views. But they do sufficiently demonstrate that Scripture played a foundational role in the development of his theology. Although his views never eliminated the Calvinist

---

[79]Matt. 13:15 and Rom. 9:21 served as two pivotal places where Wesley believed the Calvinists had grossly misinterpreted the Bible. He goes into detail refuting the Calvinist view and concluding that neither Jesus in the parable nor Paul in Romans had any view of God's sovereignty that led to unconditional reprobation.

[80]"Predestination Calmly Considered," *Works* (Jackson), 10:220.

[81]Ibid., 10:242–52.

view either from the theological landscape or from within early Methodism itself, he was exactly right (and on the same page as the Calvinists) when he concluded, "Therefore, Scripture alone can determine this question."[82]

Tradition

While clearly and repeatedly claiming the centrality of the Bible and his legitimate use of it, Wesley was not unaware of the role of tradition in the formation of theology in general and the doctrine of eternal security in particular. In the treatise he refers, for example, to Calvin's *Institutes*, but these references are usually quotations he uses as a basis to expound the differences between himself and his Calvinist detractors. He also refers to Isaac Watts and a lengthy quotation that Wesley uses to show how one inside the Calvinist tradition could nevertheless take issue with a strict electionist view.[83] For the most part, however, the treatise does not provide a substantial connection with the Christian tradition that preceded it. We must look outside the document to see how tradition may have informed his views.

For possible linkages, we recall that Wesley paid great attention to the early church Fathers. Chrysostom, for example, in his homily on Galatians, pointed out that Paul's blessing of grace and peace to the believers must be seen in relation to their "danger of falling from grace."[84] More powerfully to the point, however, was Wesley's use of a quotation from St. Augustine, who is generally thought of as advocating an unwavering doctrine of election. Augustine wrote, "He that made us without ourselves, will not save us without ourselves."[85] Wesley made the most of this statement, bringing the whole matter of conditional salvation to the forefront through a string of texts that he believed only confirmed what Augustine was saying.[86] Wesley

---

[82]Ibid., 10:242.

[83]Ibid., 10:226.

[84]St. John Chrysostom, "Homilies on Galatians, Ephesians, Philippians, Colossians, Thessalonians, Timothy, Titus, and Philemon," *The Nicene and Post-Nicene Fathers*, ed. Philip Schaff, vol. 13, First Series (Albany, Ore.: AGES Software, 1996–1997), 21.

[85]"On Working Out Our Own Salvation," *Works* (Bicentennial), 3:208. Augustine's original quotation was in Wesley's sermon 169, "The General Spread of the Gospel."

[86]In sequence, Acts 2:40; 1 Tim. 6:12; Luke 9:23; 13:24; 2 Peter 1:10.

concluded that God will not save us unless we cooperate with the salvation offered to us in Christ, and such cooperation must exist all along our journey with the Master.

With regard to later church history, we must mention a representative comment that Wesley made from Arminius, in the section in which he stated his view of the perseverance of the saints. Arminius wrote that the Bible allowed for the possibility of "some individuals through negligence to desert the commencement of their existence in Christ, to cleave again to the present evil world, to decline from the sound doctrine which was once delivered to them, to lose a good conscience, and to cause Divine grace to be ineffectual."[87]

However, more than scattered references against the notions of election, eternal security, and the perseverance of the saints, we must show Wesley's use of tradition to establish the core of his theology: holiness of heart and life. His identification with the holy living tradition provided the basis for his theology of grace and its attending beliefs about how it might be resisted and/or forfeited. To understand the role of tradition in Wesley's views of eternal security, we more rightly call attention to these sources than we do in referring to quotations here and there from church history. From these sources taken together, Wesley concluded that no human state is absolute—that one may lapse from grace at any stage or point.[88]

Reason

Returning to Wesley's "Predestination Calmly Considered," we may accurately take the document as a whole as an example of how he used reason to construct his views. For him, reason is no single entity. It is more properly the tapestry of clear thinking that results when the Bible, tradition, and insights from one's own time are brought together in a dynamic relationship. When viewed in this way, "Predestination Calmly Considered" becomes an example of a reasoned construction of Wesley's belief concerning eternal security.

We must also note some particular examples of sustained

---

[87]James Arminius, *The Works of James Arminius*, 3 vols. (Albany, Ore.: AGES Software, 1997), 1:229.

[88]Outler, *John Wesley*, 31–32.

reasoning that give the treatise its substance. In a lengthy section of the document, Wesley argues in a reasoned way that election (including reprobation) damages God's justice, truth, sincerity, and love. The result inescapably damages the very sovereignty the Calvinists are so intent on preserving. Again, we must remember that Wesley is able to conclude this because he cannot imagine violating one aspect of God's nature without harming another. Thus, to speak a damaging word about justice, sincerity, and love is automatically to erode a theology of sovereignty.

Following this section of the treatise, Wesley turns immediately to respond to those who object to his views. Again, with reasoned clarity (drawn from a variety of sources) he refutes these caricatures of his position: (1) that those who have any free will necessarily rob God of the total glory of salvation, (2) that he does not ascribe the whole glory of salvation to God, and (3) that God's glory is diminished unless we hold to irresistible grace. In each case he shows how his critics fail to describe his views accurately. Wesley knew there will always be those who believe differently than he did, but he wanted them to understand his position correctly and represent it to others accurately. In the context of a reasoned argument, nothing is served by misunderstanding or caricature.

Wesley then calls on his readers to put the whole issue on the table—that is, put free will on one side and reprobation on the other. Using a "both sides" examination of the doctrine of predestination, he examines how free will and reprobation play out in relation to God's wisdom, justice, and love, obviously concluding that a belief in free will is better than one in reprobation. Then, realizing that critics will call him to account for other divine attributes such as sovereignty, unchangeableness, faithfulness, and covenant, he turns to show how his beliefs uphold each of these doctrines as well.

At the end of it all, Wesley draws the razor-sharp lines of reasoning together into a single point: "I declare just what I find in the Bible, neither more nor less; namely, that it [salvation] is bought for every child of man, and actually given to every one that believeth."[89] And lest the treatise be misinterpreted as merely for the sake of debate or differentiation, he concludes the

---

[89]"Predestination Calmly Considered," *Works* (Jackson), 10:254.

work by appealing to all sides to devote themselves to one common goal: "to assist each other to value more and more the glorious grace whereby we stand, and daily to grow in that grace and in the knowledge of our Lord Jesus Christ."[90]

Experience

Although it may be properly said that "Predestination Calmly Considered" is not a grand illustration of Wesley's use of experience in formulating his theology, nevertheless it is not devoid of it. Contained within his use of Scripture, tradition, and reason are explicit and implicit references to the actual experiences of people of faith from Old Testament times to Wesley's own day. And the final sentence quoted above is one way to show that in the actual experience of the body of Christ, Wesley wanted to join forces with all true Christians to work with people in ways that enabled them to grow daily in the grace and knowledge of Jesus Christ. For him, this was the ultimate experience.

This is why so many of his subsequent interpreters have used terms like "folk theologian" to describe him and phrases like "practical divinity" to understand his system best. And it is why, in the final analysis, after it was clear that the controversy with the Calvinists would not be fully and finally resolved through reasoned debate alone, he began to publish *The Arminian Magazine*. Despite the shortcomings of the journal, which we spoke of earlier in the chapter, it was Wesley's way of recognizing that experience (i.e., experience resting on faith, not creating it) must be included to show that what he had believed and taught for more than fifty years was, in fact, what people were finding in their relationship with God. He could never be content with "dangling belief" but only with what clearly proved itself in the lives of real people.

THE CONCLUSION OF THEOLOGY

Theology cannot be chopped into pieces, because to do so is to destroy it. Theology is a living thing—given to us by a living God for the sole purpose of effecting the life of Christ within us. It can never be exclusively speculative or even largely philo-

---

[90]Ibid., 10:259.

sophical. When God chose to make the ultimate demonstration of the divine nature and will, "the Word became flesh and made his dwelling among us ... full of grace and truth" (John 1:14).

For Wesley, true theology must become "flesh" through the proper interpretation of the Bible and through the lived witness of all who seek to live by its revelation. In that regard, he remained steadfast in his conviction that his view of eternal security held the divine-human relationship in a better dynamism than did the Calvinist doctrine of eternal security. Despite those who fervently disagreed with him, he continued to maintain his conviction to the end of his life. In doing so, he left to the larger and subsequent Wesleyan tradition one of the clearest expressions of his theology.

A CLASSICAL CALVINIST RESPONSE TO STEVE HARPER

Michael S. Horton

It was a pleasure to read Steve Harper's contribution. Just as Stephen Ashby has challenged us to take a closer look at Arminius in his own words without reading later Arminianism back into his thought, Steve Harper thinks we should take a second look at that later development in John Wesley as we seek to answer this important question. His irenic posture enables him to engage with critics in a fair-minded and constructive manner.

It is undoubtedly true that a certain set of caricatures of Arminianism circulates in Calvinistic circles from time to time. This is partly due to the fact that the Arminianism some Calvinists have encountered and perhaps even embraced in the past actually held positions that Wesley, for instance, would never have countenanced. As an elementary student at a Pentecostal school, I was taught that if I were returning home from school entertaining a lewd thought and happened to be hit by a car before I had time to confess it, I would be damned. Experiences such as these are myriad, and I can see how they can be logical conclusions from the Wesleyan Arminian scheme. But the way our views are represented on the street certainly does not always conform to the way they actually appear in our formal theologies. Harper helpfully reminds us of the latter with respect to his own tradition.

Calvinists should recognize that Arminians are not Pelagians. (My own view is that the various dominant "Arminianisms" usually fall somewhere between semi-Pelagian and semi-Augustinian views.) That is to say, Arminian theology insists on the seriousness of the condition of sin and the necessity of grace before human beings can move in the direction of God. Prevenient grace is a central category in Wesleyan theology, as it was in Arminius's work. However inconsistent we believe our Arminian brothers and sisters to be in working it out, we have to take them at their word: Grace is necessary for salvation.

At the same time, Roman Catholic and Eastern Orthodox theologies have also insisted on the necessity of grace. It was grace *alone*, not grace in and of itself, that was the battle cry of the Reformation. Here is where the Calvinist and Arminian understandings of salvation become incommensurable. Harper explains:

> For Wesley, a proper understanding of grace begins in God's ultimate intent, expressed through this unchangeable fact: "He that believeth shall be saved; he that believeth not shall be damned." God sovereignly establishes the way of salvation. Nothing supersedes it, and no one can resist it. However, this saving intention is not initiated or maintained by election, but rather by God's judgment as to whether or not a person has met the condition for salvation—that is, faith in the Lord Jesus Christ. . . . This perspective understands God's sovereignty more in terms of governance, not of predeterminism.

Calvinists heartily concur with the importance of Jesus' statement of the case that Harper cites. Yet they cannot resist (!) the impression that Arminianism, at least theoretically, leads believers away from resting in God alone and his saving work in Christ alone. To say that God's "saving intention is not initiated or maintained by election" but by "whether or not a person has met the conditions for salvation" seems to me to be the same as saying that salvation is initiated and maintained by us rather than by God.

One thing that the Arminian doctrine of prevenient grace does is to allow advocates to hold as strong a view of total depravity as any Calvinist without having to say that the unregenerate are right now in that condition. As Harper puts it, "prevenient grace prevents the Fall from being so *intensive* that even the ability to respond is lost." In this scenario, then, one can say that unbelievers are able, of their own free will, to accept or reject God's forgiveness without saying that this is done apart from grace.

The question, of course, is whether Scripture does in fact teach that (1) the unregenerate are universally able now to respond affirmatively and (2) those who do come to Christ do so without any other grace than that with which God has also favored every other person. Scripture represents believers as having at one time been "dead in . . . transgressions and sins," hostile to the things of God, and unable to seek or even comprehend saving truth until God makes them alive (Eph. 2:1–5). Given this, it seems that we are faced with a dilemma: Either all people are alive in Christ or Scripture exaggerates the reality of the sinful condition prior to regeneration.

In both Ashby's and Harper's chapters, the atonement receives a large place, and that is as it should be. We cannot talk about the believer's assurance and security apart from the cross of Christ. Harper shows Wesley's affirmation of the substitutionary view of the atonement, but with a Wesleyan twist: "His substitutionary death for our sins totally accomplishes our deliverance, *but the efficacy of that deliverance must include our ongoing appropriation of it*" (italics added). Although Wesley accepts the evangelical doctrine of the atonement, "it is true that on another front he deals with penal substitution differently from his Reformed friends."

> In fact . . . Wesley does not place the substitutionary element primarily within a legal framework. Christ's satisfaction of God's demand for justice is not the satisfaction of a demand based on an eternal and unchangeable decree. Rather, it is the justice that resides in God's own nature— that is, the need to bring into proper relationship the "justice" between God's love for persons and God's hatred of sin. . . . It is not the satisfaction of a legal demand for justice so much as it is an act of mediated reconciliation.

As with many challenges to a forensic understanding of the cross and justification, this construction appears to me to rest on a false antithesis. Legal justice and mediated reconciliation are hardly alternatives, at least in Scripture. Harper himself seems unsure about this in the above quote. He refers on the one hand to "Christ's satisfaction of God's demand for justice" and on the other hand concludes, "It is not the satisfaction of a legal demand for justice so much as it is an act of mediated reconciliation."

As for the antithesis between "the satisfaction of a demand based on an eternal decree" versus the satisfaction of a loving God's justice, I can only respond that Reformed theology does not conflate predestination and the cross. In other words, the legal demand for justice is not anchored in election per se but in the divine nature (precisely what Harper argues). Election is the decision of God to select out of the "children of wrath" a great family who, though justly condemned, will be reconciled to him because at the cross he was able to reconcile his love and his justice in Christ's sacrifice.

As recent Old Testament scholarship has demonstrated, redemptive revelation takes place in the context of a covenant—more specifically, a suzerainty treaty. It is a legal arrangement, with a historical prologue, stipulations, and the announcement of sanctions (blessing and curse). It was on this constitutional basis that the prophets were God's prosecuting attorneys to arraign God's people. Far from being an imported category from Roman jurisprudence, this "Hear, O Israel, the Lord has a charge to bring against you" is legal to the core, as is the announcement of what God will do to deliver his people. But to set the legal and relational aspects against each other is to violate that covenantal structure. Without God's covenantal justice being satisfied, there is no possibility of a redemptive relationship with God.

Harper next turns to the "appropriation" of Christ's benefits to the believer. Reformed theology has preferred the term *application* to the term *appropriation*, owing, of course, to its monergism, as this is represented in Scripture. Apart from the Holy Spirit's work of applying the benefits of Christ's active and passive obedience as well as his resurrection, those benefits would remain external to us. While sinners turn to Christ in repentance and faith, this free decision is the result of God's work (application), not our work (appropriation).

Harper gets to the point: "While not minimizing the many elements that figure into the discussion, the simple difference between Wesley and his Calvinist friends lies at this very point: A Calvinistic view of appropriation rests on the basis of decree (predestination), and Wesley's view of appropriation rests on the basis of choice (graced-enablement)." But when God so frequently declares that the Spirit gives repentance and faith to the elect and that this grace is anchored in an eternal and unchangeable decree, we are not permitted to rest our salvation on our action—even if it is "grace-enabled." Harper is correct, therefore, in identifying the two radically different bases of the Christian confidence.

It is not the graciousness of grace that Wesley and his followers object to, Harper says, but the issue of its irresistibility. Resistible grace means that "its effectiveness is dependent on human cooperation." Traditional evangelical theology has held that faith is the instrument of justification—only those who believe are justified. God does not believe for us; it is a genuine human response to God's act in Christ. Nevertheless, the effectual cause of regeneration and the faith that receives is God alone. "Appropriation" transforms faith into an active rather than passive instrument. We confess that while sinners must "accept this gift of God with a believing heart," "it is not because of any value my faith has that God is pleased with me. Only Christ's satisfaction, righteousness, and holiness make me right with God."[1] From the Reformed point of view, Arminian theology compromises the gospel by making human response "effectual" rather than receptive. Therefore, it risks its stated commitment to Christ's work as the only sufficient ground and the Spirit's work as the only efficient cause of human redemption.

Ashby has already cited a number of references from Wesley and subsequent Arminian theology that directly challenge the classic evangelical doctrines of grace, atonement, and justification. Harper appears to justify this concern especially in his discussion of justification:

> Justification is not falsification or fantasy but is again the mysterious and marvelous blending of imputed and imparted righteousness. God can authentically justify us because of Christ, and because of Christ we are *being transformed* from one degree of glory to another. And because justification is viewed by Wesley as initial sanctification, it is also the ongoing means by which God pardons and forgives us.

---

[1]The Heidelberg Catechism, *Ecumenical Creeds and Reformed Confessions* (Grand Rapids: Christian Reformed Board of Publications, 1979), Lord's Day 23, Q. 60–61.

This quote illustrates the problem with Wesleyan "prevenient grace." As Harper reiterates throughout his paper, grace makes human decision for Christ possible. The atonement of Christ makes salvation possible; our faith makes it effective. Yet this is not to say "God saved me." It is to say instead that I could not have done the thing that saved me apart from God's clearing away the obstacles. Standing in a neutral position (by prevenient grace), capable of going either way, I decided to accept Christ. In normal conversation, we do not ordinarily allow the sentence, "I made such-and-such possible" to be equivalent to the sentence, "I did such-and-such." If the effectiveness (not merely the reception) of redemption is at any point ascribed to human action, then salvation cannot be said to rest entirely on God's work and Christ's merit.

Harper claims that Wesley held to imputation just as the Reformed understand it. "However, as time moved on and Wesley saw increasing misuse and abuse of 'imputation' language, he decided not to use it anymore." Even if Wesley, as Harper argues, was dissuaded from using this term because of what he perceived as Reformed antinomianism, the reticence to use "imputation" in reference to justification in fact substitutes a Roman Catholic for an evangelical doctrine of justification. As is well known, the Council of Trent, while clearly affirming the importance and necessity of grace, confused justification and sanctification—God's external, objective declaration and his internal, subjective application of that declaration.

Harper reasons, "if we are eternally secure because of God's election, which includes the permanent imputation of Christ's righteousness, then Wesley believed it was possible to 'justify the grossest abominations.'" This concern was anticipated by Paul's famous rhetorical question: "Shall we go on sinning so that grace may increase?" (Rom. 6:1). His resounding "By no means!" rests not on the believer's victory over sin but on Christ's victory applied to believers in their baptism into Christ (6:2–23). Harper emphasizes that Wesley was above all a practical theologian, and this may account for his aversion to classical evangelical categories at times. But should we not at least try to do theology on the basis of texts rather than on the basis of our own fears of what such teaching may lead to or how it might be abused?

If Scripture assures us that "we are eternally secure because of God's election, which includes the permanent imputation of Christ's righteousness," who are we to say that this should not be widely confessed and proclaimed simply because we are afraid that it will be taken the wrong way by some? The fact that Paul felt that he had to address this wrong conclusion in Romans 6:1 indicates that his argument to that point might occasion it. D. Martyn Lloyd-Jones used to say, on the basis of this passage, that if our hearers do not ask that question, we have probably not really preached the gospel. It would seem that Wesley did not even want that question to arise, so he curtailed the graciousness of grace.

The Reformed suspicion that Wesleyan theology confuses justification and sanctification is justified by Harper's explanation: "When viewed horticulturally, imputed righteousness is the implantation of righteousness, which requires daily nurturing if it is to continue to live. Consequently, Wesley put the emphasis on imparted righteousness." Again, it is difficult to see how this represents an evangelical rather than a Roman Catholic understanding of justification. If justification is an impartation of righteousness or the implantation of righteousness, then it is not an imputed righteousness. This was the issue of the Reformation: whether justification (unlike sanctification) was a once-and-for-all imputation of righteousness or a regeneration and progressive Christlikeness.

Reformed theology emphasizes the reality of the new birth and God's persevering grace in sanctification, in contrast to the view represented by Norman Geisler. Because both are God's works (for us and in us), we maintain that external justification and internal renewal are inseparable yet distinguishable. But from the subsequent citations that Harper makes from Wesley, one may be inclined to think that Wesley distinguishes imputed (justification) and imparted (sanctification) righteousness more clearly and sharply than does Harper. Like the Christological controversies, the debate over the relation of justification and sanctification is best settled by affirming that these realities, like Christ's two natures, are inseparably united without being confused. Confusing justification and sanctification appears to Calvinists to be a typical mistake of Wesleyan Arminian theology, preaching, and praxis.

Given the foregoing premises, it is not surprising that "Wesley saw two primary pathways that could result in a permanent fall from grace: unconfessed sin and the actual expression of apostasy." Here we see an indication of the insecurity of believers in the Wesleyan system. Ashby offers convincing evidence that Arminius himself limited the possibility of falling away to apostasy. (Indeed, original Arminianism left a question mark over the possibility of losing salvation.) This is true also of Lutheran theology. The covenantal approach of Reformed theology takes apostasy seriously without throwing the believer's perseverance into doubt.

However, once moral failure is seen as a source of a loss of salvation, the believer is left in much the same existential situation as the medieval monk Martin Luther before the sheer freeness of the gospel dawned on him. Harper even calls unconfessed sin "mortal sin," invoking the mortal/venial categories of Roman Catholic penance. One's experience of standing in grace is easily compromised in this scheme, as it was for me in the Pentecostal school to which I referred at the beginning of this response.

More important, the objective and definitive character of Christ's saving work is compromised if God's wrath against sin is finally satisfied, not only by Christ's obedience but also by that of weak and sinful Christians. So what about those who go on in voluntary sin without repentance? Ironically, the "eternal security" position outlined by Geisler (and more radically, by Charles Stanley, Zane Hodges, and Charles Ryrie) and the position of Wesley and Harper share the belief that this condition can be true of a regenerate Christian. They also agree that even in those who fall away, "the seed of faith remains planted. The Spirit remains active. The seed may yet be revitalized by repentance and faith." Both, then, hold that a "backslidden" Christian's faith and repentance may become dormant and unproductive—yet not outside of God's grace in some sense. The difference between these views is that the former maintains that such a believer forfeits only rewards, while the latter maintains that he or she forfeits salvation (at least until repentance is renewed).

Reformed theology, by contrast, holds that this does not describe a genuine believer at all but merely one who professes faith and belongs to Christ, his covenant, and his community externally. Genuine believers cannot become dormant, having "been born again, not of perishable seed, but of imperishable, through the living and enduring word of God" (1 Peter 1:23). Thus, we would encourage the sort of preaching that announces to the church, "You have been born of imperishable seed. You have been baptized. However deeply you will struggle with doubt and sin, you will never return to Egypt because God has delivered you." This seems to be more biblical and gospel-driven than inspiring believers with the fear of losing reward or salvation. The New Testament warnings based on the distinction between those who are physical descendents of the covenant community and those who are also true children of Abraham by faith plays a large role in our interpretation.

In Harper's view, Wesley "did not want to maintain the Lutheran view of *simil justus et peccator*, which seemed to him to put too little emphasis on God's power to deliver us from sin." Again, it would appear that—at least in Harper's construction (which confirms my own reading of Wesley)—reaction to practical circumstances is Wesley's driving motive. It is certainly true that in many of our Lutheran and Reformed circles "simultaneously justified and sinful" sometimes becomes the only category for understanding the Christian life. But surely this is corrected, for instance, by the fact that Paul's discussion moves from total depravity and human helplessness, to justification by grace alone through faith in Christ alone, to the reality of the new life we have in Christ.

While evangelical theology sometimes fails to regard Romans 6 as definitive of Christian existence as Romans 7, Wesley's rejection of *simul justus et peccator* represents a one-sided emphasis on the former at the expense of the latter. "So long as we live in faith ... we are not committing sin," says Harper. But does this not trivialize both faith and sin? If grace is greater than our sin and "in this life even the holiest have only a small beginning of this obedience,"[2] we must live with the paradox that Scripture describes so realistically. Is it not the measure of faith's greatness (or better yet, God's) that it is not ultimately threatened by the believer's enemies but rather overcomes the world? It is at least the attempt of Reformed theology to do equal justice to the reality of the new birth and the reality of indwelling sin.

---

[2]Ibid., Lord's Day 44, Q. 114.

Because of the truth of Romans 6, there can be no such thing as a "carnal Christian"—someone who is justified but is dormant in sanctification. (Ironically, both dispensationalists and Wesleyans seem to embrace a view of justification and sanctification in terms of two different stages requiring separate acts of faith.) Justified sinners are sinners who are alive in Christ. While justifying faith is only passive and receptive, its essence is immediately to set about finding good works to do for God's glory and the neighbor's good. Any other kind of "faith" is something other than true faith. Yet, while this accounts for the believer's constant striving to mortify sin, the weakness of the believer's faith, hope, and love throughout the Christian life bar any expectation of perfection—even "perfect love"—this side of the anxiously anticipated next stage of our redemption: glorification.

Some concluding observations may be offered, although in this space we cannot do justice to the arguments that Harper raises. First, he points up Wesley's exegesis of Romans 9, a classic Calvinist text. At the center of Wesley's criticism of Reformed exegesis is the concern that the latter abstracts God's sovereignty from his other attributes. I have seen this done in Calvinistic circles from time to time, just as I have seen (more often) the abstraction of God's love from his other attributes in Arminian preaching. But in terms of typical Reformed theology and exegesis, commitment to divine simplicity constrains this temptation.

God's love is essential to his being, while showing mercy in a particular situation is not. Otherwise, it would not be mercy—dependent on God's freedom—but would be necessary. God's justice is essential to his being, while his wrath against sinners is not. In Christ he has freely chosen to save sinners from his wrath, but he cannot freely choose to act contrary to his justice. God's sovereignty is essential to his being, while election (contra Barth) is not. God shows wrath and even a just hatred of sinners because that which is essential to God's nature requires it. One cannot use God's love as a means of neutralizing a statement such as "Jacob I loved, but Esau I hated" (Rom. 9:13). God would be love even if he did not elect anyone from the rebel race that he created as the mirror of his holiness. Marvelously, God cannot help being love, but he is not thereby bound to show only love to everyone, as numerous texts witness.

266 | Four Views on Eternal Security

Wesley rejected the clear biblical teaching that God chooses not only a way of redemption but particular sinners to redeem—even "before [they] were born or had done anything good or bad—in order that God's purpose in election might stand" (Rom. 9:11). By so doing, Wesley grounded the actual salvation of individuals in the human rather than the divine will. Election is simply God's choice of a plan in which whoever believes will be saved. Yet Scripture indicates that God "chose us in [Christ] before the creation of the world" (Eph. 1:4), not merely a plan. "Those he predestined, he also called" (Rom. 8:30), and so forth.

It does not matter whether we can figure it out or whether it offends our moral sense, as Romans 9 clearly asserts. God is free to be God—merciful to the elect and just to the rest. Although he does not take pleasure in the death of the wicked (Ezek. 18:32), God is glorified in both ends (Prov. 16:4; Rom. 9:14–25). And while we are forbidden to probe God's secrets, we have reason enough to conclude with Paul's exultation in Romans 11:34–35:

> "Who has known the mind of the Lord?
>   Or who has been his counselor?"
> "Who has ever given to God,
>   that God should repay him?"
> For from him and through him and to him are all things.
>   To him be the glory forever! Amen.

A MODERATE CALVINIST RESPONSE TO STEVE HARPER

Norman L. Geisler

AREAS OF AGREEMENT

Although Moderate Calvinism rejects the central thesis of Wesleyan Arminianism, there are, nonetheless, a number of common features between the views. First of all, we agree that each doctrine must fit consistently into an overall theological system. In the context of eternal security, this is particularly true with regard to one's view of God and of human free choice. These must be kept in harmony.

Further, we agree that humans are not robots or puppets but are free in a libertarian sense that they could have done otherwise. That is, they have the power of contrary choice in relation to accepting or rejecting God's gift of salvation.

Of course, we have this power, like everything else, by the grace of God. We agree that grace is a radical gift that is wholly unmerited by us.

What is more, we concur that human beings do not have any "natural" free will that can attain salvation, unaided by God's grace. The first move in salvation is God's, not ours. We love him because he first loved us.

In addition, we agree that fallen humanity is utterly incapable of doing any spiritual good on its own. Thus, Pelagianism is wrong. However, the Fall is not intensive but extensive. As a result, even in this fallen state, the unbeliever, by God's grace, is capable of recognizing and responding to God's offer of salvation. We also agree with Augustine's statement cited that "he who made us without ourselves, will not save us without ourselves."

We also concur that God's grace is not irresistible on the unwilling. God does not force anyone to believe. Acceptance or rejection of the gospel is a free act. Indeed, we agree that the concept of irresistible grace produces a deficient anthropology. At least the two go hand in hand, whichever produces the other.

Furthermore, Moderate Calvinists agree with Wesleyans that the atonement is not limited. God loves all in a saving way, and Christ died for all human beings, not just for the elect. Salvation is for everyone who believes. In short, God is truly omnibenevolent.

We also believe with Wesleyans that Christ died for our present as well as our past sins. It is, however, difficult to see how Wesleyans reconcile this with their belief that salvation can be lost, since Christ died for all our sins before we had committed any of them, including those alleged to precipitate the loss of salvation.

Another point of agreement is that strong Calvinists are wrong in assuming that something is true because it brings more glory to God. This is an error called theologism, and it is akin with the error of voluntarism—that something is good simply because God wills it rather than God's willing something because it is good, in accordance with his unchangeable nature.

Regarding the nature of faith, we also agree that saving faith is more than intellectual assent; it involves the heart's trust. The disagreement comes in the Wesleyan claim that those who truly have saving faith can ever lose their salvation. We hold, contrary to the free grace view, that those who turn away from the faith never had true saving faith to begin with but possessed merely nominal faith or intellectual assent.

There is also agreement that a mere act of sinning is not the ground for the loss of salvation. Salvation is not here today and gone tomorrow. However, not all Wesleyans seem to agree with this in practice, since their insecurity regarding salvation often seems to be connected with a now-I-have-it and now-I-don't attitude. Indeed, statements such as the following reinforce that notion: "Involuntary transgressions (i.e., sins we commit without the awareness that we have done so) are not held against us by God, unless we discover them and do nothing about them. Voluntary sins—deliberate violations of known laws of God—do, however, become mortal if we do not repent of them."

With the Wesleyans, we also reject strong Calvinism's separation of God's attributes—it focuses on sovereignty to the neglect of others. This neglect, we may add, extends to strong Calvinism's view of human beings who for all practical purposes are deprived of truly free choice.

Finally, we concur that "Scripture alone can determine this question." We have endeavored to show in our chapter that Scripture supports the Moderate Calvinist's view. However, we fail to see how the Bible upholds the view that salvation, which is the work of God from beginning to end, can ever be lost.

AREAS OF DISAGREEMENT

Contrary to the implication of the Wesleyan claim, not all views can be true. Some clear contradictions exist between the views, and contradictory positions cannot both be true. For example, a true believer either can or cannot lose his salvation, but not both.

Further, it appears to be inconsistent to claim, on one hand, that tradition, reason, and experience, along with Scripture, are parts of the basis for a doctrine, and yet on the other hand, to maintain that the Bible "alone" is the sole basis for doctrine. It often appears to a Calvinist that Arminians interpret the Scripture by their experience rather than understanding their experience in the light of the Scripture.

In addition, as we argued in our chapter, neither Scripture nor logic demands that the choice to reverse our salvation exists after conversion. The Bible declares that the choice for salvation was final, and sound reason shows how this can be so, with God prompting, confirming, and supporting our free choice.

Further, it is inconsistent for Wesleyans to use Hebrews 6 to prove believers can lose their salvation and yet believe they will gain it back, since the text says "it is impossible" to renew such a one to repentance (Heb. 6:4–8).

Furthermore, the belief in eternal security, as held by the Moderate Calvinism defended here, does not make it possible to justify the grossest sins. For we hold that a true believer who so sins will be disciplined by God and lose his or her rewards (1 Cor. 3; Heb. 12). Moreover, anyone who continues in sin was not a true believer to begin with (1 John 2:19; 3:9).

What is more, as noted earlier, predestination is not conditional, as Wesleyans claim. God gives saving grace unconditionally (Rom. 11:29). The only condition is for our receiving it, not for God's giving it.

Finally, contrary to Wesleyan claims, God would not be unjust in sending all to hell, for all have sinned and deserve it. But contrary to strong Calvinists, while there is nothing in fallen humanity that demands God not justly condemning them, nevertheless, there is something in God that prompts him to attempt to save all of them (namely, his omnibenevolence).

SOME CONCLUDING CONTRASTS

In summation, the Arminian does not altogether understand omnibenevolence, and the strong Calvinist denies omnibenevolence altogether. For the Arminian believes that God gives his love to all, but not unconditionally. The strong Calvinist believes that God has unconditional love but does not give it to all. Moderate Calvinists, however, affirm that God offers his unconditional love to all, and those who receive it by faith are never separated from it (Rom. 8:38–39); they are eternally secure.

Further, Arminians assert that God's love is only persuasive but not irresistible. Strong Calvinists believe God's love is irresistible on the unwilling. Moderate Calvinists, however, affirm that God's love is irresistible only on the willing. For God's love never works coercively, even though it works effectively and eternally.

In the final analysis, strong Calvinists affirm God's complete sovereignty but deny humanity's complete freedom. Arminians affirm humanity's complete freedom but deny God's complete sovereignty. Moderate Calvinists, however, affirm both God's complete sovereignty and humanity's complete freedom.

As for confidence in our salvation, strong Calvinists have eternal security but no present assurance. Arminians have present assurance but no eternal security. Moderate Calvinists, however, possess both present assurance and eternal security—the best both now and forever more.

A REFORMED ARMINIAN RESPONSE TO STEVE HARPER

Stephen M. Ashby

Dr. Steve Harper has endeavored to present the Wesleyan view by setting forth John Wesley as his primary spokesperson rather than by examining later luminaries of the Wesleyan theological perspective. Harper is certainly correct when he says regarding Wesley studies that "one of the problems in doing theological study is that the primary spokespersons can easily get lost or misrepresented by their 'interpreters.' ... [Hence] we must read the words of the primary person before we use the words of subsequent interpreters to color (or cloud) our thinking." Harper's approach to Wesley is a noble undertaking. One might only wish that this approach would not be so rare when Wesleyan theologians deal with the writings and ideas of Arminius.

Harper is also right to point out that Wesley's use of the term *Arminian*, for example in his *Arminian Magazine*, "erroneously made it appear that Arminius was a more substantial theological source than he actually was.... John Wesley was a 'Church of England man.'" Unfortunately, this misunderstanding has had a far-ranging effect on the history of Protestant theology, since people have typically set forth Wesleyan thought as being Arminian while never actually reading Arminius. Perhaps some "Phase 3" Arminius studies are needed.

Harper is correct to point out the areas where Calvinists and Arminians agree. He says, for example, "First, we all agree on the sovereignty of God.... For all Christians, 'God's *fundamental* designs of creation and redemption cannot be finally frustrated.'" This statement provides a needed corrective, given the emphasis of some Calvinists who apparently think that Arminians do not believe in the sovereignty of God. Further, as I said in my chapter, Reformed Arminians stand with traditional Wesleyans on their disagreements with Calvinistic views regarding particular grace and predestination. We agree with Wesleyans on conditional election, the universality of the atonement, the resistibility of grace, and the possibility of apostasy. Finally, Harper is on the right track when he says that "we agree that equally genuine and devout Christians may nevertheless disagree on the matter of eternal security and the perseverance of the saints, [or] to restate Wesley's words ... we agree that 'wise and holy men' stand on different sides of this issue."

SOME TENSIONS EMERGE

Despite the common ground that Reformed Arminians and Wesleyans share, many subtle and also not-so-subtle differences emerge between my treatment of the subject and Professor Harper's. These differences belie the tensions that have always inhered in Wesleyan thought.

In their view of depravity and human inability, for example, Wesleyans have always struggled with a tension between semi-Pelagianism and a more Augustinian approach to this subject, albeit the vast sweep of Wesleyan theology over the past two centuries has tended toward the former. Harper exemplifies this tension. While he, like Wesley, commendably tries to distance himself from notions of "natural free will," seeking to avoid outright Pelagianism, he moves away from that commitment in statements like the following:

> Prevenient grace literally means the "grace that comes before." Before what? Before our first conscious awareness of God's existence or God's love. ... First, it is grace that "prevents." But what does it prevent? The absolute, "tee-total depravity" of the human being ... [it] prevents the Fall from being so *intensive* that even the ability to respond is lost.

I have no problem with differentiating between *intensive* and *extensive*, as both Harper and Geisler do. We are not *abso-

lutely depraved; our every act is not as bad as it could possibly be. However, I must emphatically state that the Fall *does* render us *unable to respond rightly* to God. Fallen humanity is always responding to God *wrongly*. Reformed Arminians differ from Wesleyans in our understanding of prevenient grace. It is not like a dense fog settling over a city in which everyone equally shares, hence, canceling out the effects of the Fall for all of humanity. Rather, it is individually directed and brings with it God's enablement as he draws human beings to himself. Though Reformed Arminians insist that God universally provides his salvific grace, they at the same time resist the notion that prevenient grace reverses the effects of the Fall. Rather, such grace, though universal in scope, acts in enablement and drawing on an individual human level.

This same problem is seen in Harper's statement that "by gracious provision, *human nature is preserved*, including the necessary capacity to recognize and respond to God—or to refuse to do so" (italics added). According to this Wesleyan approach, God's prevenient grace is scattergun, undoing the effects of the Fall. Given this approach, it does not sound like the Fall at all—rather, a slip. One is not rendered unable to please God, merely infirmed. One is not left blinded by sin—just confused. From this Reformed Arminians respectfully demur. Instead, because of the Fall, human beings are lost, blind, dead, and hardened against God. So, with Arminius and in the words of Christ himself, "Without me [Christ] you can do nothing."

A MISREADING OF WESLEY?

Another area of divergence between Reformed Arminians and Wesleyans centers on the atonement. While Wesley held a view of atonement that was unique to him, most Wesleyans have, more consistently, held a governmental view of the atonement. Harper correctly shows that Wesley held a modified penal substitution view. Yet I find it a sad omission by Harper that he vaguely alludes to "some [who] have mistakenly concluded that Wesley modified the classic penal substitution theory by holding to a belief that Christ atoned only for the believer's past sins, not for the *condition of sin* (original sin) or for sins committed by believers after their conversion." I wish he had openly identified those individuals. I would have certainly congratulated them. Indeed, *it is not they but he who misreads Wesley*. Harper says:

> This error springs from a misreading of two statements in Wesley's writings. The first misreading occurs in "A Dialogue Between an Antinomian and His Friend," in which Wesley (the friend) replies to the Antinomian: "Did he then heal the wound before it was made and put an end to our sins before they had a beginning? This is so glaring, palpable an absurdity, that I cannot conceive how you can swallow it."

Harper goes on to comment:

> But such a false reading is quickly seen if the statement is placed in its context. For just before it, Wesley affirms that Christ died to "take away, put an end to, blot out, and utterly destroy *all our sins for ever*" [italics Harper's]. There is no distinction between past, present, and future sinfulness. . . . Perhaps most unfortunate is the fact that this misreading leaves open the question of what kind of "atonement" is required and/or sufficient for sins that believers commit after their conversion. Or to say it more clearly, nothing in Wesley's writings supposes anything other than the all-sufficiency of Christ (through his atoning death on the cross) for our redemption from whatever condition, expression, or timing of sin.

Respectfully, I must insist that Professor Harper is the one who misreads Wesley here. Harper says that the supposed "false reading is quickly seen if the statement is placed in its context." So it would behoove us to look at the context.

> Ant.[inomian]—Do you believe, then, that the "whole work of man's salvation was accomplished by Jesus Christ on the cross?"
>
> Friend.—I believe, that, by that one offering, he made a full satisfaction for the sins of the whole world.
>
> Ant.—But do you believe that "Christ's blood and our sins went away together?"
>
> Friend.—To say the truth, I do not understand it.
>
> Ant.—No! Why, did not Christ, "when he was upon the cross, take away, put an end to, blot out, and utterly destroy, all our sins for ever?"

Friend.—He did then pay the price, for the sake of which, all who truly believe in him are now saved from their sins; and, if they endure to the end, shall be saved everlastingly. Is this what you mean?

Ant.—I mean, He did then "heal, take away, put an end to, and utterly destroy, all our sins."

Friend.—Did he then heal the wound before it was made, and put an end to our sins before they had a beginning? This is so glaring, palpable an absurdity, that I cannot conceive how you can swallow it.[1]

Who is the real misreader of Wesley here? A casual reading of this passage shows that it completely undercuts Harper's point and makes mine. Wesley held that only the believer's past sins are atoned for. It is *not Wesley* but the Antinomian who says *twice* that the atonement utterly destroys all our sins forever. Wesley disagrees with not only those statements but also the Antinomian's belief that "Christ's blood and our sins went away together" (*this* is the Reformed view of imputation).

Harper goes to great lengths to mitigate Wesley's clear-cut views on this subject. He does this by claiming that interpreters like me are "misreading" Wesley. However, Harper misreads him drastically. In fact, his misreading reinforces the Reformed Arminian's point. Wesley did *not* subscribe to the Reformed view that through the believer's identification with the atonement of Christ, the condition of sin, not just past sins, is atoned for, indeed, remitted, and so the atonement does not have to be reappropriated every time a believer sins and gets forgiveness.

We see Harper's own tension on this point in another place where he says that Christ's atonement "totally accomplishes our deliverance, but the efficacy of that deliverance must include our ongoing appropriation of it." What does this mean? Harper goes on to define this appropriation as "immediate repentance." Is *immediate repentance* every time one sins the basis for remaining connected with the atonement? In this system, each sin requires our ongoing appropriation of the atonement. The question is this: Has the atonement been applied to the individual or not? Is he or she justified or unjustified?

---

[1]"A Dialogue Between an Antinomian and His Friend," in *The Works of John Wesley*, ed. Thomas Jackson, 14 vols. (London: Wesley Methodist Book Room, 1872; repr. Grand Rapids: Baker, 1986), 10:266–67.

JUSTIFICATION AND THE IMPUTATION
OF CHRIST'S RIGHTEOUSNESS

Harper exemplifies another Wesleyan tension in the tendency (which he shares with Wesley) to use the *language* of imputation while emptying it of its content. Harper says, "Along with the Calvinists, Wesley affirmed imputed righteousness.... In terms of philosophical theology [on imputation], he was one with believers in the Reformed tradition." These statements are either misleading or confused. Wesley clearly did not mean by "imputation" what Reformed believers have meant by it for almost five centuries.

As I quoted in my chapter, Wesley diverged sharply from the Reformed consensus on the imputation of the righteousness of Christ, believing it to be a *legal fiction*. "The judgment of an all-wise God," Wesley argued, "is always according to truth; neither can it ever consist with his unerring wisdom to think that I am innocent, to judge that I am righteous or holy because another is so. He can no more confound me with Christ than with David or Abraham."[2]

Here again, however, Harper is himself in tension. No matter how much he wishes to claim oneness between Wesley and the Reformed tradition, Harper cannot escape his Wesleyan roots. Both Wesley and Harper deny the imputation of Christ's perfect obedience to the believer. Harper says that "it is important to note that for Wesley justification is not something God does that is contrary to the real state of things.... Justification is not falsification or fantasy but is again the mysterious and marvelous blending of imputed and imparted righteousness."

The Reformed Arminian could not disagree more. Imputed righteousness relates to justification. Imparted righteousness relates, not to justification, but to sanctification. Yet like all traditional Wesleyans, Harper wrongly confuses imputed and inherent righteousness: "When viewed horticulturally, imputed righteousness is the implantation of righteousness, which requires daily nurturing if it is to continue to live. Consequently, Wesley put the emphasis on imparted righteousness."

The reason Wesley moved away from any use of imputation language in his later years is his polemics with antinomi-

___
[2]Sermon "Justification by Faith," *Works*, 5:57.

anism. Harper argues, "Wesley's problems emerge when Calvinists combine the idea of imputation with a belief in election. If God has predetermined who will be saved, and if all such persons have been clothed in the righteousness of Christ (the eternally sinless Son of God), then it only stands to reason that their security would be eternal." The answer to antinomianism, however, is not to back away from a forensic understanding. For, indeed, the justified one is justified by the righteousness of Christ, Christ's righteousness being legally imputed to him or her. Rather, the answer is to point out what the problems actually are: antinomianism and decretal salvation. If Wesley were *truly Arminian* at this point, he would not have backed away from imputation language.

Harper goes on to say that Wesley changed his language because "what he observed in the eighteenth century was a host of people who used Calvinist theology to rationalize inappropriate behavior." Of course, this sort of rationalization is unconscionable. Nonetheless, Wesley's answer was the wrong one. Contrary to Wesley and Wesleyanism, salvation is provided by *Christ's righteousness alone*, that is, his active obedience and his passive obedience imputed to the believer's account. Indeed, I cannot add one thing to what Christ has done. My salvation is not just *for the sake of* what Christ has done (Wesley's definition of imputation) but what Christ *actually* did, placed on my account.

SIN AND THE LOSS OF SALVATION

Harper's tension is seen again in the way he deals with sin after conversion and how it relates to the loss of salvation. On the one hand, Harper seems to want to say that sin in the life of the believer is not the cause of the loss of salvation. Yet on the other hand, he indicates that if sin is not confessed, the Christian will lose his or her salvation. The following quotations illustrate Harper's tension:

- Our standing with Christ and in Christ is not so fragile that a temporary lapse into sin cancels everything God has done for us up to that point.
- The loss of salvation is much more related to experiences that are profound and prolonged.

- Involuntary transgressions (i.e., sins we commit without the awareness that we have done so) are not held against us by God, unless we discover them and do nothing about them. Voluntary sins—deliberate violations of known laws of God—do, however, become mortal if we do not repent of them. The subject of eternal security rests (in both categories of sin) on the matter of ongoing repentance.
- As long as we live in faith . . . we are not committing sin.

How can one say that temporary lapses into sin do not cause loss of salvation while also affirming that voluntary sins *become mortal* if we do not repent of them? Or, what does it mean to say that God holds it against us when we discover involuntary sins and do nothing about them? Furthermore, Harper's statement that "so long as we live in faith . . . we are not committing sin" implies a definition of faith that is at odds with the doctrine that justification comes by the imputed righteousness of Christ to the believer. This notion of saving faith is simply different from the Reformed view. This is the heart and soul of the Reformed Arminian disagreement with Wesleyanism. It is tantamount to saying that if a person is living a life of faith, he or she is sinless. Yet in another place, Harper states that Wesley "could not follow groups like the Moravians, who were teaching 'sinless perfection.'"

Harper is at cross-purposes with himself. On the one hand, he says that one who is in faith is "not committing sin." Yet on the other hand, he dismisses the doctrine of sinless perfection. Writing from within the Wesleyan tradition, Harper cannot simply give a *one-sentence dismissal* of sinless perfection. If he is going to talk about sin in the life of the believer, then he must deal with the doctrine of *entire sanctification*. Historically, Wesleyans have not wished to skirt this issue, but Harper is willing to brush it aside without further comment.

Wesley himself did *not* see loss of salvation as being related to profound and prolonged experiences with sin. In fact, the passage Harper cites at that point in his discussion comes from Wesley's sermon "The Great Privilege of Those That Are Born of God." In this sermon, Wesley gives examples of believers in the Bible who were children of God at one moment and then committed a sin and at that moment lost their salvation and became children of the devil. Wesley wrote:

To explain this by a particular instance: David was born of God, and saw God by faith. He loved God in sincerity. He could truly say, "Whom have I in heaven but thee? and there is none upon earth," neither person nor thing, "that I desire in comparison of thee." But still there remained in his heart that corruption of nature, which is the seed of all evil.

"He was walking upon the roof of his house," (2 Sam. 11:2) probably praising the God whom his soul loved, when he looked down, and saw Bathsheba. He felt a temptation; a thought which tended to evil. The Spirit of God did not fail to convince him of this. He doubtless heard and knew the warning voice; but he yielded in some measure to the thought, and the temptation began to prevail over him. Hereby his spirit was sullied; he saw God still; but it was more dimly than before. He loved God still; but not in the same degree; not with the same strength and ardour of affection. Yet God checked him again, though his spirit was grieved; and his voice, though fainter and fainter, still whispered, "Sin lieth at the door; look unto me, and be thou saved." But he would not hear: He looked again, not unto God, but unto the forbidden object, till nature was superior to grace, and kindled lust in his soul.

The eye of his mind was now closed again, and God vanished out of his sight. Faith, the divine, supernatural intercourse with God, and the love of God, ceased together: He then rushed on as a horse into the battle, and knowingly committed the outward sin.[3]

Also, as I quoted in my chapter,

Wilt thou say, "But I have again committed sin, since I had redemption through his blood?" . . . It is meet that thou shouldst abhor thyself. . . . But, dost thou now believe? . . . At whatsoever time thou truly believest in the name of the Son of God, all thy sins antecedent to that hour vanish away. . . . And think not to say, "I was justified once; my sins were forgiven me:" I know not that; neither will I dispute whether they were or no. Perhaps at this distance in time, it is impossible to know. . . . But

---

[3]Sermon "The Great Privilege of Those Who Are Born of God," *Works* , 5:230.

this I know, with the utmost degree of certainty, "he that committeth sin is of the devil." Therefore, thou art of thy father the devil.[4]

Since I have already dealt with this in my chapter, I see no need to reiterate the problems that Reformed Arminians have with this kind of approach to sin in the life of the believer. People are either justified or unjustified. If one is justified, his or her sins are laid on Christ. Christ's righteousness is credited to him or her. This is a legal designation. Thus, as long as people continue to be justified *by faith*—as long as they continue to be *in Christ*—they remain in a state of grace. It is only by making shipwreck of that faith that they will lose their salvation.

THE REMEDIABILITY OF APOSTASY

The final area of tension in Wesleyan thought is seen in Harper's (and Wesley's) view of whether or not apostasy can be remedied. Reformed Arminians believe that it cannot be. Certain passages in Wesley indicate that some instances of apostasy may be final and irremediable. Yet Wesley, in the end, argues that renewal is possible, even for those who have committed the apostasy discussed in passages such as Hebrews 6:4–6 and 1 Timothy 1:19:

> If it be asked, "Do any real apostates find mercy from God? Do any that have 'made shipwreck of faith and a good conscience,' recover what they have lost? Do you know, have you seen, any instance of persons who found redemption in the blood of Jesus, and afterwards fell away, and yet were restored,—'renewed again unto repentance?'" Yea, verily and not one or an hundred only, but, I am persuaded several thousands.... Indeed, it is so far from being an uncommon thing for a believer to fall and be restored, that it is rather uncommon to find any believers who are not conscious of having been backsliders from God, in a higher or lower degree, and perhaps more than once, before they were established in faith.[5]

Harper holds this same position, saying, "Even when we fall *from* grace, we do not fall *beyond* grace." The Reformed

---

[4]Sermon "The Fruits of the Spirit," *Works*, 5:95.
[5]Sermon "A Call to Backsliders," *Works*, 6:525.

Arminian position, conversely, believes that apostasy—that decisive act of defection from faith in Christ, the once-for-all sacrifice for sin—is without remedy. I have developed this position
more fully in my chapter.

Finally, I am bewildered by Harper's statement that "Wesley's theology of grace comes very close to being the same as
eternal security." Wesley believed that those he described as
fallen were *lost* while they were fallen. I would be interested to
know what eternal securitist Harper might cite who would agree
with him that Wesley's theology of grace comes very close to
being the same as eternal security.

GLOSSARY

antinomianism. A view that appeared among Lutherans and Calvinists in the sixteenth and seventeenth centuries. It emphasized that since Christians are saved by grace alone through faith alone, they are freed from the moral obligations of the law. Its critics blamed antinomians for being morally lax and underemphasizing sanctification and confession of sin.

a priori. A Latin phrase meaning prior to or independent of experience.

effectual calling. A term Classical Calvinists use to denote the irresistible drawing of the elect by the Holy Spirit.

forensic. Pertaining to legal or judicial matters. The Reformers emphasized forensic notions of atonement and justification, teaching that Christ's righteousness and death satisfied God's justice and wrath against sin and legally credited believing sinners with the righteousness of God in Christ.

intra-Trinitarian. Refers to something that takes place among the three persons of the Trinity.

Molinism. The view of sixteenth-century Jesuit theologian Luis de Molina. Also called "middle knowledge," this perspective says that God foreknows what his free creatures would do in any given set of circumstances. So he creates the optimal possible world, thus preserving human freedom and divine sovereignty.

monergism. Distinguished from synergism, from the Greek *monos* (alone) and *ergon* (work). This view holds that salvation is the work of God alone, from start to finish, and that the human will does not cooperate in the salvation process.

ordo salutis. A Latin phrase, meaning order of salvation.

Pelagianism. A theological movement with origins in the thought of the British monk Pelagius (c. 354–c. 402). It

284 | Four Views on Eternal Security

denies original sin and depravity, emphasizing the priority of human free will in attaining salvation. According to Pelagius, human beings by nature can will to attain righteousness before any operation of God's grace. Christians can likewise achieve sinless perfection. Augustine opposed this system, and the Council of Ephesus condemned it in 431.

Remonstrants. Followers of Jacobus Arminius, many of whom strayed far from Arminius's own theology. In 1610 they issued the "Remonstrance," which denied a Calvinistic understanding of salvation. The Calvinistic Synod of Dort, which met in 1618–19, condemned the Remonstrants and their teachings.

simul justus et peccator. A Latin phrase, at once justified and yet a sinner. This is a phrase Martin Luther and other Reformers used.

sola fide. A Latin phrase, by faith alone.

sola gratia. A Latin phrase, by grace alone.

soteriology. From the Greek *soteria* (salvation). The doctrine of salvation.

supralapsarianism. From the Latin *supra* (before) and *lapsus* (fall); hence, before the Fall. A Classical Calvinist doctrine that God decreed election and reprobation before he decreed the Fall. This system proposes the following order of the divine decrees:

1. the decree of the election of some and the reprobation of others
2. the decree of the creation of the elect and reprobate
3. the decree of the Fall
4. the decree of salvation in Christ for the elect

suzerainty-vassal treaty. An ancient Near Eastern covenant or agreement between a lord and his underlings. Many scholars see this as representative of the biblical covenants between God and his people.

synergism. Distinguished from monergism, from the Greek *syn* (together) and *ergon* (work). A view associated with sixteenth-century Lutheran theologian Philip Melanchthon, which says that the human will cooperates with the Holy Spirit in bringing about salvation.

Synod of Dort. The international council of Calvinists that convened in Holland in 1618–19 to deal with the problem of Arminianism in the Reformed churches. The Synod condemned Arminius's successors, the Remonstrants, and their Arminian views. It produced the Canons of Dort, which hold what has popularly become known by the acrostic TULIP: Total depravity, Unconditional election, Limited atonement, Irresistible grace, and Perseverance of the saints.

typological interpretation. A traditional method of biblical interpretation that interprets Old Testament people, events, rituals, and so forth as "types" that symbolize or prefigure Christ and his new covenant.

ABOUT THE CONTRIBUTORS

Stephen M. Ashby is assistant professor of philosophy and religious studies at Ball State University in Muncie, Indiana. Dr. Ashby holds graduate degrees from Grand Rapids Baptist Theological Seminary (M.Div., M.R.E.), Lynchburg College (M.Ed.), and Bowling Green State University (Ph.D.). His publishing projects include many articles as well as his forthcoming commentary on *The Acts of the Apostles* (Randall House).

Norman L. Geisler is president and professor of theology and apologetics at Southern Evangelical Seminary in Charlotte, North Carolina. Dr. Geisler holds graduate degrees from Wheaton College (M.A.) and Loyola University of Chicago (Ph.D.). He has authored, co-authored, or edited over fifty books, including *Chosen But Free: A Balanced View of Divine Election* (Bethany House), *Baker Encyclopedia of Christian Apologetics* (Baker), *Unshakable Foundations: Contemporary Answers to Crucial Questions About the Christian Faith* (Bethany House), and *Christian Ethics: Options and Issues* (Baker).

Steve Harper is vice president and dean and professor of spiritual formation and Wesley studies at Asbury Theological Seminary in Orlando, Florida. He has also served as dean of the Chapel of the Upper Room in Nashville, Tennessee. Dr. Harper holds graduate degrees from Asbury Theological Seminary (M.Div.) and Duke University (Ph.D.). He has authored such books as *John Wesley's Message for Today* (Zondervan), *Prayer and Devotional Life of the United Methodists* (Abingdon), and *Devotional Life in the Wesleyan Tradition* (Upper Room).

Michael S. Horton is associate professor of apologetics and historical theology at Westminster Theological Seminary in Escondido, California. He serves as vice-chairman of the Alliance of Confessing

Evangelicals and editor of *Modern Reformation* magazine. Dr. Horton holds graduate degrees from Westminster Seminary, California (M.A.R.), and Coventry University, U.K. (Ph.D.). He has authored and edited several books, such as *We Believe: Recovering the Essentials of the Apostles' Creed* (Word), *Putting Amazing Back Into Grace* (Baker), *Power Religion: The Selling Out of the Evangelical Church?* (Moody), and *A Confessing Theology for Postmodern Times* (Crossway).

J. Matthew Pinson is president of Free Will Baptist Bible College in Nashville, Tennessee. Mr. Pinson holds graduate degrees from Yale University (M.A.R.) and the University of West Florida (M.A.) He is completing his Ph.D. at Florida State University, where his dissertation topic concerns the diversity of English Arminianism in the seventeenth and eighteenth centuries. Mr. Pinson's writings include *A Free Will Baptist Handbook: Heritage, Beliefs, and Ministries* (Randall House).

SCRIPTURE INDEX

SUBJECT INDEX

We want to hear from you. Please send your comments about this book to us in care of the address below. Thank you.

GRAND RAPIDS, MICHIGAN 49530

WWW.ZONDERVAN.COM